Building Feminist Movements and Organizations

Global Perspectives

Edited by

Lydia Alpízar Durán, Noël D. Payne and Anahi Russo

Zed Books

LONDON & NEW YORK

Building Feminist Movements and Organizations: Global Perspectives
was first published by Zed Books Ltd, 7 Cynthia Street, London N1 9JF, UK,
and Room 400, 175 Fifth Avenue, New York, NY 10010, USA
www.zedbooks.co.uk

Published in association with

The Association of Women's Rights in Development (AWID)
215 Spadina Ave, Suite 150, Toronto, Ontario, M5T 2C7, Canada
and Zamora 169, Casa 2, Colonia Condesa, Mexico DF, CP 06140, México

Designed and typeset in Monotype Bembo
by Long House Publishing Services, Cumbria, UK
Cover designed by Andrew Corbett
Printed and bound in Great Britain by Biddles Ltd, King's Lynn, Norfolk

Distributed in the USA exclusively by Palgrave Macmillan, a division of
St Martin's Press, LLC, 175 Fifth Avenue, New York, NY 10010

A catalogue record for this book is available from the British Library
Library of Congress Cataloging-in-Publication Data available

ISBN 978 1 84277 849 4 Hb
ISBN 978 1 84277 850 0 Pb

CONTENTS

Acknowledgements   vi

1   **Introduction** *Building Feminist Movements and Organizations: Learning from Experience*   1
Lydia Alpízar Durán

Part 1   Challenging Power and Revisioning Leadership   13

2   **Repoliticization of the Women's Movement and Feminism in Argentina**   15
The Experience of Pan y Rosas
Andrea D'Atri

3   **A Jewish Orthodox Women's Revolution**
The Case of Kolech   25
Margalit Shilo

4   **An Insight into Feminist Organizations**   35
Yamini Mishra and Nalini Singh

5   **Empowering Womanspace**
Power Distribution and Dynamics in Christian Feminist Community   44
Kelsey Rice and Ann Crews Melton

Part 2   Revisiting Organizational Practices   55

6   **New Democratic Exercises in Mexican Feminist Organizations**   57
Adriana Medina Espino

7   **Linking Empowerment and Democracy**
A Challenge to Women's Groups in Quebec   67
Nancy Guberman, Jennifer Beeman, Jocelyne Lamoureux,
Danielle Fournier and Lise Gervais

8 **Gender Mainstreaming in Development Organizations**
Organizational Discourse and the Perils of Institutional Change   78
Nicholas Piálek

9 **Feminists, Factions and Fictions in Rural Canada**   87
Leona M. English

Part 3 Building Organizational Capacity and Resources   97

10 **A Model for Social Change**
15 years Investing in Mexican Women   99
Emilienne de León, Amanda Mercedes Gigler,
Lucero González and Margaret Schellenberg

11 **Reflections on Strengthening Leadership in Community-based
Organizations in India**   109
Pramada Menon

12 **Virtual Seminar on Gender and Trade**
An Innovative Process   119
Verónica Baracat, Phyllida Cox and Norma Sanchis

Part 4 Broadening the Support Base of Movements   129

13 **Zimbabwe Women Writers**
1990–2004   131
Mary O. Tandon

14 **Amnesty for Women**
*Building Mechanisms to Integrate and Empower Migrant Women
in Hamburg, Germany*   140
Sol Viviana Rojas and Raquel Aviles Caminero

15 **The Korean Women's Trade Union**
A Foothold for Women Workers' Rights   150
Jinnock Lee

16 **Power in Bridges**
A Romanian Story about Spreading Feminist Values   159
Camelia Blaga

17 **Widening the Base of the Feminist Movement in Pakistan**   167
Shahnaz Iqbal

Part 5 Sustaining Work in Situations of Conflict   179

18 **The Women's Emancipatory Constituent Process for Peace in Colombia**   181
Yusmidia Solano

19 **From Individual Struggle to National Struggle**
Palestinian Women in the State of Israel   190
Trees Zbidat-Kosterman

20 **Equal Representation in a Divided Society**
The Feminist Experience in Israel   200
Dalia Sachs and Hannah Safran

21 **The 'Motherhood' Strategy of Indonesia's Suara Ibu Peduli**   209
Monika S.W. Doxey

Part 6 Campaigns as a Means for Movement Building   219

22 **Remobilizing the Algerian Women's Movement**
The 20 Ans Barakat Campaign   221
Caroline Brac de la Perrière

23 **Advocating Sexual Rights**
The Campaign for the Reform of the Turkish Penal Code   230
Liz Ercevik Amado

24 **An Inter-American Convention on Sexual Rights and Reproductive Rights**
We're Campaigning!   239
Elizabeth C. Plácido

25 **A Matter of Life or Death**
Campaigning to Build Support for the Defence of Women's Rights in Nigeria   250
Titi Salaam

26 **The Evolution of Discourse**
The Campaign to Change the Family Law in Morocco   258
Alexandra Pittman
with Lucero González and Margaret Schellenberg

Editors and contributors   270
Index   276

ACKNOWLEDGEMENTS

One of the greatest pleasures of working on this project has been the opportunity to engage with the many dedicated and passionate women who shared their wisdom and experience, and who inspired us daily with their courage and unflagging dedication to the belief that it is not only possible to create sustainable women's movements, but that it is both necessary and urgent to do so.

Our thanks first to the women's rights advocates who participated in the selection committee for the project: Bisi Adeleye-Fayemi (African Women's Development Fund, Ghana), Filiz Bikmen (Third Sector Foundation, Turkey), Geetanjali Misra (Creating Resources for Empowerment in Action, CREA, India), Sanja Sarnavka (Be Active Be Emancipated, B.a.B.e., Croatia), Indai Sajor (Human Rights Advisor, the Philippines), Virginia Vargas (Centro de la Mujer Peruana Flora Tristán, Peru) and Barbara Williams (Consultant on Diversity and Organizational Development, Canada). Barbara in particular deserves kudos for seeing the project through from inception to completion, watching carefully over the project at every stage. We cannot thank any of them enough for their patience and wisdom, their willingness to trust in the process, and for their solidarity and friendship.

We also want to thank the staff at Zed Books (Anna Hardman, Susannah Trefgarne, Anne Rodford) and at the Association for Women's Rights in Development (Lina Gómez, Fernanda Hopenhaym, Caroline Sin, Zazil Canto) for their many contributions and advice at different stages in this process. In particular, we would like to thank Joanna Kerr, the Executive Director of AWID during this project, for her vision, trust in the initiative, constant support, and her ever present boldness and creative energy. We are also grateful to Marina Bernal, who put in many, many hours of volunteer work and whose ideas helped shape this initiative and get it off the ground in its earliest stages. Their collective editorial insights, their willingness to share time and expertise, and their many smart recommendations have contributed in immeasurable ways to the outcome and success of this project.

We would also like to recognize all those who responded to our Call for Contributions, particularly those whose contributions were selected for the book. We cannot begin to count the number of hours we spent together on the phone and on Skype, on e-mail and in person, talking and revising, shaping and reshaping their contributions. It goes without saying that this initiative would not have been possible without their hard work and significant insights and inputs. This book has been inspired and shaped by their collective generosity, and their willingness to be bold and take risks.

Finally, we would like to acknowledge the funders who believed in and supported this project: HIVOS and Oxfam Novib from the Netherlands, the Swiss Agency for Development and Cooperation (SDC), the Sigrid Rausing Trust from the United Kingdom, and the Network Women's Program of the Open Society Institute in the USA. Their leadership within the funding community and their support for movement building and organizational strengthening is critical to sustaining and advancing women´s rights and gender equality worldwide.

1

INTRODUCTION
Building Feminist Movements and Organizations
Learning from Experience

Lydia Alpízar Durán

Why do we still want to talk about building feminist movements and organizations when they have been around for several decades? The Association for Women's Rights in Development (AWID) believes this to be an urgent task for feminist and women's movements. The context in which we carry out our work, the enormous external challenges we currently face – increasing forms of fundamentalism, unilateralism and militarism, the pervasive violence against women, rising poverty and exclusion – as well as challenges relating to the internal organization and mobilization of movements, merit serious attention.

Contemporary women's and feminist movements and organizations, like other social movements, have been through a variety of trans-formations over recent decades – sometimes in response to changes in context and specific historical moments, sometimes due to evolution in feminist thinking and a new understanding of how to make organiza-tional change happen.

Worldwide, a rich diversity of processes and movements has emerged from the work of individuals, awareness-raising collectives and other groups, organizations and networks at a variety of levels. Evolving beyond 'the personal is political', feminist organizations have taken up highly complex struggles that have resulted in some of the most significant societal changes of the last century.

But women's victories are usually hard–won and highly vulnerable. Rising fundamentalism, resistance from right-wing interest groups and forces, as well as increasing inequalities and forms of exclusion threaten not only past achievements but also our transformative agendas for women and girls all over the world. In order to continue our struggle we thus need to be more effective, to become stronger actors in diverse arenas and at different levels, to adapt to changes and to reinvent ourselves. And in this process, we need to ensure consistency with our values and principles.

In this introductory chapter, we address three main questions. Why do we see building feminist movements and stronger organizations as so important to social, economic and cultural change? What are the key issues and insights that have emerged while putting this book together? And how are we to move forward?

The importance of our task

In 2003, AWID launched its new Feminist Organizational Development programme, but subsequently decided to expand its scope to include feminist and women's movements. It thus broadened its range beyond that of organizational development itself to include the movements out of which many of our organizations emerge. The change in name to Feminist Movements and Organizations Programme was not cosmetic. It arose from a strong belief in the need to apply this broader perspective to the agendas not only of feminist and women's movements and organizations, but also to those of funding agencies. This is particularly important if we are to take advantage of the opportunities for change and respond effectively to the challenges we face. At a critical turning point for strengthening feminist movements, both creating spaces for discussion and developing tools that address organizational efforts and movements to build collective power are more urgent than ever before.

Many initiatives have already been taken 'in the field'; discussions and debates among women in all regions have generated a rich store of knowledge and experience. Our task now is to share all these experiences in order to build stronger movements and organizations for the advancement of gender equality and women's rights. We therefore wanted to complement all these initiatives in movement building and organizational strengthening by making a compilation of feminist thinking, knowledge, experience, projects, cases, methodologies, publications and tools from different regions. AWID's Feminist Movements and Organizations Programme was thus built on what was already available and involves the identification of gaps and processes that require strategic responses and support. This book is the result of such a process. It presents a selection of the brilliant and provocative array of essays and case studies – 144 contributions from 42 different countries – that reached us from all over the world.[1] We think these contributions show how much is happening on the ground. As feminist and women's movements, we need to build on our legacy and organizational capacity by learning from these valuable experiences.

We were surprised to find that some contributions took the form of reports to donor agencies. They tended to be descriptive of the work carried out, with little analysis of the experiences involved. They did not identify the key lessons learned or the insights gained from their initiatives. A variety of factors could have influenced this result: more experienced women may have been unable to find the time to document processes or carry out analyses; resources may have been lacking; or donor agencies may have exerted a strong influence on the way these feminist and women's organizations chose to talk about work and experiences. 'Where is the Money for Women's Rights?', an online survey carried out by AWID in 2006, revealed that 87 per cent of almost 1,000 women's and feminist organizations who responded had been created within the last 16 years; and, of those, about 40 per cent had been created within the previous six years. If the results of this survey are representative, we can conclude that most active women's and feminist organizations are relatively new and that institutional memory is being lost.

Given this reality, analysing and documenting our experience of organizing and movement building is key to ensuring the transfer of knowledge and experience. This can happen in a variety of ways, but it is clear that global feminist and women's movements are likely to lose much accumulated experience – so jeopardizing the future – if we are unable to take advantage of institutional memory and to transfer experience and knowledge beyond our borders and to other social movements. Loss of memory also denies newcomers to our movements their sense of belonging to a historical transformation process that has been taking place for centuries, and of which we are all part.

We consider this book to be a valuable resource for feminist and women's organizations, networks, campaigns, groups, collectives and individuals. We can assure you that, regardless of the direct relevance of each contribution to your work, and whether you agree or not with the author(s), each chapter will help you reflect on our central theme. The variety of contributions shows that there is neither one definition for movement building and organizational strengthening nor one single way to go about it. We recognize the need to promote spaces for reflection, debate and discussion of what we understand by movement building and how this is evolving, so that the movements and the organizations themselves are able to develop organically.

The very nature of our work as feminist and women's advocates challenges the normative practices that diminish, erode or deny women's rights and the kind of change processes we promote. As a result, building organizations and movements is imbued with power dynamics that frequently result in tensions and difficulties that are difficult to comprehend, identify or effectively challenge as we enhance our conceptualization of and practices in building movements and organizations. Several contributions present examples of how women's organizations are struggling with these issues. They analyse their implications and come up with different ways to deal with them that are effective and consistent with feminist values.

Some key insights from work on this book

The different contributions to this book enable us to learn from women (and one man) who discuss movement building within feminist and women's organizations and networks, all the way up through development institutions and even in traditional patriarchal structures such as unions and religious institutions. It is clear that all of the authors perceive their work and their experiences as related directly to movement building or organizational strengthening. Thus we discover that *building a strong organization can, in itself, contribute to strengthening the movement.* Under such circumstances we note how important it is to be clear on role of the organization and its contribution to the larger collective power building process if social change is to be achieved. Although it is easy to see how movement building is able to contribute to organizational strengthening, organizational strengthening does not necessarily lead to movement building. If we are to build collective power, it is indispensable that we consider how to go about developing an organizational strengthening model that includes movement building.

Feminist values and organizational practices

Many of the contributions raise issues of how feminist values are integrated in organizational practices and, for example, in work with coalitions. We see that ensuring participation through inclusive or democratic decision-making processes and mechanisms continues to be a major concern.

The fact that groups from feminist movements engage in such debates is a reflection of their commitment to dealing with these and other related issues. For example, the translation of these values into a feminist practice that ensures inclusion, participation and accountability, while at the same time producing results, is just one of the many challenges faced. It is also clear from some of the contributions that, although discussing processes and how we go about our work is important, it is not enough. We note that there are broadly institutionalized organizational practices in diverse women's groups and NGOs that tend to replicate the same patriarchal structures and values we are trying to deconstruct. So, although values can orient us in the building of our organizations and movements, it is no good simply talking about how important they are or how much we believe in them. Clear principles, mechanisms, internal policies and resources need to be in place in order to make them a reality.

Grappling with power, leadership and empowerment

Closely linked with the concern for consistency with feminist values, issues of power, leadership, empowerment and decision making continue to be a major concern. Different contributors explore practices of leadership development, decision-making structures and leadership styles, and raise key questions on which to reflect and act.

For example, it is clear that there are different and highly nuanced positions on the best decision-making models for feminist organizations. Some organizations appear to support models of consensus building as being the most consistent with feminist values, while others acknowledge the limitations of the consensus model and opt for majority-vote decision-making mechanisms. However, several organizations point out that practice has taught them to use both, making a choice according to the processes and issues at stake. Themes that go beyond the discussion of decision making include those of representation, leadership change, and optimal organizational structures, as well as that of how to balance process with the achievement of goals.

Organizational structures were discussed in several of the contributions, within a discourse dating back to the 1960s and 1970s on how best to structure an organization in line with feminist values and how to advance alternative practices in handling power in non-patriarchal ways. The book demonstrates strong positions in favour of flat or horizontal models and includes a debate on hierarchical structures and how 'feminist' they can be. Some of the theses presented by Jo Freeman in her famous text of the 1970s, *The Tyranny of Structurelessness*,[2] emerge as still valid today. For example, her argument that apparently flat or non-hierarchical organizational (power) structures are not inherently democratic or inclusive finds support in some of our case studies. Although there have been different experiences with diverse results, women's organizations continue grappling with questions of hierarchy, inclusion, participation, responsibility, ownership, representation, and so on. Are participatory democratic hierarchies possible? How are organizations larger than twenty people to be structured? Is co-responsibility an option in feminist organizations? Clearly the responses vary with the contexts, organizational characteristics and processes involved.

As new actors and contexts emerge, the way leadership is defined and understood, and the way women and feminist organizations construct leadership and imbed it in practice, are also changing. Several examples are to be found in the following chapters. These range from understanding leadership development with a focus on the individual – which has been a predominant vision in feminist movements – to understanding leadership as a more collective process, and seeing different forms of leadership as necessary for the advancement of the agendas that support women's rights.

Discussions also cover changes in key leadership positions in organizations. The challenges posed by leaders who remain for many years in their organizations, and limit opportunities for continued growth, innovation and openness to different leadership styles, emerge in several of the contributions. Some questions that are both relevant and often painful relate to where older leaders of organizations and movements go, when they move on. In many cases, with very limited or no social benefits (such as pension funds and health insurances) many older women leaders have difficulty in moving out of organizations around which their lives have been built. How are we to respond to these important issues by creating spaces that honour, recognize and harness the knowledge and experience of these leaders and at the same time create spaces for the support and emergence of new leaders and the recognition of new leadership styles?

Other leadership-related issues involve prevailing leadership styles in organizations and movements. Questions are also raised as to how democratic and inclusive they really are. And is there an ability to foster and recognize different forms of activism and leadership – that go beyond the older models of activism based on negation of personal life and needs, and full commitment to the cause – while leaving space for the personal lives and needs of activists?

Building the base of support of our movements

More than a decade after the 1995 Fourth World Conference on Women held in Beijing and other key conferences in the 1990s, we believe it is important to carry out a critical analysis of the impact these conferences and their follow-up processes have had on our organizations, agenda definition and priorities, and on the way in which we carry out our work.

Few people would deny the importance of the achievements that have resulted from the different conference processes: international organizing initiatives, the creation of new networks, inter-regional work, broader participation by women from different regions and traditionally marginalized sectors. And after all the effort, work and resources invested by women and feminist movements in these conferences, it was only logical that many follow-up efforts focused on the implementation of the international agreements at different levels. This resulted in many advocacy efforts to influence legislation and public policy development, and in the creation of government institutions – referred to today as 'gender machinery'. But somehow, during the process, constituency building and work at the grassroots were left behind – the scenarios varied from country to country, and region to region. Clearly, however, constituency building and establishing the support base of our agendas and causes have not emerged as top priorities for thousands of women's and feminist organizations.

The paradox is that many of those international and intergovernmental agreements will not gain the necessary footholds if there is no broad public support for our agendas and our demands. At AWID we firmly believe that in order to defend achievements to date and continue moving forward with our struggles, we need strong and bold women's and feminist movements and organizations grounded in a broad and solid support base.

Political sustainability of our struggles and resource mobilization

A common reality of most feminist and women's organizations and movements in different regions of the world is the difficulty they have in accessing funding. The online survey carried out by AWID in 2006, as part of its research–action initiative on funding for women's rights organizations, showed us that approximately 33 per cent of all women's organizations that responded had an annual (2005) income of less than US$10,000. We also noted that funding for women's rights and gender equality has decreased over the last decade, and that funding for women's organizations is very difficult to access and unevenly distributed.

It is clear that donors are responsible for the decrease in funding for women's rights work, that women's issues are no longer a priority, and that gender mainstreaming has not yet had the hoped-for positive impact in promoting real transformation in these institutions and the projects they fund. However, as feminist and women's organizations we must also accept responsibility for our approach to money and funding, and for a necessary depoliticization in the funding of our agendas.

Women's movements have attempted to respond to funding challenges in many ways, such as the creation of women's funds to leverage local resources in the North and the South. But women's funds alone will be insufficient to respond to the crises faced by our organizations. We need a radical transformation of how we relate to money. This relationship is affected in many ways by long-standing patriarchal beliefs and our sense of entitlement to funding ('our causes are just and therefore worthy of resources to support them and turn them into a reality for all people of the world'). It has also been affected by our move away from practices of fundraising or resource mobilization that weakened our movements by encouraging competition, fragmentation and even confrontation among women and feminist organizations. Finally, there is a need to repoliticize the relationship with donors by creating spaces in which we can discuss funding priorities and align terms of engagement with support for a women's rights agenda, and thus contribute to strengthening women's and feminist movements throughout the world.

Importance of campaigning to build collective power

It is no coincidence that several of the following chapters are case studies of different types of campaigns carried out in different regions around the world. Advocacy of normative and cultural changes has increasingly assumed a pivotal role in the strategies of feminist and women's organizations and movements since the mid-1990s.

We have said that not all forms of organizational strengthening necessarily contribute to movement building, and the same applies to campaigns. Nevertheless, campaigns have considerable potential in contributing to key movement-building processes such as constituency building, establishing alliances with actors from other social movements, providing visibility to key issues within the public discourse and modifying this discourse when it obstructs or hinders the full enjoyment and advancement of women's rights. It is also clear that campaigning can contribute to leadership development – including the emergence of new leaders, and new forms of leadership – as well as to the exploration of diverse ways of working together.

Some key questions posed by the experiences presented in this book relate to how campaigns are planned. Some may be designed to go beyond just changing a law or a public policy, but give little thought to building power to ensure implementation. Others may be planned explicitly to contribute to building collective power, or even have this as their main goal. We must also ask ourselves what kind of language and communication is needed in order to reach out successfully to a broader public and contribute to building constituencies.

And after all this ... what's next?

This is the time, we at AWID believe, to open proactive debates and reflections on all these issues. We must generate creative thinking about the organizations we need and the strategies that would benefit feminist and women's movements. This will allow us to adjust to considerable changes of context at local, national, regional and international levels, and to respond to challenges delaying the advance of feminist agendas in different parts of the world.

As feminist and women's movements, we need to reinvent ourselves in order to become stronger and continue growing – we have done this successfully in the past, and would do well to learn from such experiences. (For example, at the end of the 1970s changes took place in several regions of the world with the organization of small awareness-raising groups or circles and the creation of broader organizations within movements. In the 1980s, likewise, some regions with movements rather than formal organizational structures started creating NGOs and networks.) Only thus will we be able to address the form feminist and women's movements and organizations should take in this new century. We need to invent new ways of organizing ourselves, and yet see what can be learned from our long and rich history of organizational development. There are several institutional forms in which we might be able to find some answers. However, we are mainly interested in creating spaces for political debates that relate directly to building our collective power to defend and continue advancing our vision of the worlds we would like to build as women.

We also believe in the need to develop new discourses, frameworks and tools that will help us link organizational strengthening processes to movement building. This represents a new way of looking at how organizations – rich in colour, flavours and forms – should be linked explicitly to collective power building processes. There is a need to resist approaches, often imposed by funding agencies, that see women's groups and organizations as isolated units devoid of social context and expected to work with the narrow efficiency of separate production units in a given market. Under such constraints, groups easily become excessively technocratic, bureaucratic and devoid of political vision and strategy. These approaches originated mainly in the North and within corporate perspectives of organizational and social change processes. They bear little relation to the needs and visions of the work carried out by feminist and women's organizations and movements around the world – work requiring a capacity to alter the power structures it sets out to challenge.

So it is time for us to create new ways of thinking and operating in this area. We need to build on our history and experience, and respond to the new characteristics of today's movements, as well as to the new opportunities and challenges of the current global context. How do we build feminist movements and organizations that continue to grow and become stronger, that defend our achievements and advance women's rights and gender equality worldwide? What issues do we need to revisit or reconsider as part of this process? And what are the areas we need to change if we are seriously committed to organizing ourselves to radically transform the lives of women and girls throughout the world, and to build other possible worlds? Are we up to the challenge of reinventing ourselves as stronger political actors able to transform the public and private spheres of our societies? We have accepted the challenge. And we invite you to join us!

NOTES

1   The contributions included in this volume were selected from an open call for contributions on feminist organizational strengthening and movement building launched by AWID in late 2003 to early 2004. An international committee composed of women with experience in feminist organizing selected the contributions presented in this book.

2   Freeman, Jo (1970), *The Tyranny of Structurelessness*, first printed by the women's liberation movement, USA, in 1970. It was reprinted in the *Berkeley Journal of Sociology* in 1970 and later issued as a pamphlet by Agitprop in 1972. The electronic version of this article is available at:
    <http://www.jofreeman.com/joreen/tyranny.htm>

Part 1

Challenging Power and Revisioning Leadership

2

Repoliticization of the Women's Movement and Feminism in Argentina

The Experience of Pan y Rosas

Andrea D'Atri

Pan y Rosas (Bread and Roses) came into being as the initiative of a group of young women within the context of the unique climate of repoliticization that emerged in Argentina after the social, political and economic crisis at the end of 2001. Protests on 19–20 December shook the country and toppled the government. In the days before and the weeks and months that followed, we witnessed desperate men, women, girls and boys pillaging stores and supermarkets in search of food in the outlying districts of Buenos Aires and other cities. Later, workers occupied factories in an attempt to avoid closures and lay-offs as a consequence of the economic crisis, while middle-class sectors promoted the formation of neighbourhood assemblies to support protesting workers and the unemployed demanding real jobs. Prompted by university students and professors, hundreds of research projects, case studies and projects were developed around this massive political process that travelled the globe via televised images and inspired films and books.[1]

Formed in mid-2003, Pan y Rosas was created in the heat of the processes that started unfolding in our country after that emblematic December, as an inheritor of that climate of struggle, organization, fraternization and repoliticization. We especially identify ourselves as the daughters of the fifty women workers at the small Brukman textile factory in Buenos Aires. When the failing plant was abandoned by its owners, these women took it over, made it produce, paid off the debts and resisted police repression – supported throughout by thousands of neighbours who surrounded them in solidarity. National encounters were organized with other workers in the same situation; the women

withstood three eviction attempts; and, when the last one was successful, they set up camp outside and spent several months exposed to the
elements. Finally, after months of resistance, they recuperated the factory
– *recuperar* means 'to take back' as well as 'to put in good condition' – and
are now back in it, producing 'without employers'. The 'Workers
without Employers' movement became a symbol of the country's
struggles as well as of the Argentinian women's movement and feminists
in general. For several months many banded together around the
emblematic struggle of these textile workers, recalling those others who
gave rise to the commemoration of International Women's Day on 8
March 2002.[2] In encounters, interviews, meetings, forums and other
activities carried out with the women workers, we discovered and got
to know one another – and thus it was that we proposed the creation of
the group Pan y Rosas.

Workers and students on the streets

There were no more than ten of us then, all 20–35-year-old workers
and students who were acutely aware of the fragmentation of the
women's movement and of feminism into dozens of non-governmental
organizations. We had points of agreement with some, and little in
common with others, but what really concerned us was that, as a
whole, they had become depoliticized. Absorbed in seeking funding for
their projects, some small groups had even distanced themselves from
the problems afflicting women on a day-to-day basis. Hope in a
government that presented itself as an alternative to the 'neo-liberal
decade' had also worn down the fighting spirit of some feminists, who
now preferred to frequent the corridors of Parliament. Most had
migrated during the previous ten years from the street to academia and
other institutional spheres.

Those of us who later formed Pan y Rosas agreed on one basic point:
the struggle against patriarchy is inextricably linked to the struggle
against capitalism. And so it was that in the course of 2002 we un-
expectedly met up in worker meetings and mobilizations, convinced
that 'something' was missing from the women's movement: a voice to
denounce the miseries to which women were doubly subjected by
capitalism; a voice speaking clearly for women workers and the lower-
income sectors of the population. Feminist groups displayed little
concern about what seemed of vital importance to us.

During the meetings of workers of the recuperated factories organized by the Brukman women workers, we proposed that they form a women's commission where the women workers and unemployed who were participating would have their own space in which to share experiences and have debates on their specific needs. Afterwards, when the workers were evicted in an act of violent police repression, we organized feminist support in solidarity with the workers, contacting all of the activists and groups we knew by word of mouth and alternative media. To our surprise, the reaction was broad and colourful, with almost a hundred women from different groups and sectors answering the call to mobilize.

We continued as an unorganized group of no more than ten young women, until we later found ourselves promoting a feminist 'contingent' against the war in Iraq to denounce the consequences of the war on the Iraqi people, and particularly on women and girls. And on 28 May, the International Day of Action for Women's Health, we coordinated a debate with the women workers of Brukman, women from the *piquetero*[3] movements, health professionals, feminists and students, among others.

Finally, in mid-2003, during the run-up to the eighteenth National Women's Meeting[4] in the city of Rosario, a crisis arose when the local bishop condemned the meeting, sexual and reproductive rights, the right to abortion, and various other feminist causes. In response, older, pro-choice activists called on all feminists and Leftist parties to organize and confront this attack from the ecclesiastical hierarchy. Once again we met, and agreed about what needed to be proposed. That was when we decided the time had come for us to create a more formal group.

Before and after the National Women's Meeting

We knew what we wanted to say at that Women's Meeting in Rosario:[5] 'Right to free and legal abortion!' and 'Support for the rights of women workers!' We denounced, among other things, the situation of unemployed women, of workers forced to occupy factories to keep them open, and of those who had no union rights. But our main concern was that the meeting make a statement supporting the right to abortion and challenging the accusations, abuse and even physical violence inflicted by fundamentalist sectors of the Catholic Church.

So it was that we arrived in Rosario with two flags. A lilac flag, inspired by the 1912 US textile workers' strike, said: 'We do not ask, we *demand* our right to bread … but also roses!'[6] The other flag, seven metres long and coloured deep violet, bore the slogan 'For the right to free and legal abortion', the rallying cry of approximately a thousand women as they stood before the cathedral in repudiation of the bishop's misogynous statements. The impact was so great that the demonstration was pictured on the front page of a prestigious national daily the following day.[7]

When we got back to Buenos Aires, we no longer had any qualms. At a meeting of around thirty young students and workers, we decided to call ourselves Pan y Rosas and drafted a manifesto that included our core protests against capitalism and patriarchy.[8] This was towards the end of August 2003, and we proposed to take part in a demonstration for the right to abortion planned for 28 September. This was to be the Latin American and Caribbean Day for the Decriminalization of Abortion, in which around four thousand women would participate. In November we organized talks and films – followed by debates – on violence against women. Experts, renowned feminists, women workers and young students participated in these events in neighbourhood halls and cultural centres throughout the country. More than five hundred women gathered for these activities throughout the country.

On International Women's Day (8 March) in 2004, the women's and feminists' movements were divided. Some urged confidence in the new Kirchner government,[9] which was making certain political gestures that appeared to benefit the situation of women in the country. Others thought we needed to confront the government and continue alongside the social movements in support of their struggles and protests. Pan y Rosas finally decided to publish a special newspaper setting out our positions, with articles written by members in different cities around the country. Three thousand copies were printed for distribution at the demonstrations and events held that day in Argentina's principal cities.

The book and travels within the country

By summer new *compañeras*[10] had joined after learning about us at the Rosario encounter or through the Internet, since we posted our publications and press releases on the website of the Argentinian women's information network (RIMA) and on Indymedia, an alternative information website.[11]

As one of the original promoters of the group's creation, I had written a little book about women's history, feminism and the participation of working women in strikes and other workers' struggles. We decided to print this work ourselves,[12] and income from its sales enabled presentations in various cities. The participation of prominent feminists and activists at each presentation contributed to extensive exchanges of ideas and debate among respected representatives of our country's feminist movement. Inspired by our project, many young women started to form their own Pan y Rosas groups in their own cities. One year after the group was founded, it had almost a hundred members in eight different cities.

Free the butterflies!
The struggle for women political prisoners

The nineteenth Women's Meeting (Mendoza, October 2004) was approaching. The country was no longer the Argentina of December 2001, when we had first met one another at the strikes, neighbourhood assemblies and worker protests. The President, who many people believed would change the course of Argentina, had earned the sad distinction of detaining the greatest number of political prisoners since the last military dictatorship. It was estimated that as many as four thousand social activists were being prosecuted in October 2004; at the international level this situation was referred to as the 'criminalization of social protest'.

Boldly, we called a meeting of all the women's groups, feminists and leftist parties to prepare the next Women's Meeting. During this process, three unemployed women – together with dozens of *compañeros*[13] – were jailed. They had been promised work in a remote oil production area in the south. However, when the companies went back on their word the three women blockaded the entrance, and were subsequently arrested. The situation was clear: we could organize a meeting in Mendoza ... but there were three women who wouldn't be there because they were imprisoned! This was why Pan y Rosas proposed that the flags should say: 'Freedom for all political prisoners! For the right to abortion! For the rights of women workers!'

In the end, not everyone wanted to challenge the government. But we did not give up. Our group carried an enormous flag denouncing the government's repression and demanding that the jailed women be released. Together we shouted the same cry: 'No more the drudge and idler – ten that toil where one reposes'[14] and 'Free the imprisoned women and join the fight with Pan y Rosas', interrupted only by the slogan 'Woman worker, listen, your struggle is our struggle'.

Back in our respective cities, we each printed a poster to put up in streets, schools and factories during a week-long campaign, the 'Fight against Violence toward Women in Latin America and the Caribbean'. The poster remembered the three Mirabal sisters in the Dominican Republic, assassinated in November 1960 during the time of the Trujillo dictatorship,[15] and the three unemployed women jailed in our country because they asked for work: 'Freedom for the imprisoned women of Caleta Olivia'.[16] Today, as yesterday, our call is to 'free the butterflies'.

A tent was also set up in front of the National Congress by a group of workers who had taken over a factory in Zanon in the west of the country[17] and were protesting against the government. We presented our video *Tiempo de Mariposas* (Time of the Butterflies), filmed during the Women's Meeting in Mendoza, to over a hundred spectators.

Year-end tragedy

As the year came to a close, more than 4,000 young people celebrated the arrival of 2005 at a rock festival in Buenos Aires. The concert came to a disastrous end shortly after it began, when a fire broke out. Almost 200 young people died, making it one of the worst tragedies in the history of our country.[18] As the news broke on Argentinian television channels and in the international media, we spectators were horrified at reports of the number of babies and children who had perished at the site. Immediately there were voices condemning the 'irresponsible mothers' who had taken their children with them to such an event. But the truth was very different. The audience at this event consisted of people from poor neighbourhoods, most of them young and unemployed or with only temporary jobs. So we spoke out against the hypocrisy of those who dared blame the victims as, although public authorities had set up the concert site, it failed to meet basic safety requirements.

All of this was taking place in a country with extremely high rates of adolescent pregnancy, and many young mothers who were themselves children. According to official statistics, 14.6 per cent of live births in Argentina are to mothers under 20 years of age, most of them from poor households: a ratio of 17:1 compared to those from higher income brackets. There are almost one million adolescent mothers; every five minutes a woman under 20 gives birth; and only 32 per cent of adolescents use a safe method of contraception. One out of every three adolescent deaths is a consequence of clandestine abortions performed without proper hygiene, aseptic conditions or professional assistance. Furthermore, not even girls who have been abused and raped – usually by adults in their own family setting – have the right to a voluntary termination of pregnancy. Despite these dramatic numbers, only a few days before the tragedy of the fire, the majority political parties – pressured by fundamentalist sectors – had blocked the passage of the Law on Sexual Education.

The fire revealed the grim reality of adolescents and young people, especially the poorest. It occurred in a city where paying for childcare is a luxury no woman who is unemployed or with unstable work can afford. Pan y Rosas added these specific denunciations when outraged victims, their families and large sectors of the population took to the streets to demand JUSTICE. We were there for the girls and adolescents with their babies and small children – victims not just of the fire but, even more fundamentally, of hypocrisy, sexual discrimination and gender oppression.

Conclusions

Membership of Pan y Rosas ranges between a hundred and two hundred *compañeras* in different cities of Argentina, depending on the particular political climate. The structure of our group is highly flexible yet operational. Only our ideas unite us. We have no by-laws or obligations for our members, because each one acts on the basis of personal convictions. Those of us who promoted the creation of this group did so because we had some ideas in common, that we later expressed in a manifesto. The *compañeras* who joined subsequently did so because they could identify with Pan y Rosas's manifesto or actions – they shared our feelings, beliefs and ways of thinking.

We receive no funding. When we need money to print a book or the manifesto, make a film, posters or other materials, we all contribute or seek loans that can be paid back with income from sales. Our conclusion is that economic independence requires a small sacrifice, but brings enormous satisfaction.

We currently have two ongoing projects. First, a group of Pan y Rosas history and literature students is researching the biographies of women workers, experts, anarchists and feminists who have contributed to the struggle of working women. We hope to compile and publish these so they can be disseminated widely among activists in our country. It has always been difficult for women to reconstruct our history and even more difficult for the activists to recognize themselves as part of the genealogy of women who made history by being rebellious.[19]

The second project involves a team of women workers and Pan y Rosas sociology students who are collaborating in the design of a gender-sensitive survey on the situation of the Argentinian working class. This survey, which has already been carried out in some segments of the economy, is aimed at highly feminized sectors such as telephone companies, health care and the food industry. We believe the results will enable us to gain an in-depth understanding of the day-to-day reality of women workers in the most exploited sectors, and a greater awareness of their needs, so as to engage them in what we hope will be a mutually enriching dialogue.[20]

We know that these two projects were something we wanted to do. We know that once we were just ten women who wanted to take decisive action against exploitation and oppression. We were unable to find a political niche among existing feminist groups which were often afflicted by infighting over leadership and trivialities. We did not imagine that in such a short time and without financial support we would grow to become a hundred-strong group of women from all over the country. We also know that there is much more to do. We are going to fight for our dreams because, as the pioneering feminist Julieta Lanteri said, 'Rights are not won by begging, but by conquering.'[21]

NOTES

1   The best-known was the Naomi Klein/Avi Lewis film *The Take*. See <http://www.thetake.org/> (last accessed 13 September 2006).

2   See <http://www.boedofilms.com.ar/peliculas/trilogia.htm> (last accessed 2 August 2006).

3 From the English word 'picketers'. *Piqueteros* are people without work who block roads and highways as a way to protest and demand their rights.

4 The National Women's Meeting (Encuentro Nacional de Mujeres) was initiated by feminist groups in 1986 and is held each year in a different city. The event currently attracts more than 10,000 women representing different groups, social movements and political parties, or attending independently.

5 Held in August 2003.

6 For more about Bread and Roses and the 1912 textile workers' strike see: http://www.lucyparsonsproject.org/iww/kornbluh_bread_roses.html   (last accessed 15 October 2006).

7 See <http://www.pagina12.com.ar/diario/principal/index-2003-08-18.html> (last accessed 13 September 2006).

8 Among others: equal pay for equal work; distribution of work hours among employed and unemployed, with the same pay; free 24-hour child care provided by employers and the state in factories and workplaces; contraceptives to avoid abortions and the right to free and legal abortion to prevent death; and independent (from the police, the judicial system and the state) investigative commissions on crimes committed against women, to include people close to the victim, human rights organizations and other concerned parties.

9 Néstor Kirchner is the current President of Argentina, and is aligned with the Peronist party.

10 The Spanish-language term for female companions or partners. It is a term associated with comradeship.

11 See <http://www.rimaweb.com.ar> (last accessed 2 August 2006) and <http://www.argentina.indymedia.org> (last accessed 13 September 2006).

12 D'Atri, A. (2004), *Pan y Rosas. Pertenencia de género y antagonismo de clase en el capitalismo* (Bread and Roses: Gender Belonging and Class Antagonism in Capitalism), Las Armas de la Crítica, Buenos Aires, Argentina.

13 The Spanish-language term for male companions or partners. It is a term associated with comradeship (cf. *compañeras*).

14 This was a quote from James Oppenheim's poem 'Bread and Roses', inspired by one of the demonstrations which took place during the 1912 workers' strike in the United States. It is a poetic presentation of the demands of women workers. Martha Coleman set the poem to music, and the song has become part of the singing tradition of the American working class.

15 The Mirabals came to be known as 'the Butterflies' – the literal translation of their surname.

16 The location of the oil company in Patagonia that had promised to provide work for the women.

17 Zanon is a small town in the province of Neuquen, bordering on Chile.

18 See <http://www.quenoserepita.com.ar> (last accessed 13 September 2006), the official site of the victims' families.

19 D'Atri, A. (ed) (2006), *Luchadoras. Historias de mujeres que hicieron historia*

(Fighters – Stories of Women Who Made History), Instituto del Pensamiento Socialista, Buenos Aires.

20   In addition to the survey, and thanks to AWID's innovative seed grant, we have produced a video of interviews with women workers from different parts of the country.

21   See <http://www.cddc.vt.edu/feminism/arg.html>

3

A Jewish Orthodox Women's Revolution

The Case of Kolech

Margalit Shilo

The plight of Orthodox women in modern society

Notwithstanding the well-known verse 'The king's daughter is all glorious within',[1] from time immemorial it was exactly those women in Jewish society who 'came out' – such as the prophetesses Miriam and Deborah, and Queen Salome Alexandra – who earned the greatest recognition and esteem. However, traditionally and throughout history Jewish women have been excluded from the power bases of society: institutions of Torah[2] study, public service and communal religious services. In traditional Jewish society, women were regarded as a 'people unto themselves', credited mainly with enabling their menfolk to achieve greatness: 'Behind every successful man stands a woman.'

In the twentieth century, with the establishment of new societal norms, throughout the world many new opportunities arose for Jewish women – Orthodox[3] women included. The possibility of obtaining higher secular education in all disciplines, coupled with the almost unlimited prospects of advance in one's profession, only emphasized the remaining limitations and barriers to Orthodox women's progress in a patriarchal Orthodox society. In synagogues and Orthodox leadership, as well as institutions of Torah study, doors have been closed to women throughout history, and they have remained closed in modern times. The desire of Orthodox women to continue to observe religious tradition and frameworks has brought them face to face with a dissonant reality: impressive progress in secular society, but submission and self-effacement in the Orthodox one.

Is this paradoxical situation a ticking time bomb? While Orthodox women feel obliged to observe Orthodox law and adhere to frameworks dictated by patriarchal institutions, they also strive to re-examine the attitude of Jewish law (Halakhah) towards women. Some women have even gone so far as to attempt to penetrate and challenge this patriarchal system. The goal of creating a new social order in consonance with the feminist revolution as a whole is a characteristic of the Orthodox women's revolution. There is, I believe, a desire to reshape rather than seek a total break with Orthodox society as a whole.[4] In other words, an uncompromising loyalty to the overall framework (family, congregation, community) is sought while exhaustive efforts are made to modify that framework, and invest it with a new, egalitarian content. One might say that this feminine revolution is epitomized by the desire to have the best of both possible worlds.

This essay relates the activities that have led to the establishment and development of the first Orthodox feminist women's organization in Israel, discusses some of its goals, and outlines some of its important work and proposed strategies for success.

First steps towards an Orthodox women's revolution[5]

Over the last thirty years, Orthodox society in the land of Israel has witnessed several innovations that have challenged male hierarchy within the system. These have been of great significance in empowering Orthodox women, heightening their sense of empowerment, and stimulating their desire to organize themselves and fight for the achievement of their goals. Four important innovations should be mentioned.

The first of these was the establishment of *midrashot*, or centres for women and girls to study oral law at the post-secondary level. These sometimes included the study of the regular Talmud or oral law, and, since the 1980s, have spread rapidly throughout the religious Zionist camp.[6] Although Jewish women have been excluded from higher Torah study throughout the ages, it has now been accepted that there are no solid Halakhic grounds for such exclusion.

The second important achievement since 1990 has been the training of women as rabbinical lawyers. In Israel, matters relating to matrimony are dealt with in the rabbinical courts with the assistance of male rabbinical lawyers. The initiators of the concept of female rabbinical lawyers had two objectives in mind: to reinforce the voice of women who felt they were being silenced and discriminated against in the courts; and to support women in Halakhic negotiations and increase their awareness of their rights according to Halakhah. To date, about seventy women have been trained as rabbinical lawyers.

A third important innovation *vis-à-vis* Halakhic advice relates to *niddah* rules (regulations on matters regarding the ritually 'impure' state of a woman during and after menstruation). Until quite recently women in need of an Halakhic ruling on such matters have had to consult male rabbis, which was of considerable discomfort and embarrassment. It is now clear that women will more readily seek advice from other women on this issue, and that women are able to provide authoritative Halakhic answers to queries of this nature.

The appointment in 1988 of an Orthodox woman to the religious council in Yeroham, a town in southern Israel, was the fourth important achievement. Religious councils are charged with providing religious services to the community, such as ritual baths, advice regarding *Kashrut* (dietary laws), supervision, and burial facilities. Until then, all members of religious councils were men. However, the pioneering work of one Orthodox woman, Leah Shakdiel, managed to breach the hierarchy of this religious framework, and resulted in the Israeli Supreme Court ruling in favour of female membership of religious councils.

These achievements have been due to cooperation between Torah-educated women and a small number of rabbis in favour of an egalitarian approach. Despite arousing harsh opposition from the rabbinical establishment, they have become operational, and their success has proved not only that they are possible, but also that they answer a real need.

The founding of 'Kolech'

The formation of women's organizations, as distinct from co-opting women into men's organizations, is perceived as an extremely effective strategy for the achievement of women's goals.[7] It is in this way that women are able to strengthen their own self-awareness and refrain from adopting masculine norms.

The example of the Jewish Orthodox Feminist Alliance (JOFA),[8] founded in 1996 in the United States of America, inspired a few dozen Orthodox Israeli women to form Kolech: Religious Women's Forum to serve as a platform for a new initiative. One of the most important assets of the Israeli organization from its inception was its leader, Hanna Kehat. Kehat, in her late thirties, raised in a distinguished family of *haredi* (fervently orthodox/ultra-orthodox) Torah scholars and who later became a 'religious Zionist', proved to possess extraordinary leadership qualities. Over and above her intellectual capabilities and her knowledge of Halakhah and Jewish thought, she demonstrated tremendous sensitivity, perseverance, and dedication to the organization and its goals. A gifted speaker and mother of a large family, She had a personality that captivated all those who met her. Representatives of the press frequently interviewed her, seeking and airing her views on a wide variety of topics affecting women and Halakhah. The organization was virtually identified with her persona.

The name of the organization, Kolech: Religious Women's Forum, was chosen with the express intention of bringing the female voice to centre stage, inspired by a famous verse from Solomon's *Song of Songs*: 'let me hear thy voice; for sweet is thy voice'.[9] The address of the lover to his beloved 'may be interpreted ... as the unique promise of the Almighty, throughout human history, to listen to the female voice'.[10] The female voice must be restored to its proper place in history. This basic demand is being repeated again and again by women throughout the world, who have been silenced by patriarchal societies for centuries.

Kolech was created with the intention of having a fairly broad and flexible agenda that could respond to women's needs. The founders entertained the somewhat messianic hope that, in keeping with the religious belief in *tikun olam* – the imperative to repair the world – and the centrality of Torah values, women also wish to be part of this process through their spiritual contribution.[11] In a lecture delivered at the First International Kolech Conference (1999), the philosopher Yehuda Gelman cogently expressed the concept, implying that equality of women 'brings us toward the future realization of an absolute morality'.[12] The religious ideas advocated by Kolech, he argued, not only pose no threat to modern Orthodoxy, but could be considered as an aspect of *tikun olam*. Gelman convincingly conveyed the message that Kolech's mission is to purify Judaism, to transform it from a situation of 'temporary morality' – a deficient world – to a situation of 'absolute morality' – a perfect world – rather than simply improving the lot of women in religious society.

From theory to practice

Kolech's main goals are to alert Orthodox society at large to the inferior legal status of Jewish women, and to solve some very pressing specific problems mainly relating to marital laws. I shall briefly elaborate on these.

The organization first attracted public attention with a pamphlet – also called *Kolech* – discussing the weekly portion of the Torah reading. The novelty of these pamphlets was that they were generally both written and edited by women. These voiced their thoughts on the weekly Torah portion, Halakhic issues, homiletics, and various Torah subjects, which, up until 1998 had rarely been within the purview of Orthodox women. The articles published in *Kolech* placed the emphasis on issues of interest to women. However, their innovative focus aroused antagonism on the part of both a *Yeshiva*[13] teacher[14] who attacked them as 'not objective', and the former Sephardi Chief Rabbi Mordechai Eliahu, who actually ruled that it was forbidden to read them.[15]

Kolech achieved its most impressive public presence at four international conferences, held in Jerusalem between 1999 and 2005. Each of these was attended by more than 1,000 active participants. They received media attention in the general and Orthodox press, as well as through the electronic media. The questions that engaged all those following the progress of this new phenomenon were: Would it be possible to carry out a revolution without creating a total break with the Orthodox establishment? Or, put differently: Would women be able to modify the male-hierarchical character of Orthodox thinking? Would they be able to change the patriarchal character of religious society without infringing the integrity of Orthodoxy?

At the first conference, lectures were given on the subject of Torah learning for women, pointing out the possibilities and inherent dangers,[16] and presenting the question of how to relate to women's creative thought on Torah subjects and how it could be integrated with men's writings.[17]

The plenary sessions of the conferences also dealt with practical issues concerning women and family law, such as the problems of *agunot* (abandoned women) and women denied divorce, as well as sexual harassment and abuse, and the attitude of Orthodox society to abusers. These issues were deliberated at both the theoretical and practical levels. At the 2003 conference a battered wife told her life story, and another woman, a victim of long-standing sexual abuse, related how she came to grips with her situation. Problems were presented from a personal, emotional viewpoint, as well as examined from a theoretical perspective. This enabled Kolech to powerfully demonstrate its role, not just as an organization for academic deliberations, but also as a supporting arm for Orthodox women who refuse not only to remain silent but also to abandon their Orthodox way of life.

When an abused woman approached Hanna Kehat, Kolech's leader, she not only received a sympathetic ear but also had her story widely publicized. And although the Orthodox establishment responded with a veritable flood of condemnation of Kolech, the incident had a catalytic effect on attitudes to the problem. Kolech joined a colloquium of rabbis – including some not identified with its goals – and Orthodox women from several women's organizations, and contributed to drawing up a 'code of ethics' which served as a guide to rabbis and communal workers on how to provide advice to women on intimate and other matters. The mere convening of this colloquium was an open admission that relations between women and those in authority in Orthodox society were no longer under wraps. Henceforth, they would be totally transparent and subject to critical scrutiny. Guidelines were also drawn up on dealing with sexual abuse in religious institutions. These were formulated by a Kolech lawyer along the lines of a law enacted by the Knesset (the Israeli parliament) in 1998 on the prevention of sexual abuse.[18]

In addition to the concern for the legal aspects of sexual harassment, an educational team was established to draw up curricula for different age groups, to teach girls and boys egalitarian concepts – for Kolech members realized that the only way to ensure their adoption would be through education. Likewise, many other problems plaguing the Orthodox community, such as the large number of women who remain unmarried or marry late,[19] point to the need for innovative education that will help young men and women to maintain relationships in the new egalitarian society.

We still have a long struggle ahead as our goals are far from being fulfilled. Some of the most difficult questions that remain to be answered relate to the most effective strategy for their achievement.

Is the Orthodox revolution possible?
And what strategy should we adopt?

Is a new social order that alters women's image and status within Orthodox society a 'mission impossible'? Perhaps the opponents of Kolech are correct in their claim that one cannot change the Orthodox framework and, at the same time, expect to preserve it. Over the last eight years, there have been some positive developments in many of the areas dealt with by the organization. However, the fear that the feminist initiative would undermine the Orthodox framework has not declined, and opposition to Kolech in the religious community is as virulent as ever. The expression 'Hold back your voice,' a misquoted citation from the prophet Jeremiah, is heard more frequently than the original one, 'Hear ye my voice.'[20] Orit Kamir has pointed out that the women's revolution as a whole suffers from a split personality as it challenges patriarchal notions but refrains from calling for war against men.[21] This, she believes, explains the slow pace of the revolution. Indeed, while the preliminary achievements of Kolech are promising, they are also disappointing. The most serious problems, such as relief for *agunot* and the denial of divorces for women are still, to our disgrace, awaiting solutions. One wonders whether the slowness of the campaign is not an indication of an inherent defect.

An analysis of the radical changes that have taken place within the Israel Defence Forces over the past decade reveals that they were conditioned by several factors. A handful of women who untiringly demanded reform of the military system and were even ready to lead the way; cooperation with part of the male sector (in this case, the judicial system); and current social perceptions elsewhere (for example, in the US Army) as to the priority of egalitarian considerations even in the military framework, all contributed to these changes. A similar analysis of the efforts of religious women reveals that their revolution is clearly dependent on three main conditions. These are women's accomplishments in Torah learning and their consequent demand for real equality; close cooperation with at least some part of the male sector;[22] and acceptance throughout the western world of the principle of an egalitarian society.[23] As I have endeavoured to show, the religious women's revolution did not issue from a vacuum; it was and continues to be distinctly influenced by the achievements of women in society at

large. The various 'glass ceilings' that still block women's progress need
to be shattered. Only then will it be possible to dismantle the male-
rabbinical hierarchical system.

What is the correct strategy? Will organization, loud protests, and
publicity promote the desired goal? Or should we opt for intensive, non-
threatening, behind-the-scenes activities?[24] At a first glance, the success of
the *midrashot* might indicate that underplaying their importance is
effective; inroads are being made slowly but surely. However, the status
of women in the rabbinical courts is perhaps a counter-indication, as
cooperation with the system has brought only slight and slow results.
Can conclusions be drawn from other women's struggles? Esther Yeivin,
one of the active members in the secular Federation of Women for Equal
Rights, founded in Eretz Israel (the Land of Israel) in 1919, whose motto
was 'one law and one constitution for men and women in Israel', wrote
in no uncertain terms: 'In this battle [for voting rights for women in
Eretz Israel] women have learned an important lesson, namely, that the
solution of important problems cannot be postponed, and that one
cannot depend on others, always remembering [the saying], "If I am not
for myself who will be for me? And if not now, when?"'[25] In the struggle
for women's suffrage, the 'winning strategy' of elitist women consisted
of focusing exclusively on that issue, avoiding radical feminism, and
having faith in one's ability to bring about an overall change in the social
order.[26] Moreover, besides appreciating the leadership, the 'foot soldiers'
must also be taken into consideration, as well as the connection between
the specific struggle and other social changes.[27]

A wide-ranging review of history reveals that various significant
revolutions occurred in Jewish religion – such as the abolition of slavery.
May we hope that, in our time too, it will be possible to replace the
religious hierarchical system with an egalitarian one, or is this merely a
messianic, Utopian hope? We may assume that the three conditions
mentioned previously – women's achievements in the field of Torah,
cooperation with the male establishment, and society's general acceptance of egalitarianism – will facilitate this longed-for revolution. The
Kolech organization can work, together with the Orthodox establishment, towards the fulfilment of the first two conditions; the third lies
beyond our control. Although the struggle has focused on several
specific matters, its significance lies in the general revolt against the
gendered hierarchy. This revolt, which is the core of the struggle, is also
the root cause of the opposition it has aroused.[28]

NOTES

1   Psalms 45:14.
2   Torah is the entire body of Jewish religious law and learning, including both sacred literature and oral tradition.
3   Henceforth, the term Orthodox refers to Jewish Orthodox.
4   See Kamir, O. (2002), *Feminism, Rights, and Law* (Hebrew), On-Air University, Ministry of Defence, Jerusalem, p. 21; and Ruth Abrams (2000), *Jewish Women in the International Woman Suffrage Alliance 1899–1926*, Bell and Howell, Michigan, p. 10. Ruth Abrams does not believe that discrimination against women in Judaism was the cause of the particularly intensive activity of Jewish women in the struggle for suffrage.
5   Ross, T. (2004), *Expanding the Palace of Torah: Orthodoxy and Feminism*, Brandeis University Press/University Press of New England, Hanover and London, pp. 1–45.
6   So far there are 25 *midrashot* in Israel. See *Makor Rishon* (a weekly magazine), 27 January 2006, Section 5, p. 4.
7   Ross, T. (2004), *Expanding the Palace of Torah: Orthodoxy and Feminism*, Brandeis University Press/University Press of New England, Hanover and London, pp. 1–45.
8   See <http://www.jofa.org> (last accessed 9 September 2006).
9   *Song of Solomon*, 2: 14.
10 Chana Kehat, Opening Address, in Margalit Shilo (ed.), *To Be a Jewish Woman: Proceedings of the First International Conference, Woman and Her Judaism, 1999*, Jerusalem 2001 (hereafter *Jewish Woman*), p. 13.
11 *Ibid.*, p. 14.
12 Yehuda Gelman, 'Religious feminism and the theological challenge' (Hebrew), *Jewish Woman*, p. 41.
13 *Yeshiva* or *yeshivah* is an institution for religious studies attended by males.
14 Rabbi Gigi, in a public debate held in January 2004 under the auspices of the Zalman Shazar Center and the Israel Historical Society.
15 See: *Hozofe* (a daily newspaper), August, 2004.
16 Yuval Cherlow, 'Women's Torah learning – prospects and dangers' (Hebrew), *Jewish Woman*, pp. 67–72.
17 Rachel Keren, 'Scholarly women – where from and where to?' (Hebrew), *Jewish Woman*, pp. 77–82.
18 See *Kolech* No. 89, 2005.
19 Raising a family and giving birth are two of the fundamental aims of a practising Jew.
20 Jeremiah, 11: 4
21 See Kamir, O. (2002), *Feminism, Rights, and Law* (Hebrew), On-Air University, Ministry of Defence, Jerusalem, p. 21.

22   On the need for at least some assistance from the authorities see Introduction in Baker, J. H. (ed.) (2002), *Votes for Women: the Struggle for Suffrage Revisited*, OUP, New York, pp. 3–20.

23   The situation with regard to universal suffrage was similar as it is dependent on an overall societal transformation; see Susan Kingsley Kent (1987), *Sex and Suffrage in Britain 1860–1914*, Princeton University Press, Princeton, p. 195.

24   The question of the correct way to wage the struggle arose specifically in connection with the violent nature of the struggle for women's suffrage in England in the first half of the twentieth century. See Smith, Harold L. (1998), *The British Women's Suffrage Campaign 1866–1928*, Seminar Studies in History, Longman, London, pp. 15–20.

25   Yeivin, E. (1944), 'Twenty-five years of the federation for equal rights in Eretz Israel' (Hebrew), *The Federation of Jewish Women for Equal Rights in Eretz Israel. Twenty-Fifth Anniversary Volume*, December 1944, p. 10.

26   Fowler, R. B., and S. Jones, 'Carrie Chapman Catt and the last years of the struggle for woman suffrage: "The Winning Plan"', in Baker, J. H. (ed.) (2002), *Votes for Women: the Struggle for Suffrage Revisited*, OUP, New York, pp. 130–42.

27   Baker, J. H. (ed.) (2002), *Votes for Women: the Struggle for Suffrage Revisited*, OUP, New York, pp. 3–20.

28   Purvis, J. and S. Holton (eds) (2000), *Votes for Women*, Routledge, London and New York.

4

An Insight into Feminist Organizations

Yamini Mishra and Nalini Singh

This essay is not a formal work based on organizational development or feminist theories; nor does it target any particular organization or individual. More simply, it reflects on several years' experience working with a wide variety of women's, feminist and other organizations – some national, others regional and international, and all in the non-profit sector with a commitment to human rights and social justice. We wish to do no more than share personal experiences, perceptions and analyses.

This essay draws the reader's attention to some of the pressing issues that challenge feminist organizations. Although it discusses some of the broader socio-political developments that define the external environment, the focus is on challenges posed from within. It also proposes some avenues to be explored in seeking solutions to some of these challenges.

Feminist organizations?

Feminist organizations are a rare species. There are organizations that work on women's issues, gender issues and women's rights but only rarely refer to themselves as feminist. There is a general feeling that feminism has become vilified in many parts of the world, with its protagonists being perceived as man-haters, bra-burners, fundamentalists, home-breakers, women–with–their–hair–cut–short, women–who–don't–wax–their–legs, etc. How simple it would be for those of us

35

who have struggled tirelessly for women's rights and waged difficult battles, if all our problems could be boiled down to such simple misconceptions!

While on the one hand there are individuals and organizations struggling for the same causes for which we in the feminist movement are struggling, but who shy away from the term *feminist*, on the other, there are those others who call themselves 'feminist' but who clearly do not embrace feminist principles. For example, there was a woman in one of our training sessions who insisted she belonged to a feminist organization but argued passionately against abortion, considering it totally wrong under any circumstances. This left us wondering: who is a feminist? There are those who do not want to be called feminists – although they defend feminist causes (such as women's rights, gender justice, and dismantling patriarchy), share feminist values, challenge all sites of power and oppression, and struggle to create a world that is more just. Are we to consider them as feminists? Or should any woman who wants to call herself a feminist be considered one – even if she is opposed to something as basic as abortion rights for women?

The external challenges we face

In order to understand the challenges from within it is necessary for us first to take a look at some external ones, and particularly those of a socio-political nature that are tending to compound women's struggles. Today, the resurgence of fundamentalist forces in several countries, particularly in the Asia-Pacific region, and the coming to power of military and right-wing regimes are resulting in more blatant violations of women's human rights. In our experience, Malaysia, India, Pakistan and Iraq are a few of the countries which offer sad examples of the growing power and influence of fundamentalist groups that are increasingly defining what is culturally 'acceptable' and morally 'right' – and even, in some cases, institutionalizing these norms through national laws and policies.

Such forces have led to government-sanctioned oppressive practices against women, including restrictions on mobility, the denial of access to education, and the curtailment of freedom of expression as well as other fundamental freedoms. In conflict situations, battles are being fought over women and their bodies, seen as symbols of the honour of their cultures and communities. Fundamentalist religious forces appear to be uniting in an 'unholy alliance' against women. This reality became clear at the 1994 International Conference on Population and Development, when the Roman Catholic Church joined conservative Islamic forces in opposing women's rights. The conservative government in Japan is also pushing to amend Article 24 of its constitution on gender equality in the interests of 'protecting the family'. The US-led wars in Afghanistan and Iraq have resulted in innumerable deaths and scores of other forms of human rights violations, and women are now frequently used to justify these conflicts that are being carried out 'to save imperilled Muslim women'. In addition, the efforts of the United States of America to undermine the International Criminal Court, by, for example, its attempt to dilute the text of the Beijing Platform for Action, and by denying women the right to abortion, have a direct impact on women in Third World countries. There is strong evidence to suggest collusion between the US, the World Bank, the International Monetary Fund and the World Trade Organization in defending their positions and attempting to create a unipolar world in which the voices of the least-developed countries, the poor and women are not heard. The market logic of unfettered globalization has had a direct impact on the lives of women and resulted in aggravated – and sometimes new – forms of violence. Deregulation, privatization and liberalization have led to the erosion of traditional livelihoods and the displacement of communities. A greater number of conflicts over increasingly scarce resources have made women more vulnerable both to domestic and other forms of violence and violations of their rights as human beings.

Challenges from within

While external factors have an impact on major issues such as social justice among women, modes of internal organization and power structures within groups represent a whole range of equally debilitating challenges. As these challenges are many and vary considerably between organizations, this chapter only considers those of relevance to feminist organizations.

It is our opinion that feminist organizations, by their very nature, attract a particular kind of individual. Of course there is diversity, but there are also some basic commonalities. For example, women attracted to and keen to work with feminist organizations generally have strong characters and are defiant; they are frequently single and are united in their willingness to take a stand against an all-pervasive patriarchy. Our interaction with women working in feminist organizations also persuades us that they are more motivated by social aims than materialistic ones. It is also our opinion that the management of women who are attracted to feminist organizations is often more challenging due to their strong characters, as mentioned above.

We have also observed that some feminist organizations place excessive emphasis on processes often to the detriment of ends. When so many perspectives need to be considered, it often takes too much time and energy to decide on the means by which something needs to be done. Debates on processes – on whether something was done correctly or incorrectly – have a tendency to become overbearing, time-consuming and inefficient from the managerial perspective. Effective managers, therefore, need to have a variety of skills: to be democratic but not let themselves be swayed by popular opinion; to respect diverse viewpoints and build consensus; to decentralize operations but ensure targets are met; and, finally, to deal with the likelihood that, at the end of the process, there are still likely to be voices of dissent.

Feminism is a fight against all types of abuse of power and oppression: against hierarchy, subordination, and power structures. While in principle feminist organizations aspire to these goals, in reality, individuals and women are products of the societies in which they grow up, and are often unprepared for life within non-hierarchical egalitarian structures. We have observed that most feminist organizations thus have a matriarch who seeks control over the organization, and has little tolerance of challenges. Heads of women's organizations and their management structures often play power games with subordinates which run counter to the ideals of feminist thinking, and double standards abound. Programme officers, for example, have their work mandates – or 'territories' – clearly delimited, and are averse to intrusions into what they regard as exclusive domains. An administrative officer, for example, might respond to or interact with an executive director, a programme officer or anyone else higher up the hierarchical ladder in one manner; while those 'below' her on that same ladder might well be treated according to a different set of standards. Another example is the testimony of secretaries, who frequently feel the real brunt of their power-wielding 'superiors' and have often been heard to say they were happier with their male, non-feminist boss than with their female feminist one! Another common form of abuse of power that runs against the feminist grain is the ill-treatment of domestic staff.

This flagrant conflict between principles and practice is typical of women who are not yet ready to assume responsibility for the implementation of the principles to which they aspire. This represents one of the greatest challenges facing the feminist movement. Although, thankfully, this is not the norm, there are many aspiring feminists who are disillusioned by this state of affairs and who recognize the urgent need to build consensus on feminist principles and practice. This is so critical that the very essence of feminist organizations is at stake.

A fine line along which to walk

Another delicate issue is the fine line along which many non-governmental organizations (NGOs) have to walk. Unlike private enterprise, which charges for its products or services, NGOs are answerable to two distinct stakeholders: the people and communities they serve, and the funding agencies on which they depend for sustenance. Although balancing answerability is complicated and has always created internal conflicts, there is a permanent need to seek this compromise: if one stakeholder is sacrificed for the sake of the other, the organization falls into crisis.

While this holds true for many NGOs, the challenge is doubly difficult for feminist organizations, as experience with several of them has shown that fundraising for feminist organizations is particularly onerous. In the case of Scandinavian countries, in which gender equality has been achieved, they are no longer interested in funding feminist organizations as they consider the battle to be already won. So if we persist in promoting a feminist agenda they tend to feel that the issue is now being overstated. However, we have noted that organizations have a better chance of funding if they are presented as proponents of women's rights.

As several funding agencies consider the issue of gender as simply one type of project among others, we need to work harder to ensure that it is understood as an integral part of our perspective on life that informs each and every aspect of our work.

Another challenge is that feminist organizations are also under constant pressure from aid agencies to hire men, being instructed 'not to burn your bridges with men' and to include them in their projects. However, we fail to understand why, if the patriarchal world in which we live ensures a blanket discrimination against women – with innumerable workplaces consciously hiring no women – people are so upset when there are just a few all-women workplaces. These represent a form of affirmative action prompted by the community of women that historically has been marginalized and discriminated against. History has shown that rights are not granted: they usually have to be torn from those in power. With limited resources, the focus needs to be on empowering historically discriminated-against communities so they are in a position to demand their rights. It cannot and should not be the other way round. Men need to come to terms with relinquishing some of their privileges.

Reporting to funding agencies also poses difficulties as quantifiable indicators to check levels of efficiency usually take precedence over qualitative ones. Yet processes – such as learning – are themselves often more important than the end (quantifiable) results, as they add important qualitative value to the organizations. For example, an organization might create 100 income-generating or micro-credit groups for women and meet the proposed indicator. But what has really been achieved if the women are using the income to pay a higher dowry, or are unable to control increased domestic violence that results from their contributing to income generation and thus upsetting the power distribution within the households?

With whom should we form alliances?

Another challenge facing women's organizations is the choice of collaborating organizations. One of the major criticisms of the feminist movement is our tendency to be introspective; we only work with the converted. In the past, one of the women's organizations with which we were professionally related attempted to work with a mainstream human rights organization that had little interest in the issue of gender. Sometimes the engagement was fulfilling, sometimes not. It is important for us to assess the real rationale behind the male-dominated organizations that try to work with us. Are they really seeking our collaboration as a result of their commitment to gender issues, or are they simply responding to their donor's criteria which require that gender concerns be addressed? Engagement in situations such as these is rarely satisfactory, and in the end feminist organizations often feel they would have done better to focus their limited resources elsewhere.

God, I am tired...

The pervasiveness of patriarchal systems makes it all the more important for feminist organizations to assess their priorities critically and choose their battles accordingly. Overextending ourselves and exhaustion are problems that affect many feminists and the organizations they represent. The continuous pressure for us to be different, to set higher standards and to meet higher expectations also adds to the levels of stress. How we manifest our feminism is also an issue that we need to address: 'you are not feminist enough', or the one-upwomanship of 'more feminist than thou' and the accompanying ethos places constant pressure on women to prove themselves and their commitment to feminist ideology. While it is important to develop a critical perspective on mainstream feminist issues, it is important that space be given to those who wish to criticize something, even if to do so is deemed 'un-feminist.'

What remains to be done?

Thankfully, feminists have also provided the solution to most of the above-mentioned problems. 'Personal is Political'[1] was the call from feminists who considered that the appropriation of this message would save and strengthen the feminist movement and its organizations. It is important that we stop believing that one can become a feminist by reading books or forming part of feminist circles, which can, at best, provide stimulation. One can become a feminist only from within, as the saying goes: 'the greatest battles are fought within'. Living from inside out is important. Gandhian principles of non-violence, peace, truth, love and above all, living one's own life according to the principles one advocates, could be one direction to consider.

Equally important is the need to respond creatively to the challenges of an ever-changing world through new approaches to and forms of feminism. Many feminist organizations have started to work on issues such as globalization, militarism and various forms of fundamentalism, and to address such contemporary challenges with fresher, innovative approaches and new perspectives.

To adequately face these challenges some feminist organizations are working towards ensuring that processes and systems are established so that important decisions are not taken arbitrarily or on an *ad hoc* basis, and that discretionary powers of heads of organizations are limited and saved for strategic interventions. It has also been discussed that the rationale behind decisions needs to be explained as far as possible, and that transparency and accountability need to be built into decision-making processes. Monitoring and control systems should be established to ensure these processes function adequately and are not abused or circumvented for personal gain. In this sense several organizations have developed clear procedural guidelines in a participatory manner, and for the use of all concerned. Such guidelines are not set in concrete but require periodical reviews in the light of the changing situations in the workplace and elsewhere. Regular independent evaluations of processes and decisions have also been observed as a positive step in ensuring effective accountability.

Feminist women also need to remember that the future of the movement is in our own hands. The kind of image we project will either expand and strengthen the movement or leave people dis-illusioned and desirous of abandoning it. Feminists – and especially the more experienced ones – are becoming increasingly aware that there is a need to inspire, motivate, mentor and encourage younger women to keep the fire burning in the next generation. Most importantly, as feminists we need always to practise what we preach and not just pay lip service to the movement.

We cannot afford to be anchored in the past and should not discount or discredit new and innovative ideas with proclamations such as 'What do you know of how it was before?' or 'What would you know of the battles we fought to bring the movement to where it is today?'

It has also been suggested that strategic planning should be undertaken as part of a participatory consensus-building process within and between organizations to identify suitable partnerships, prioritize issues of importance, define work programmes, and thus facilitate decision-making processes so as to optimize our chances of making a real difference. It is this strategic planning process that will enable us to choose the battles that we can and need to win.

One question with which we often grapple is: if patriarchy were indeed to be replaced by a feminist social order, would we be able to give the world anything better? On a bad day, we would say 'no' and on a good day 'we hope', – but today we have told ourselves with conviction, 'Yes'!

NOTE

1   'Personal is Political' is a phrase that is widely used within the women's
    movement. At the risk of oversimplification, we think this means that
    everything that is personal also has a political aspect. It challenges the divide
    between 'the home', historically the site of most of women's experiences, and
    'the outside politicized world'. It 'authorizes the private, subjective experience
    of the individual woman to be read in terms of/for its significance with respect
    to larger issues, to stand as/for "the issues" of contemporary society'. See Mary
    S. Leach (1987), 'Is the personal political?' *Philosophy of Education*, ed.,
    Nicholas Burbules, Philosophy of Education Society, Illinois. Vol. 1987,
    169–81.

5

Empowering Womanspace

Power Distribution and Dynamics
in Christian Feminist Community

Kelsey Rice and Ann Crews Melton

Finding womanspace:
one woman's coordinating committee experience

My[1] first year of university included the clichéd experience of losing my faith, as I emerged from an East Texas Christian evangelical bubble into a liberal arts microcosm of expanded horizons. I reluctantly attended a Presbyterian-affiliated conference the following summer, and was delightfully surprised to meet several trendy Christian feminists belonging to the National Network of Presbyterian College Women.

After that event, I applied for a position on the coordinating committee of the National Network of Presbyterian College Women (NNPCW). I sought to connect better with the cool women I had met; it was only later that I began to understand that the safe spaces facilitated by NNPCW were the outcome of intentional work toward inclusiveness and conscious decisions to level power dynamics. During my tenure on the coordinating committee, I served as co-moderator of the network for a one-year term, facilitating meetings with another woman as we overlapped in a fluid model of shared leadership.

My experience with NNPCW taught me ways to facilitate consensus-model decision making, encourage mutual invitation in meetings, and model mutuality within a patriarchal corporate hierarchy. I began a chapter of NNPCW on my local college campus, creating a safe space for women to connect and explore spirituality. I am only one woman changed by finding a spiritual feminist home within NNPCW, and, due to that time of nurture and growth, will continue to expand the web of non-hierarchical organizing as women everywhere challenge all forms of oppression and struggle toward a truly inclusive, beloved community.

The National Network of Presbyterian College Women

The National Network of Presbyterian College Women is a ministry sponsored by the Presbyterian Church (USA),[2] comprised of up to 500 'young women in college, connected by our belief in God, seeking to understand what it means to claim a Christian faith that empowers women'.[3] It is a nationwide network of collegiate Christian feminists from the Presbyterian Church and other Christian traditions, including United Methodists, Moravians, and Roman Catholics, to name just a few of the backgrounds represented. This organization hopes to provide opportunities for young feminists of faith to integrate their spiritual experience with an analysis of oppression based on gender, race, class and sexuality.

This unique outreach to young women began as a pilot project in 1993. At that time, twelve young women from colleges and universities around the country came together to form the network's coordinating committee, an officially recognized governing body of the Presbyterian Church that carries out the mission, commitments and objectives of the network at the national level.

The coordinating committee exists as the locus of a far-flung and non-hierarchical web of connections between campus groups, individual members, and other various components of the network. This same committee also functions effectively within the traditional structure of the Presbyterian Church. This case study focuses on the use of power-equalizing tools and strategies in the coordinating committee from 2000 to 2005, highlighting the group's triple functions as a feminist 'woman-space',[4] a governing council, and a spiritual community, and demonstrating a dedication to shared leadership as a model for change. Its commitments to inclusive community and non-hierarchical leadership, nestled in a corporate organizational hierarchy, effectively show how feminist groups can model power sharing to established structures from within.

Coordinating committee as womanspace

The coordinating committee has always been considered a governing body within the larger structure of the Presbyterian Church, under the auspices of the Church's General Assembly. Yet its relationship with a patriarchal institution is problematic. As Anna Fels points out in her psychological study of women and ambition, 'girls and women change their behaviors when their interactions involve men' by being more deferential and less assertive.[5] Generally, forces of sexism, ageism and, in many cases, racism work against individual young women if they attempt to speak out within the Church, driving them away from religious institutions altogether. Young women have a low level of perceived power to influence the Church, leading to either acceptance or abandonment of the established patriarchy. Neither response leads to transformative social change within the institution.

When minority groups experience a low level of perceived power, change only occurs when the minority comes together to speak to the established order.[6] This necessitates a place for young women in the Church to share their stories with one another and strategize action. As a result, the coordinating committee functions first and foremost as 'womanspace': a place where young women enter into the feminist ethic of personal experience.

The committee creates a safe space for leadership development by intentionally eliminating several sources of hierarchy. Its meetings are restricted to female-only space, thereby diminishing the potential for a power imbalance with male presence. Although the committee recognizes the role men play in a united struggle for gender justice, it also acknowledges the way women are socialized to interact in the presence of men. They therefore choose to create a safe space for nurture and woman-only care.

As the committee is also comprised of young adult women, systemic inequities such as ageism are reduced, with no older matriarchal influences to command an authoritarian presence even within a community of women. The young women find empowerment through leadership amongst perceived equals – a safe space through which to explore their own identities, form spiritual community and gain experience in speaking out on issues of importance in a Church business setting. Through this model of empowerment, the women can then venture forth into other arenas and maintain a voice of legitimacy and self-confidence, even when the added dynamics of older adults and males are present.

A third component integral to the coordinating committee's construction of womanspace is creating a safe space for women of differing sexual orientations and racial or ethnic backgrounds. The committee is aware that historically the women's movement all too often has been dominated by upper-middle-class, white, heterosexual Western women. The committee also struggled through affiliation with a denomination that is likewise comprised of predominantly privileged white individuals, and has sought to model a safe space for women of colour and queer[7] women within the larger Church that may not always be so welcoming. The committee consciously seeks to incorporate members of diverse racial and ethnic backgrounds in its application process, and, in an effort to circumvent tokenism, facilitates open dialogue around issues of race and white privilege. The committee has also consistently included women of varying sexual identities, and maintains a commitment to inclusion of queer and straight women even while the larger denomination holds an ambivalent policy regarding civil unions for queer couples and does not endorse lesbian, gay, bisexual or transgender (LGBT) ordination.

Through levelling all of these dynamics within womanspace, the coordinating committee intentionally challenges the power inequities that broader society has come to accept as normative, specifically hierarchies of gender and age, while being conscious of systems of privilege such as heterosexism, racism and classism.

Coordinating committee as governing council

The Presbyterian Church conducts its business using a parliamentary system. Committees of the Church debate policies using *Robert's Rules of Order*[8] and make recommendations to larger decision-making bodies, who then vote on recommendations. The system, while honouring individual conscience in the voting process, focuses on conflict and combat as the way to reach decisions. One side always wins and one side loses. Moreover, the 'majority rules' ethic limits the ability of this process to incorporate the views of minorities. Women, people of colour, and other socially marginalized groups often lose to the white male majority. The parliamentary system ultimately perpetuates the *status quo*.

Like all other committees of the Church, higher governing bodies give the coordinating committee the authority to make decisions for the membership of the National Network of Presbyterian College Women. However, the committee deviates from the parliamentary norm as it is infused by the feminist ethic of non-hierarchical leadership models, and several power-distributing methods for dialogue and decision-making are built into the group's manual of operations.

Two co-moderators, nominated by a sub-committee of the larger coordinating committee, facilitate meetings. The leadership position is quite fluid. With staggered terms of service, power is never concentrated in the same two members of the committee from meeting to meeting.

It is the task of the co-moderators to ensure that the diverse voices of twelve women are heard in all discussions. Yet for the coordinating committee and its parent denomination, lifting up the voices of the marginalized can be problematic. Even with the levelling dynamics of womanspace, how can women of widely varying backgrounds and sexual identities facilitate dialogue without white, heterosexual women dominating the conversation? Such an environment perpetuates those same cycles of patriarchy and dominance that feminism struggles to overcome. For example, in 2004 the coordinating committee counted one-quarter of its student membership as women of colour. These women included two African-Americans and two Latinas.[9] Yet the committee, which also nominates college women to other leadership positions in the Church, struggled to find women of colour when called upon to staff several task forces. Nor does the mere presence of women of colour change the level of perceived power those women hold in a predominately European American group.

The coordinating committee has worked to address this issue through the use of mutual invitation as a tool for dialogue in Church business sessions.[10] Mutual invitation, outlined by Chinese-American priest Eric H. F. Law,[11] works to break down barriers that prevent effective communication by eliminating power differentials. Within the committee, the model works as follows: a co-moderator poses a question for the group to consider. She then invites another student in the circle to speak. This woman has the option to pass on the question, but when she is finished, she must invite another woman to speak until all have had an opportunity to address the issue at hand. As Law says in *The Wolf Shall Dwell with the Lamb: a Spirituality for Leadership in a Multicultural Community*: 'Mutual invitation gives everyone the experience to exercise power. It also offers the opportunity to use power again and again. The repeated experience of power enables powerless people eventually to claim their share of power with ease and comfort.'[12]

Not only is this experience crucial to ensuring that women of colour in the group have an opportunity to exercise power, but it functions as a model in which every woman, used to being silenced in the larger Church structure, claims a voice.

The committee's use of mutual invitation relates very closely to its main method of coming to decisions, the consensus model of decision making.[13] Crucial to this alternative governing procedure is the balance between individual voices and communal decisions. When a group chooses to make a decision by consensus, the co-moderator poses the decision under consideration to the group. The group discusses the issue, often using mutual invitation to ensure that all voices are heard. If members seem to be moving toward agreement, a co-moderator conducts a 'consensus check': after stating the decision that seems to be emerging, the co-moderator asks each woman whether they consent to this choice. If there is still dissent, the group continues to consider. When all can agree to a particular decision, the group claims consensus. Though a slow process, consensus usually results in a decision that all participants personally own.

In the consensus model of decision making, members block consensus only as a last resort. The ability to block means that no one person can be coerced into supporting a decision that contradicts her conscience. Her voice will be heard and honoured by the process. The result of a consensus block is a majority vote, as in the parliamentary process. Yet the group must officially acknowledge that they did not reach consensus, and that not everyone supported the decision. In the coordinating committee's experience, even blocked consensus helps build a communal ethic that recognizes the marginalized.

Mutual invitation and consensus decision making are models that the coordinating committee spreads not only to the denomination, but also to its own college-age constituents in an interconnected informational web. This committee does not 'head' NNPCW, but rather coordinates the work of all members through non-hierarchical connecting strands. It circulates materials and information, provides the impetus for a national leadership-training event, and directs new initiatives of the network. It certainly does not tell members or Christian feminist groups on campuses what they need. The committee attempts to relate to NNPCW's members with the same type of autonomy that it claims from the denomination, empowering young women to find their own solutions to struggles of gender justice in their lives.

Coordinating committee as spiritual community

The basis for the coordinating committee's equitable power distribution is unique in that the committee integrates a feminist ethic of non-hierarchical organization with the spiritual tenet that all are equal in the eyes of God. Thus it operates as a spiritual community, ardently striving to include rather than exclude, while creating a safe space to explore questions of personal belief.

Business meetings of the committee open with a devotion or prayer, frequently featuring feminine imagery of God, women-focused songs or wisdom from non-canonical texts marginalized within patriarchal Christianity. The committee grounds its spiritual practice in a theology derived from women's experience, utilizing the work of academic theologians and the writings of women who express their own unique images of the divine forged from diverse life perspectives. The committee, in its own practice and interaction with other Church bodies, intentionally lifts up and celebrates the works of womanist,[14] *mujerista*[15] and feminist theologians. This asserts that such theologies are integral, rather than marginal, to the life and spirit of the Church.

The coordinating committee recognizes its positioning not only within the broader women's movement, but also within a pluralistic society. It thus creates space for women of diverging beliefs within the Christian theological spectrum, as well as respect for interfaith concerns. The by-laws of the coordinating committee require the inclusion of a non-Presbyterian, which illustrates a commitment to ecumenical voices. Moreover, the coordinating committee networks groups that allow for spiritual exploration, and so welcomes those whose belief systems may or may not align with mainstream Christianity. Because the committee facilitates a decentralized network of local campus groups and individual membership, each group can self-determine how to identify as a spiritual community. For example, the campus group mentioned in the introduction is a spiritual women's community affiliated with NNPCW, but includes individuals who identify as Wiccan, agnostic, and Christian. Members may agree to disagree on specific doctrine or even on affiliation with organized religion, but can find common ground in recognizing a nurturing, spiritual entity connecting each woman to an interdependent community much larger than herself.

At each gathering of the coordinating committee – usually held at a conference or retreat centre over a number of days – the women have a chance to interact not solely through the Church business meetings, but through sharing communal space and the responsibilities that further the common good. One night of the meeting is devoted to 'check-in', during which women share reflections, joys or concerns about their lives – once again modelled through mutual invitation, where each woman is granted unique space to speak and be heard. During the final meeting of the year, committee members completing their terms receive a candlelight ritual of affirmation, where other members who name the strengths that she brings to the group honour each woman. These simple rituals remain vital in the formation of a spiritually empowered community that models egalitarian respect, whether taking turns doing the dishes or highlighting unique spiritual gifts.

Finally, the coordinating committee strives not just to facilitate a womanspace of nurture and rest, but moves upon the spiritual tenet that enacts a vision of God's equitable love and justice. It speaks with a prophetic voice to the larger Church, calling it to recognize ways in which its own exclusionary patriarchy denies the Gospel of Christ. Central to this broader outreach is the merging of God's inclusive, egalitarian love with feminist goals of deconstructing systems of patriarchy.

Conclusion

As a small enclave of non-hierarchical feminism entrenched within a patriarchal institution, the coordinating committee of the National Network of Presbyterian College Women takes advantage of the system to create revolutionary change. By intentionally creating a womanspace that operates with egalitarian tools for dialogue and decision making, buttressed by a theological ethic affirming equality, the committee provides a working example to the Presbyterian Church of new direc- tions for spiritually and socially active communities of faith. However, the structure of the coordinating committee need not be limited solely to spiritual communities. Within feminist organizations, the strategies the committee uses to level power differentials can apply to working groups, grassroots organizing collectives, and governing boards. The key lies in intentionality; by recognizing the intersecting levels of inequality at work in all social interactions and using the coordinating committee's tools to address them, women can create proverbial mustard seeds of empowerment that transform patriarchal structures.

NOTES

1 Although this chapter describes the experiences of both authors with the National Network of Presbyterian College Women, the first section relates specifically to Ann Crews Melton as a student participant.

2 This and all further mentions of the Presbyterian Church refer to the Presbyterian Church (USA), the largest of several Presbyterian denominations in the United States.

3 'National Network of Presbyterian College Women Mission Commitments and Objectives' (2002), *Women's Ministries Area*, 2002: 2, Louisville, Kentucky.

4 We use this term in NNPCW to refer to the woman–only space created for dialogue and worship among participants. See the section 'Coordinating committee as womanspace' for a further discussion of the term.

5 Fels, A. (2004), *Necessary Dreams: Ambition in Women's Changing Lives*. Pantheon Books, New York, p. 41.

6 Law, E. H. F. (1993), *The Wolf Shall Dwell with the Lamb: a Spirituality for Leadership in a Multicultural Community*. Chalice Press, St Louis, Missouri, p. 19.

7 We use the word 'queer' intentionally, as the lesbian, bisexual and transgender constituency of NNPCW tends to prefer this term. Young adult women are reclaiming 'queer' as a positive identifier since it is less categorical [than LGBT – lesbian, gay, bisexual or transgender] and more inclusive for women who may be questioning their sexual identity.

8 *Robert's Rules of Order* is a reference handbook that standardizes and explains parliamentary law for civic organizations. Written by Henry Martyn Robert in 1876, the handbook, currently in its tenth edition, is codified in the Presbyterian Church's constitution as the reference manual for the Church's governing process.

9 A term commonly used to refer to women of Latin American origin residing in the United States of America.

10 For online resources on the use of mutual invitation in other group settings, see 'Bible Studies Using Eric Law's Community Bible Study Process', *Presbyterian Peacemaking Program*, at <http://www.pcusa.org/peacemaking/iraq/biblestudies.htm> (last accessed 15 September 2006).

11 We mention Law's ethnicity only to illustrate his exclusion within certain power structures. As authors, we find it unfortunate that omission of ethnicity means assumed whiteness, particularly within Western normative paradigms.

12 Law, E. H. F. (1993), *The Wolf Shall Dwell with the Lamb: a Spirituality for Leadership in a Multicultural Community*. Chalice Press, St Louis, Missouri, p. 87.

13   Several resources are available online to explain further the use of consensus decision making. See 'Consensus Decision Making,' *Act Up Civil Disobedience Resource Guide,* available at <http://www.actupny.org/documents/CDdocuments/Consensus.html> (last accessed 15 September 2006), and *Seeds for Change: Workshop and Training for Grassroots Campaigners,* available at <http://seedsforchange.org.uk/free/consens> (last accessed 15 September 2006); *Consensus Overview,* People and Planet Groups Guide, available at <http://noncms.peopleandplanet.org/groups/guide/guide.consensus.php>; and, of course, NNPCW's own web guide, *NNPCW Consensus Model of Decision Making, National Network of Presbyterian College Women,* available at <http://www.pcusa.org/nnpcw/resources/consensus-model.htm>   (last accessed 15 September 2006); and see also Rice, K. (2004), 'I Consent? Understanding the Consensus Model of Decision Making,' *Horizons: The Magazine for Presbyterian Women,* March/April 2004: 20–1.

14   Womanist theology is the study of God from the perspectives and experiences of African-American women. Like *mujerista* theology, it brings together elements of feminist theology, liberation theology, and cultural theology to examine the Bible in the light of the social location and cultural history of African-American women.

15   *Mujerista* theology brings together elements of feminist theology, Latin American liberation theology and cultural theology.

Part 2

Revisiting Organizational Practices

6

New Democratic Exercises in Mexican Feminist Organizations

The internal dynamics of Mexican feminist organizations have been transformed in recent years. Left behind is the idealized self-management model in which equality was considered a fundamental principle that guided the participation of all members. Also left behind is the desire to exercise a radical and unfettered participatory democracy, and the perception of feminism as a finite and acquired expression measured according to the parameters of an idealized movement. These practices had frequently led to paradoxical situations and deep conflicts as none of them took into account the contradictory processes that feminist women had to face on a day-to-day basis at the organizational level.[1]

Over time and with increasing experience, several Mexican feminist organizations have attempted to reduce friction between the ideal and reality[2] by setting out complex collective learning processes. These have included the continual reconstruction of mechanisms, tools and instruments to ensure the democratic, efficient and effective participation of all their members.

This essay explores a part of the institutional experience of Salud Integral para la Mujer (total health for the woman) known as SIPAM, a leading Mexican feminist organization that defends women's sexual and reproductive health. Its history, which began in 1987, is characterized by a multiplicity of processes interwoven in a tapestry of what could be considered vital contributions to the strengthening and burgeoning of current feminist expressions.

The history of SIPAM –
a heterogeneous mosaic

Headquartered in the Federal District of Mexico, SIPAM is a feminist and civil organization currently working with women and youth. It focuses on political promotion, and advising and lobbying around three central themes – maternal mortality, women with HIV/AIDS, and citizenship[3] – which are approached from the paradigm of sexual and reproductive health within the framework of women's human rights.

The organization emerged during the second half of the 1980s, growing from a marginal position that was disconnected from the feminist expressions of the time. Today, it has distinguished itself as a pre-eminent feminist organization in the promotion and defence of the core of women's personal, cultural and political transformation: the free and enjoyable exercise of sexuality and sexual and reproductive rights. The organization has thus become a cornerstone of Mexican feminist militancy and organization in the wider context of Mexico's democratization process.

Whether SIPAM can achieve the gender mainstreaming to which it aspires – the projection of feminist values and demands into all sectors of society – depends on the resolution of internal tensions and surmounting external obstacles.[4] It has thus been necessary for SIPAM to undergo fundamental changes in its feminist essence and the way it operates: its 'being' and 'doing'. These changes have modified the way in which the organization perceives itself, and it has moved away from a rebellious, reactive stance to an intentional, proactive one. What is important is not its capacity for feminist resistance, but its ability to subvert dominant codes through a more reflective approach to day-to-day events and a modern political practice[5] that challenges social and cultural traditions and inertias with respect to gender.

These processes have been institutionalized through a modification of the organization's structure and routine relations, in an effort to link the organization's practical needs (access and control of resources, specific projects, etc.) more effectively and efficiently with strategic feminist needs (political demands, cultural changes, etc.).[6] The synthesis of these processes and the divergences arising within SIPAM are revealed in what we refer to as institutional milestones.

Institutional milestones

The most important moments of change in SIPAM's history have been registered in its collective memory as three institutional milestones that are, according to *Sipameras* (women members of SIPAM) highly illuminating.

These milestones have revealed an institutional complexity that has challenged members' unity. They have exposed multiple conflicts, imbalances and vicissitudes and have obliged the organization to examine internal processes creatively in an effort to resolve or adapt these issues to collective needs.

The first of these milestones, in 1996, involved the organization's first effort at strategic planning. This resulted in a plan that formally charted the organization's direction and course in the medium and long terms. The formal withdrawal from the organization of its founders (beginning in 1999) marked the second milestone. This involved a complex process and an extremely difficult change in leadership that resulted in an institutional crisis. The final milestone was identified with the breaking away of several SIPAM staff members in March 2002. This had its origin in a 1995 internal leadership crisis – the *Cocoyocazo*[7] – that resurfaced in 2002 and led to the resignation of the organization's director and eleven other members. These moves obliged the founders to take charge of the organization once again. This break-up, which current SIPAM staff members refer to as *el Sipum*, seriously jeopardized the organization's institutional viability.

These milestones are considered emblematic moments that obliged the collective to take controversial decisions that generated tension, problems and challenges. Although their resolution involved excisions and ruptures, there was no discussion of the subjective dynamics of daily operations or of leadership dynamics inside feminist collectives.

Power and leadership

In examining the various leaderships within SIPAM, it should be noted that the organization in its formative period was recognized as a small, tight-knit collective that generated an all-absorbing enthusiasm among its most committed members. This was largely due to internal experiments with and expressions of feminist and democratic identity. In sharing everyday life, particular rules emerged based on friendship, trust and respect for the opinions, preferences and ideas of all members.

In the early years of SIPAM, issues relating to internal democracy were immersed in a sort of denial of authority in an attempt to maintain rigidly egalitarian practices among staff. The organization was considered a vital space, not just in the conception, design and implementation of actions, but also in the sharing of transcendent experiences, and even in the awakening of feminist consciousness. Meetings were informal and flexible, a model that was often compared to a meeting of friends. From this perspective, democracy was not perceived as a matter of representation or responsibility, but as an authentic levelling out of power.

With respect to work dynamics, the idea among early members was that of sharing tasks, skills and abilities so that everyone could decide on all types of issues relating to the organization. For many staff members SIPAM became more than a workplace, and for others it became impossible to draw the line between their private lives and participation in the organization.[8] The constant extra time required by the organization was not considered excessive because the experience was considered as 'a friends' space'. However, as SIPAM grew[9] it became increasingly difficult to maintain egalitarian treatment and the limitations of friendships became apparent as internal leaderships began to consolidate.

What seems to have occurred in SIPAM is that as time went by and with the incorporation of new members it became impossible to include the entire collective in the circle of friends, and therefore the majority of the group remained *de facto* outside the space created by the handful of founding members who held greater leadership powers.

The internal strength and core identity of SIPAM, based on sisterhood and solidarity, reflected in the union of work and friendship, commitment and enthusiasm, the absence of formal rules, the prevalence of informality, insider jokes and even shared holidays, began to imply the exclusion of those who were not or did not feel part of the circle of leaders. For newcomers, these patterns were forms of internal selection, exclusion and hierarchy that created a differentiated status among staff members, giving the impression that 'all members were equal, but some were more equal than others'.

In the routine of daily organizational life, these situations caused degrees of discomfort that became accentuated as there were no means in place through which disagreements, internal conflicts and differences of opinion could be dealt with effectively without damaging the collective. The emphasis placed on an assumed shared experience and common interest discouraged tolerance of disagreement. This made it difficult and highly complicated to understand, process and find adequate solutions to internal problems, given the prevailing fear of offending or hurting 'friends' – synonymous with *compañeras*[10] – as well as the desire not to violate the principles of a militancy based on commitment to the feminist cause.

Decision making within SIPAM usually took place face-to-face in the context of meetings in which differences were considered to fly in the face of consensus. This, of course, contradicted the principle of participatory democracy, as this type of decision making is invariably defended by those with the self-confidence to satisfactorily articulate their position, and exercised by those who hold privileged positions within an organization based on their charisma, experience and/or leadership.[11] As a result SIPAM meetings were occasionally quite undemocratic, as members' proposals and opinions did not carry the same weight.

The seemingly innocent request for an opinion could turn into an uncomfortable act or a form of pressure. Open discussion, as a frequent practice in organizations, can be used as a form of censure of 'different' opinions. It may even become a source of veiled dispute in that all members not only know each other, but also share significant experiences in both their personal and work lives. Challenging 'group consensus' can thus become difficult and costly, since the subjective load and the emotional intent are likely to interfere with the day-to-day running of the organization.

In the case of SIPAM these situations came to a head at key moments – milestones – in the institution's history because some members considered conversations and agreements to be 'institutional secrets' that took place outside formal meetings among leaders who subsequently directed the agenda in meetings, constituting a powerful body with shared experiences that legitimized and strengthened their positions when facing 'the rest' of the collective.

At particular key moments, anger and disagreement by some members became vividly evident. Their position seemed to express an 'extreme' and even 'exaggerated' disgust that signalled a more 'radical' direction, almost as if it were necessary for them to accumulate an angry bravado in order to express their disagreement and shatter the apparent consensus. A closer look revealed that disagreements in SIPAM were often concealed or buried for periods of time. This resulted in their intensification and exacerbation, until they became a time bomb that would eventually reach a point of no return and explode in a thunderous way.[12] Meetings, therefore, could give either a false sense of harmony and accord, or result in exaggerated anger and disquiet.

It is necessary to identify some vital problems in the processes experienced within SIPAM. With the formal rejection of the nuances of equality in participation and an insistence on full equality in every aspect, democracy became ineffective due to the lack of definition in individual functions and responsibilities. In the absence of decision-making structures, procedures and mechanisms to control leaders' decisions were also precluded. The heavy reliance on face-to-face meetings tended to foster the concealment of possible conflicts, and false consensus as some members could feel pressured to feign agreement. The exercise of leadership and power became problematic inasmuch as it was based on ties of friendship and therefore was not necessarily perceptible as power. While recognized power can be subjected to democratic control processes, power that is denied or unrecognizable can become unlimited and capricious.

When these problems surfaced within SIPAM, members recognized the need for specialist help in individual and collective reflection on the lessons learned from the different crises with regard to structures for participatory democracy within the organization.

Constructing new democratic processes

Through the reflections that followed the institutional milestones, there is now a collective recognition that a totally democratic division of work is not viable, and any such effort is likely to be insufficient. Staff members of SIPAM have therefore focused their efforts on designing formal rules that are recognized and adopted by all members, and which define, to the extent possible, the division of labour within the organization based on specific tasks that are easily manageable by individuals or small teams, and for which there is a clear assignment of responsibilities.[13]

The underlying logic of this new internal structure is the control of resources and results through a work system that distributes specific tasks among members, endeavouring to overcome tensions and align the operational objectives (practical needs) with the institutional mission (strategic needs).

The work carried out by the *Sipameras* involves the daily exercise of feminist activism. In this regard, the organization asserts the importance of remunerating members' work commensurate with each one's responsibilities within the organization. Remuneration allows and enables the full-time dedication needed to ensure professionalism, specialization and quality, which, in turn, permits access to and diversification of the funding necessary for institutional viability.[14] Above all, remuneration is important, as a means of compensating effort, work and feminist commitment.

The *Sipameras* recognize that the enthusiasm generated by a committed militancy does not mean that women should 'forget about themselves' when they participate in a collective project. Not every feminist can be expected to live only for the collective cause; rather, each one should aspire to fill her day-to-day life with content, meaning and vitality as part of the cause.

Regarding the 'radical' equality in treatment and participation within the organization, staff members consider this an illusion, and that at the individual level each person has different experiences, knowledge, skills and abilities, which allow for the existence of leadership. This means that leaders must be held accountable to other members through the adoption of a series of mechanisms such as regular reporting, clearly delimited responsibilities, and periodical evaluations.

The reflection on the relationship between the organization and its founders is implicit in the recognition of internal leaderships. According to some authors,[15] in organizations there is a type of member for whom complete withdrawal is inconceivable because their identity is directly tied to the organization. Those who identify with organizations in this way seem to be unable to negotiate their exit effectively given their adhesion, active or influential participation, commitment and loyalty to the organization. With the greater personal cost at the subjective level the decision to leave is problematic and costly, and makes departure all the more difficult. Loyalty thus becomes a barrier to leaving the organization, and for some this represents an insurmountable obstacle given the assumption that the organization cannot exist without its identifiers and that they, in turn, cannot exist without the organization. Their eventual exit, therefore, will imply that the organization changes structurally, becoming 'another organization' in the process.

This situation is currently the subject of reflection in SIPAM and emphasis is being placed on the need to develop leadership transfer processes that would focus on the training and mentoring of new leaders over long periods of time. This would allow potential new leaders to mature and optimize the development of knowledge, abilities, and personal skills, as well as acquiring relevant experience. Part of the process also includes reflection on the correct mechanisms for recognizing the contributions of all members, including the founders, so that the corresponding exits can take place with minimal emotional cost and impact on the collective activity of the organization. The *Sipameras* have succeeded in carrying out exit processes for several of the founders, in the light of the lessons provided by the institutional milestones.

Final thoughts

The experience of SIPAM is a tapestry of complex processes that provide healthy lessons about restating ideals of participatory democracy as practised in the day-to-day operations of an organization.

The recognition that members – leaders responsible for strategic decision making, the operational team responsible for specific projects, and the administrative staff responsible for administration – have a plethora of motivations and different thresholds of collective action is evidence that SIPAM is an organization composed of a diverse collective with shared interests. This gives rise to the need to establish the appropriate mechanisms for strengthening democratic participation within the organization, and requires that *Sipameras* be willing to co-operate in the construction of these democratic processes.

In keeping with its history and experience as an organization, SIPAM represents a concrete link between contemporary feminist orientations, opportunities and challenges. It is an organization that expresses the transition from a Utopia to daily practice. Its permanent striving to overcome internal tensions and imbalances demonstrates maturity and a commitment to feminist principles. For its staff members, SIPAM means activism, diversity, participation, effort, involvement, solidarity, commitment and tenacity.[16] These elements express the renewed effort of current members to visualize the organization as a protagonist within the social movement, with all its complexity and diversity of feminist and other contributions.

NOTES

1 Muñiz, E. (1994), *El Enigma del Ser*, UAM-A (ed.), Mexico, p. 66.

2 Arizpe, L. (2002), 'Del grito de los setenta a las estrategias del siglo XXI', in G. Gutiérrez (ed.), *Feminismo en México. Revisión histórico-crítica del siglo que termina*, PUEG, Mexico.

3 See <www.sipam.org.mx> (last accessed 15 September 2006).

4 Alberoni, F. (1984), *Movimiento e Institución*, Ed. Nacional, Madrid, Spain, p. 226.

5 Gelb, J. (2002), 'Feminism. NGOs and the Impact of the New Transnationalisms', *Dynamics of Regulatory Change: Globalization Affects National Regulatory Policies*, Vol. 1 Article 9, New York.

6 See Moser, C. (1991), 'La planificación del género en el Tercer Mundo: Enfrentando las necesidades prácticas y estratégicas de género', pp. 55–124 in Guzmán, V., P. Portocarrero and V. Vargas (eds.), *Una nueva lectura: Género en el Desarrollo*, Flora Tristán, Lima, Peru.

7 *El Cocoyocazo* (the term alludes to the village of Cocoyoc in the State of Morelos, where efforts began to settle the conflict) was an internal crisis among directors in 1995. It was motivated mainly by the growth of the organization and the fear and uncertainty that achievements to date would slip out of control. Some of the members of the coordinating group left as a result of this crisis. Then, in 2002, the crisis brewed up again among its leaders. This was referred to as the *Sipum* (suggesting the impact of the crisis, a type of 'knockout' of the organization's stability): the general director left, along with most of the members. However, some returned after a process of institutional intervention to overcome this crisis, the greatest challenge SIPAM has had to confront to date.

8 Hiriart, B. and M. Del Puerto (eds.) (1997), *El aliento y los pasos, festejando diez años de SIPAM*, SIPAM, Mexico.

9 SIPAM originally consisted of four women. Three years later the team had grown to nine, and to almost 40 by 1994 (the period of greatest growth in terms of membership numbers). At the time of writing, approximately 15 people work at SIPAM on a permanent basis, and another 15 external collaborators – including students carrying out social service – work on specific activities.

10 The Spanish-language term for female companions or partners, indicating comradeship.

11 Tarrés, M. L. (1998), 'De la identidad al espacio público: las organizaciones no gubernamentales de mujeres en México', in J. L. Méndez (ed.), *Organizaciones civiles y políticas públicas en México y Centro América*, Miguel Ángel Porrúa, Mexico; and Phillips, A. (1996), *Género y teoría democrática*, UNAM, Mexico.

12 Lozano, I. and C. López (2001), 'Evaluación externa institucional SIPAM', SIPAM internal document.

13 Rivera, L. M. and M. I. Ibarrola (2004), 'Evaluación Institucional, SIPAM A'.

C. SIPAM internal document.

14   Feminist organizations in Mexico are currently facing considerable uncertainty regarding institutional viability due to cutbacks in funding from international agencies.

15   Pizorno, A. (1989), 'Algunas otras clases de otredad: Una crítica de las teorías de la "elección racional"' in A. Foxley, M. S. McPherson and G. O'Donnell (eds.), *Democracia, desarrollo y el arte de traspasar fronteras*, FCE, Mexico, pp. 370–1.

16   Loría, C. and C. Rodríguez (2002), *Intervención institucional en el colectivo salud integral para la mujer, A. C.* Final Report.

7

Linking Empowerment and Democracy

A Challenge to Women's Groups in Quebec

Nancy Guberman, Jennifer Beeman, Jocelyne Lamoureux,
Danielle Fournier and Lise Gervais

This chapter raises the issue of the necessary links between organizational democracy and empowerment, and questions practices in women's groups that reduce women to being the 'objects' of interventions while excluding them from exercising power over the group itself. It also examines the relation between women learning to exercise power over their lives and within their communities (empowerment), and learning to exercise power over the organization in which they participate (democracy), based on the experience of ten women's groups in Quebec, Canada.

Too often 'democracy', when applied to participants[1] within women's groups, is conceived of as 'helping' women, individually and collectively, gain control over different aspects of their lives, that is, to become empowered, but without this empowerment 'according' them control over the organization that is helping them. However, if empowerment is what the group does *for* its members, democracy is what it does *with* its members. Although these two conceptually different notions should go hand-in-hand, both in theory and in practice they are often mutually exclusive.

This chapter attempts to clarify the notions of empowerment and democracy, and demonstrate the possibility of essential links between them. The issues of inclusion of group participants in membership and the nature of the democratic practices implemented in women's groups are examined as essential components of our analysis.

We define empowerment as those practices aimed at accompanying women in the development of their self-determination, and their capacity to make socio-political analyses and take control of their own lives, both as individuals and collectively. By democracy, we refer to organizational democracy, or the internal formal power relations within the organization. We use the concept of democratic practices to mean those decision-making processes concerning the group's vision, management and practices, including the sharing of different types of information as well as the time and space allocated for deliberation. The building of citizenship refers to practices that provide the knowledge and skills enabling women to become actively involved in the social and especially the political processes within their communities.

We report here on an empirical study that used a qualitative design and multi-method approach aimed at understanding the organizational culture of ten women's groups in Quebec. This chapter presents a snapshot of what existed at the time we undertook our observations and interviews in 2000–2. The study gathered information and documented the practices of ten different organizations. A women's centre[2] offered educational activities, self-help groups, counselling and referrals, while also organizing and participating in collective actions such as demonstrations, briefs, and press conferences. There were four shelters, two for women in difficulty, and two for women victims of domestic violence. An advocacy group offered its services and activities to members who were workers in jobs particularly vulnerable to serious exploitation. The local chapter of a major provincial women's organization was involved in education, lobbying and advocacy on various issues. The other three organizations were a women's health centre; a sexual assault centre; and a group that served as an employment agency for women. All were non-profit local women's groups and considered themselves part of the Quebec women's movement.

Group characteristics

One of the most striking characteristics of all the women's groups was how they were constantly evolving and developing,[3] and experimentation and innovation were observed to occur constantly at all organizational levels.

All the groups had been in existence since the 1970s and 1980s, with the exception of the local chapter of the major provincial women's organization, which had no paid employees. All groups had between two and twelve core staff, and most also had part-time workers. Group operating budgets varied considerably, ranging from approximately US$1,500 for the local chapter, to upwards of US$200,000 for some of the shelters and service organizations that had recurrent stable funding.

Three of the groups worked primarily with poor women of French-Canadian origin while four others served poor women from immigrant and minority ethno-cultural groups. The others reached both poor and middle-class women. Staff were mainly, but not only, middle-class white women.

A variety of management structures were represented within the groups.[4] Seven of the groups under study (the four shelters, the women's centre, the sexual assault centre and the advocacy group) were jointly managed by the workers and the board of directors. In these cases the workers were generally responsible for day-to-day management while more substantive issues were decided in consultation with the board of directors. The division of responsibilities between the staff, director (where there was one) and the board varied from group to group, and could change within the same group over time.

At the time of the study, the health centre was controlled by workers and managed by a collective made up uniquely of permanent paid staff, as it was not a membership group. The group serving as an employment agency had no members but did have a board, chosen by the director, which comprised professionals from within the community – unlike the local chapter of the major provincial women's organization, which was controlled by rank-and-file members. While these members elected the executive to oversee its more technical affairs, programming and operational decisions were taken by members at monthly meetings.

The empowerment process

In commenting on the empowerment process, we present a brief analysis of the practices of the ten different groups with reference to the components included in the table. Although it is not possible for us to discuss in detail all the different elements that brought us to define these components, they emerged from data collected during observations, interviews and the examination of organizational materials.

An examination of the table enables us to detect the similarities between many of the observed empowerment and democratic practices, and at the same time to observe divergences in or divisions among these practices.

Table 7.1 The empowerment and democratic processes

The empowerment processes

Phase 1: Develop human relations	Phase 2: Build a sense of belonging	Phase 3: Offer feminist intervention	Phase 4: Promote active participation	Phase 5: Empower women
· ensure direct and 'warm' contact (greeting mechanisms) · see women as people not problems · go beyond a 'helping' relationship · ensure voluntary nature of participation · ensure respectful atmosphere	· organize and arrange space · provide accessibility of services (location, spaces, timetable, etc.) · minimize rules and regulations · create an alternative primary network	· demystify the expert · share personal experiences · share routine activities · validate women's experiences · collectivize situations	· benefit from services actively · encourage assumption of responsibilities · provide tools for knowledge and change · acquire learning skills	· enable growth and understanding · exercise of critical consciousness · assume control of one's life

The democratic processes

Phase 1: Develop human relations	Phase 2: Build a sense of belonging	Phase 3: Promote active participation	Phase 4: Enhance women's skills	Phase 5: Democratic participation and group control by members
· ensure direct and 'warm' contact (greeting mechanisms) · see women as people not problems · go beyond a 'helping' relationship · ensure voluntary nature of participation · ensure respectful atmosphere	· organize and arrange space · provide accessibility of services (location, spaces, timetable, etc.) · minimize rules and regulations · create an alternative primary network	· benefit from services actively · encourage assumption of responsibilities · provide tools for knowledge and change · acquire learning skills	· integrate women into the group through training and activism · develop critical consciousness · promote mobilizations and collective actions	· seek mechanisms to integrate women into formal decision-making structures · ensure alternative spaces for members to hold power · promote participation and active decision making at annual general meeting · encourage participation in group decisions as a form of empowerment

The top half of the table describes the five phases of the empowerment process.

The first four aspects in Phase 1 are aimed at providing women with the time and space to develop their capacities and take more control over their own lives. All ten organizations included a focus on developing human relations with participants from their first contact with their respective groups, as a step towards the empowerment of these women. In addition, by building a sense of belonging, offering a feminist framework and promoting active participation, the intervention in women's groups provided participants with the essential tools for individual and often collective empowerment. The phases of the process are not necessarily as linear or chronological as suggested by the table, and different levels of empowerment are achieved throughout the process.

Separating empowerment from democratic practices

In all the groups, we observed important and impressive intervention practices towards women's empowerment, although in terms of their participation within the groups, the democratic orientation was not present. It was interesting to note that there were few instances where women could influence the group's functioning and orientation. On examining the results of our research we recognized that it was essential for participants to experience and understand the complex process of re-appropriating certain fragments of power within themselves – in terms of self-confidence, motivations, family relationships, and the general orientation of their lives as part of the empowerment process. It was also important that the women develop an understanding of the general mechanisms of their alienation and subordination, and the individual and collective ways of affirming themselves as subjects and social actors. However, the knowledge and skills acquired as part of the process do not exclude the need for further knowledge and skills necessary to ensure participation in democratic processes. Democracy entails participation in the decisions affecting one's life. If one is a participant in a community group, this means being involved in its important decisions. While empowerment is a key component of the democratic process, the two are not synonymous, as they are sometimes represented in North American feminist organizational literature.[5]

The democratic process

Despite great differences in their histories, structures, orientations, and the services they offered, it was observed that four of the groups under study shared a variety of basic practices – such as attempting to integrate women into the group, including its decision-making processes – that contribute to fostering internal democracy (see Table 7.1, second half). It was noted that for these groups – that do not disassociate empowerment and democracy – the active participation of members is central to their orientations. These groups provided many different activities and forums, in addition to their normal services, in which their members could participate. They also offered many levels at which women could enter into group activities.

When the empowerment and democratic processes were compared it became apparent that the democratic process was initiated, in the case of the groups under study, in a manner that was almost identical to that of the empowerment process. Both processes were seen to begin by developing human relationships. Our analysis showed that many disenfranchised women need to feel welcomed, comfortable and secure in their first contacts with the group prior to developing a sense of belonging and before feeling they have a stake in the group. This was identified as an indispensable step prior to getting involved in decision making or in management activities. As one staff person described the process:

> For the women who decide to become activists, they have one thing in common; the group was a turning point for them. They say that it was really a revelation when they began to understand all sorts of things. They experienced intense moments and now they say they want to give back what they received.[6]

Both empowerment and democratic processes were observed to promote active participation; this helped reinforce participants' sense of belonging, allowing them to experiment with and develop various skills, and to emerge as subjects within the group. It was found that these skills subsequently enabled them to participate more effectively in deliberations and decision-making processes. The advocacy group, for example, required that women seeking services from the group first become members and attend a training session. It was during such sessions that the women received an introduction to their rights as workers and were made aware of their rights as members of the group.

It also emerged from our observations that in order for women to become full and active participants in the democratic process, there was a need for two other components that were not part of the empowerment process. These were the acquisition of organizational and strategic skills, and the promotion of democratic participation and shared control of the group by members and staff.

Acquisition of organizational and strategic skills

The acquisition of organizational and strategic skills was found to be of particular importance during the fifth phase of the empowerment process, being necessary in the exercise of critical consciousness. The empowerment process enables women to become subjects and social actors with some control over their own destiny, as well as potentially active citizens who partake in social and political life. It was observed that similar skills were required in democratic participation (or Phase 5 of the democratic process) as the aim was to involve women in the life of the group so that they become concerned about and active in the issues facing the group. Participants would thus be able to act as spokeswomen for the group in public meetings or coalitions, and be trained to lead activities within the group.

Promotion of democratic participation

Groups that practised both empowerment and democracy encouraged participants to become active members of the group; joint member/ staff control of the group was held as a central value. Democracy was not reduced to the existence and functioning of the formal management structure, and democratic practices were part of day-to-day group activities. It was found that these groups were the ones that actively questioned what structures would best support the democratic management of their group. The women's centre, for example, was constantly experimenting with ways to make the board more accessible to participant members. It held regular information sessions on the role and duties of the board, and during board meetings members were invited to observe and comment on its work.

On examining the results of our study we were left with a doubt as to how those groups that do not promote the democratic participation of participants are able to limit their intervention to the empowerment process. And, is it possible for women to become fully autonomous in organizations in which their roles are limited to those of service users or activity participants, and, at the same time, have little understanding or say in their operations?

Analysis of the main issues

Three main issues emerged from our analyses that contribute to an understanding of the separation of empowerment and democratic practices. The first involves how staff and board members perceive participants. We found that some groups, which work solely on empowering women as individuals, often viewed participants primarily as service users or 'women in need'. It appeared to be more difficult for staff and board members in these groups to recognize participants as potential colleagues capable of sharing management decisions. Of these groups, a few considered women participants as 'victims', thus virtually eliminating the possibility of their being treated as active social agents or assuming roles as active members of their group. In one shelter, workers even went so far as to express distrust or disbelief in the idea that participants could ever be considered the equals, for example, of board members.

In all the scenarios described, an acceptance of participants in sharing management decisions would necessarily involve accommodating 'outsiders' (women other than team members, and in particular women with different interests and ideas) in internal decision-making practices. It was observed that such a step would be difficult when, for many staff, one of the advantages of working on projects in the community is the fact that they have control over their work processes, and would probably be reluctant to relinquish control over these and accept an increased level of accountability.[7]

The second key issue that emerged from our study was the question of whose interests actually define the common good. It was found that those women who have the opportunity to participate in democratic discussions, deliberations and decisions are able to determine the groups' mission and activities, and are therefore able to contribute to the definition of their common good. However, those groups that did not allow the involvement of participants had, in most cases, not even considered the importance of their contribution in this definition. And although their practices were often aimed at supporting women to participate as full citizens in society, this participation did not extend to their participation within the group. Reinhelt[8] attributes this situation in part to the fact that some groups, such as shelters, may provide services to women who have no specific commitment to feminist politics.

We would agree that not all women who come to a group for a service or an activity are interested in becoming involved in the management of that group, and that there should be no pressure on them to do so. We therefore consider that groups need to ensure that prior to accepting women as members, they should at least be aware of a general philosophy and have spent some time getting to know the group's work. It would therefore appear appropriate for organizations to establish mechanisms and terms for membership so that women who participate in a group's services and activities are not totally excluded from participating in decisions affecting the group. Otherwise, who is to make decisions and on what basis, and who represents the interests of the participants?

Several authors[9] conclude that the exclusion of service users from the decision-making process benefits the workers, who are thus able to better promote the interests of the organization and its users. The workers' needs come to be perceived as synonymous with the needs of the group. There is also a belief among workers that they are able to understand and respond to the needs of participants without involving the latter in decision making. Indeed, these case studies and previous experience indicate that women's groups run by women for women often serve to camouflage important differences between women in terms of their interests and power to articulate and promote those interests. Allowing participants to partake in the decision-making process increases the chances that divergent interests and opinions will be expressed and the likelihood that changes will occur. Democracy necessarily involves pluralism. It cannot be reduced to a small group of like-minded individuals who monopolize decision-making processes while excluding others who are willing to participate. Such 'paternalistic' practices contradict the feminist principles of demystifying the expertise of the workers and establishing egalitarian relations between workers and participants.

The third and final issue we observed is how the separation of empowerment and democracy processes has an impact on the promotion of full citizenship. The acquisition of skills necessary for active participation in democratic practices at the micro or group level sets the stage for participation and citizenship on the macro level, beyond the confines of the group. It was observed that the safety and security felt by some women belonging to these groups is indeed a fertile ground for the acquisition of the necessary skills and knowledge. However, the question remains: if these opportunities are not forthcoming within the organizations to which these women turn and where they start to build a relationship of trust and a feeling of belonging, where else will these opportunities be found?

Training for active citizenship does in fact 'begin at home' in the case of some groups, which reflects in the actions taken to foster the development of interests and skills towards the participants' involvement in internal deliberations. However, we found it problematic that others, despite having active participation as full citizens as an ultimate goal, only provided a limited number of tools for women, and expected them to acquire many skills and most experience outside the confines of the group.

Conclusion

We consider it relevant to question the dissociation of democracy from empowerment, as observed in six of the ten groups, because it has consequences for the role women are able to play within their groups, and also cuts off an important avenue for empowerment. As a result of our analyses, we came to believe that the two processes are indeed mutually reinforcing in exciting ways that can allow women to move from being victims of horrible situations to politically involved social actors. They can become integrated into new networks where they are able to play a valuable role in determining the orientation and functioning of organizations developed to help them. If former service participants are excluded from playing significant roles within these organizations, their voices and experiences are lost and groups, such as those studied, are likely to respond to the perspectives of workers rather than the whole range of stakeholders. We feel very strongly that women who approach women's groups must have the opportunity to appropriate the democratic deliberation process if these groups are to be truly inclusive and offer a voice to those who seek services.

NOTES

1   The terminology used to describe the relationship women have with the different groups varies, as do the statuses accorded these women within them. In order to avoid confusion, we will generally employ the term 'participant' as opposed to 'user' when referring to those who are benefiting from some form of service. In some groups, participants are automatically considered 'members' and have the right to attend and vote at the annual meetings, and to elect and sit on the board of directors, this being the body that manages the group on an ongoing basis between annual meetings. In other groups, participants cannot be members. To distinguish between the different statuses, we will refer to the former group as 'participant members'. This also distinguishes these women from other types of members, usually professional women who volunteer to serve on the board but do not participate in group activities as 'users', and staff, who in some groups are considered as members with a right to sit on the board, while in others they are simply employees.

2   The names of the groups are not provided so as to ensure anonymity.

3   Each group is structured somewhat differently. In order to help identify the different actors involved we have harmonized the terminology as follows: 'participants' and 'participant members' are described in note 1; 'workers' refers to remunerated staff; 'members' refers to all those eligible to vote at the annual general meeting, and to elect and be elected to the board of directors. These can include both 'participant members' and non-participant members as outlined in note 1.

4   In what follows, we describe only the management aspect of the groups' work. Workers also ensure the daily activities and services offered by the respective groups.

5   See, for example Ahrens, L. (1980), 'Battered women's refuges: feminist co-operatives vs. social service institutions', *Radical America*, 14 (3): 41–7; Iannello, K. P. (1992), *Decisions without Hierarchy: Feminist Interventions in Organization Theory and Practice,* Routledge, New York; and Rodriguez, N. M. (1988), 'Transcending bureaucracy: feminist politics at a shelter for battered women', *Gender and Society*, 2: 214–27.

6   Name withheld to maintain anonymity.

7   Guberman, N. *et al.* (1997), *Innovations et contraintes: des pratiques organisa-tionnelles féministes*, Centre de formation populaire et Relais-femmes, Montreal.

8   Reinhelt, C. (1994), 'Building community: the challenge for state-funded feminist organizations', *Human Relations*, 47 (6): 685–705.

9   Godbout, J. (1983), *La participation contre la démocratie.* Éditions Saint-Martin, Montréal; and Tom, A. (1995), 'Children of our culture? Class, power, and learning in a feminist bank', in M. M. Ferree and P. Y. Martin (eds), *Feminist Organizations: Harvest of the New Women's Movement*, Temple University Press, Philadelphia.

8

Gender Mainstreaming
in Development Organizations

Organizational Discourse and the Perils
of Institutional Change

Nicholas Piálek

This chapter looks at how the proliferation of organizational discourse on gender, encouraged by mainstreaming strategies and approaches in development organizations, can actually subvert the intended process of institutional change. The chapter represents one aspect of my current research into the relationship between organizational culture and policy failure. It is based on research I conducted within Oxfam GB[1] and attempts to demonstrate, through Oxfam-based examples, what can happen if we ignore how gender discourse is framed within organizational literature. I shall show that the uncritical positioning of gender terms and concepts in relation to other organizational themes can lead to a situation whereby 'ordinary' staff are disempowered from the process of putting gender and development (GAD) approaches into development practice.[2]

Oxfam GB (hereafter referred to as Oxfam) formally adopted a gender policy in May 1993. Prior to this, Oxfam had created a Gender and Development Unit (GADU) in 1984 to raise awareness of gender issues amongst staff and in the organization's activities. In one form or another over two decades Oxfam has demonstrated commitment to GAD and gender mainstreaming. Through gender mainstreaming Oxfam has developed the idea that GAD approaches to development are the responsibility of all staff. It has been supposed, therefore, that levels of understanding and actual technical capacity to implement GAD approaches in projects and programmes have been good throughout the organization.[3] However, by Oxfam's own admission, gender mainstreaming has failed to achieve as much as expected in promoting gender within the organization's work. Translating its progressive gender policy into solid practice has proved difficult and is the subject of much internal research and debate. The difficulties seem all the more perplexing given that open resistance to gender main-streaming is not significantly present. Most staff recognize the impor-tance of gender transformative goals, not just for their instrumental value in creating broader and more sustainable solutions to poverty, but also for their intrinsic value. Oxfam thus provides an interesting case study for developing an analysis of gender mainstreaming. It is quite unlike organizations and institutions where gender mainstreaming meets open hostility. In many ways it epitomizes the progressive institution, where radical policies such as GAD are nurtured and where gender mainstreaming should create positive institutional change.

Framing gender in discourse: distracting institutional change

Discourse is frequently only seen as important for what it says – the shift toward a GAD perspective and the subsequent use of appropriate language and terminology is a good example of this. However, it is also important to recognize *how* discourse says something – in what way it places an issue within the wider institutional context. Framing has a huge impact on the *what* of discourse, in terms of both how it is assumed and practised by staff within an organization. However, this aspect of organizational discourse is frequently overlooked in gender mainstreaming strategies when it is not readily visible to those who are actually working within organizations. Examining how GAD-related discourse is integrated into organizations will be key to understanding how mainstreaming strategies have regularly failed to create responsi-bility for institutional change among staff, as in the case of Oxfam. It is important to recognize that Oxfam is not alone in the problems and difficulties it faces, and this chapter should offer a warning to other organizations undertaking or considering gender mainstreaming. Throughout the process of institutional change it remains important to monitor how organizational discourses on gender issues evolve and develop, as changes that at first may seem favourable could actually lead in unfavourable directions.

The integration of gender terminology within Oxfam discourse, through the way it is positioned *vis-à-vis* other languages and issues within the organization, has a strong influence on staff perceptions of how a GAD approach applies to their work. The direct influence of this discourse on the conceptual understanding of gender issues among staff is less relevant. Rather, the important aspect of discourse that does require examination is how it builds self-awareness among staff of their roles in promoting gender equity within their projects and programmes. In this chapter, I focus particularly upon the role of discourse in the unforeseen and unplanned emergence of a technical enclave on gender within the organization.

Creating a technical enclave

Gender terminology is frequently encountered in Oxfam's publications, policy and procedural documents, internal communications and meetings. However, when the term 'gender' (or related concepts) is referred to within this discourse, it is possible to identify a number of consistent parallel themes: the explicit (over)use of the term 'expert', the endless production of 'checklists' and 'tools', and the continual creation of specific acronyms and abbreviations. As a result, gender terms and subsequent GAD approaches tend to be construed as something technical.[4] In manufacturing this image of gender as something technical there is a tendency for staff to treat GAD approaches as being the exclusive domain of the (gender) 'expert'. Gender thus becomes a knowledge enclave, with its own tools, operational frameworks, and jargon fortifying its walls. The distancing of 'ordinary' staff members by this type of discourse means that responsibility for implementing GAD is, in effect, shifted from staff members to the 'expert'.

Building the walls of the enclave

Gender toolkits, frameworks, manuals, minimum standards, policies and checklists for distribution outside the organization are all designed to increase accessibility to a complex issue. Oxfam has published a number of manuals and resource books[5] over the past decade and has been working towards publishing a second complementary set of gender tools and frameworks in 2007 in the forthcoming *Oxfam Gender Training Manual 2*.[6] Internally, gender checklists, frameworks and toolkits are even more prolific, so much so that at the recent global gender meeting all those who attended quickly agreed with a despondent gender adviser who pointed out that 'we do not need any more gender tools, we have

Case Study 1

Interview with an Oxfam Project Officer in Peru[7]

Daniel Gonzalez[8] is a Peruvian sociologist working as Project Officer in Oxfam's country office in Peru (part of Oxfam's South American regional operation – SAM). He is responsible for approving, supporting, and monitoring Oxfam-supported projects in that country. Such a position makes him a key actor in transforming gender policy into practice. He was more than willing to discuss gender issues, and stressed that despite there being 'no strong work on gender in SAM, and that Peru is no exception', he was keen to see more work focusing on gender. However, after we got beyond his initial, and perhaps routine, response to my interest in gender issues, we began to discuss in more detail his interpretation of gender as a concept and how it relates to his work. In the conversation that followed he clearly demonstrated his detailed knowledge of gender and its linkages with wider development issues.

Despite Daniel's knowledge and awareness of gender issues, the impact this has on rendering the projects with which he is involved more gender transformative stops there. Daniel did not try and change this situation in which he found himself on this particular project, but rather continued by berating Oxfam for not providing a methodology to deal with the problem. In fact, throughout the conversation he made several references to the need for Oxfam to provide a 'gender framework' with indicators and instruments to measure gender as he 'does not have the specialization' required to understand with confidence how gender relations can impact on and be changed by projects. Furthermore, as I was working for the regional gender policy adviser at the time (as a condition for conducting my research), he demanded to know when we would be coming to the country office to incorporate gender into his projects and programmes. Daniel's actual knowledge and awareness of gender is very high. However, this is at odds with his belief that he is neither a specialist nor someone who has the necessary 'technical' tools for understanding gender. It is clear that he does not see himself as responsible for incorporating a GAD perspective into his projects.

loads'.[9] With all these documents to hand, then, it is clear that the problem of implementation is not one of a lack of skills or the availability of tools.

Although Oxfam's gender mainstreaming approach does not lack materials, it could in fact be that their over–abundance is detracting from real institutional change in this area. Instead of actually integrating gender issues in the field, staff come to consider gender as a technical issue, distanced from their own development knowledge and experience (see Case Study 1). The construction of gender as a 'technical problem' separates it from the everyday development experience of staff. With this distance comes a reduced sense of responsibility.

In Oxfam it is also typical for terms, from the mundane to the technical, to be abbreviated or acronymized, as this is believed to speed up communication while at the same time remaining specific and focused. Departments, campaigns, concepts, management structures and regions all have pseudonyms. For instance, ending violence against women is referred to as EVAW; the commission on the status of women becomes CSW; and gender action research, GAR. Becoming fluent in this language of acronyms can be seen as a rite of passage for new staff. Initiation to this in-house code is virtually mandatory as, without a knowledge of it, progressing with work is almost impossible. Once accepted by individuals it becomes the normal mode of communication.

Conversations and documents are unintelligible to those who are uninitiated, creating a clear distinction between those 'in the know' and those who are not. Internally the impact of this can be devastating, particularly for gender mainstreaming. Frequently, abbreviations and acronyms are specific and unique to departments or even to individual teams on some occasions. In consequence of the adoption of the discursive practice of abbreviating and acronymizing gender and specific terms related to gender mainstreaming, a mystique instantly envelopes gender work. For those who are not 'in the know' – most staff who are not directly working on gender directly as an issue – the image of gender work/ knowledge as something technical is reinforced. Documents – even those very toolkits and guidelines developed to help – become difficult to understand, and effective dialogue among gender staff and non-gender staff is reduced.

Barring the gates of the enclave

Gender knowledge is thus developed through discourse as something technical and out of reach of 'ordinary' members of staff through the exclusionary nature of acronymization and the overuse of toolkits and frameworks. However, discourse within Oxfam further reinforces this problem through the construction of the 'gender expert' in the organization: the custodians of the enclave. Much of Oxfam's internal documentation and literature refers to gender 'experts' (or sometimes

Case Study 2[10]

Oxfam's new mainstreaming strategy

In 2004 Oxfam implemented a new mainstreaming strategy, Gender Mainstreaming Focused Accompaniment (GMFA). This was designed to provide 'consistent support and skill building to key staff and partners at the country and regional level, focusing on an identified project or aspect of a programme'. In essence it was designed to provide close support to project/programme staff who work on a specific issue, in order to help them develop their knowledge of the GAD approach. The hope is that once good practice has occurred it will then spread across the region and other programmes/projects. The first programme to receive this support was the market access programme in Nigeria.

The examination of the initial GMFA document indicates that it will provide 'advisory support at strategic level, by Global and Regional Gender Advisors or members of a "pool of gender practitioners" ... during project implementation'. This can and should be seen as a positive aspect of the programme. However, for a strategy that aims to develop project-level staff capacity and confidence for tackling gender issues, it begins to reproduce the dangerous dichotomy of 'the experts' (them) and 'the project staff' (us). This exclusionary language is reinforced in the subsequent objectives of the strategy that stress it should 'address the practical skills of the project level staff, by drawing on the expertise of a pool of gender practitioners'. This statement directly opposes the two groups involved in the process, and the person reading the document then becomes either an 'ordinary' member of staff (read: someone without sufficient knowledge of gender) or a 'gender expert'.

This is also reinforced by statements confirming that implementation of the project can only be led by people with gender expertise. For instance, we learn that 'the gender action plan will be implemented under the leadership of the Nigeria Senior Management Team with the focused support of the Global Gender Mainstreaming Advisor from PPT in Oxford, the Regional Gender Advisor for West Africa, the country gender focal point and a team of local gender consultants'. The role of the project and programme staff is not mentioned at all, giving the impression that they do not possess the technical capacity to be involved.

'consultants') who are frequently identified as part of the solution to gender mainstreaming problems. For instance, it is understood that if more gender experts were available the implementation of GAD approaches would increase. The discourse of the 'Executive summaries of the gender review evaluations' is a case in point.[11] For instance, one aspect of the review highlights that staff do not have enough understanding of gender relations to be confident enough to apply it to their work. Yet, this fairly valid criticism is worded very differently and creates a much more specific interpretation among readers of the review. This indicates that the problem lies in insufficient staff with 'necessary gender expertise' and that 'gender experts are too thinly spread'. The framing of the problem in this manner removes gender as an issue for which all staff should have responsibility, and the onus is placed on management: it is about the 'organization' of experts. As a consequence, the solution to the problem inevitably reinforces this picture of gender as an issue only concerning 'experts'.

Such discourse has two significant impacts upon the uptake and practice of GAD approaches in Oxfam. First, it constructs a group of people in the organization (an artificial group) who have legitimate access to gender knowledge. Second, in creating this group, it shifts responsibility for implementing GAD approaches away from the 'ordinary' member of staff and onto this group (see Case Study 2).

Recommendations

The experience of Oxfam offers a warning to all development organizations attempting to mainstream gender: organizational change is not a simple process. Strategies and approaches might be designed to further feminist ambitions within organizations, but their outcomes cannot be guaranteed or even predicted. Oxfam has promoted discourse on gender within the organization through toolkits, policy development and, more broadly, through GAD literature. Much of this discourse has fitted in with existing themes in the organization, such as the use of acronyms and the identification of 'niche areas' on the basis of technical speciality. However, though gender discourse is now prolific and widely accepted in the organization, the impact has been to remove responsibility from individuals to integrate GAD approaches in their work. This experience provides a few cautionary examples to those who are undertaking gender mainstreaming, or who intend to do so.

It should never be forgotten, or even downplayed, that gender mainstreaming is an essentially feminist project, and as such is inherently political. It is fundamentally about changing the values held by people: about getting them not just to see the injustices faced by women but to act on their emotions and do something about it. Organizational change is about two interconnected issues: norms and values. It should be about challenging and changing both the norms of organizations, such as policies, human resource practices, project management procedures, performance management objectives, and analyses, as well as the values held by staff within those organizations. However, all too often, within the formulaic process of organizational change, it is easy to lose sight of the fundamentally political aspect of gender mainstreaming. Organizational change strategies frequently tackle norms (which are more visible and thus much easier to change) and fail to directly challenge values. There exists an assumption that a change in norms will inevitably lead to a change in values. This cannot be assumed with gender mainstreaming, and the example of discourse within Oxfam testifies to this fact. Gender mainstreaming is a political project and must directly transform the values of staff. Only when this value transformation occurs will the norms of an organization – that have been altered to promote GAD approaches – be taken up and put into practice. Gender mainstreaming approaches must be diverse and multiple, but most of all they must explicitly and directly tackle staff values.[12]

NOTES

1   Oxfam GB is an international development organization that works in over 75 countries, including the UK. It has offices and staff within nearly all of the countries in which it works. It is involved both directly and through partners in advocacy, development, and humanitarian work. It is called Oxfam GB to distinguish it from other Oxfam International members.

2   Throughout the research process Oxfam GB and the staff with whom I have worked have been fully aware of my research. On several occasions I have consulted staff on its implications and the conclusions drawn therein. Oxfam GB provides an important case study for gender mainstreaming as many organizations seek its advice on this process of institutional change. It is hoped that recognition of the problems faced by Oxfam GB in its pioneering gender mainstreaming strategies will benefit others.

3   Dawson, E. (2005), 'Strategic gender mainstreaming in Oxfam GB', *Gender and Development: Mainstreaming – A Critical Review*, 3 (2): 80–9, available at <http://www.oxfam.org.uk/what_we_do/issues/gender/gad/gad_contents. htm#mainstreaming> (last accessed 10 September 2006).

4   I am not suggesting that gender is not a technical area of knowledge, but rather highlighting that discourse within the organization consistently builds up gender as something technical rather than something accessible and knowable

by all.
5   Good examples of these are: Cummings, S., v. H. Dam and M. Valkl (eds.),
    (1998), 'Gender Training: the Source Book', *Gender, Society, and Development*,
    Oxfam GB, Oxford; March, C., M. Mukhopadhyay and I. Smyth (1999), *A
    Guide to Gender Analysis Frameworks*, Oxfam GB, Oxford; Williams, S., J. Seed
    and A. Mwan (1994), *The Oxfam Gender Training Manual*, Oxfam GB, Oxford.
6   Oxfam (2006), 'Aim 5 gender equity global meeting: developing a shared
    vision and making a compelling case for putting gender equity at the heart of
    the Oxfam agenda'. Oxfam internal document, Oxfam GB, Oxford.
7   Based on an interview conducted by the author in Lima, Peru, July 2003.
8   All names are fictitious to protect the identities of individuals with whom I
    have worked.
9   This comment was made during the 15–17 March 2006, Oxfam GB Global
    Gender Meeting. It can be referenced in the document cited in Note 6.
10 Oxfam (2004), 'Draft TOR for gender focus accompaniment to Nigeria (for
    discussion)', Oxfam internal document, Oxfam GB, Oxford.
11 Oxfam (2002), 'Executive summaries of the gender review evaluations',
    Oxfam internal document, Oxfam GB, Oxford.
12 Gender training should not be mistaken for a strategy for value change among
    staff. Frequently, gender training merely informs staff of changed organiza-
    tional norms while never truly tackling their values. There is a need to look at
    more innovative approaches, such as action research whereby project and
    programme staff transform their own values and beliefs through the process of
    conducting research on gender issues themselves. Value change by its very
    nature is a long-term process. There are no quick fixes.

9

Feminists, Factions and Fictions in Rural Canada

Leona M. English

Community-based feminist organizations work in the community as physical and metaphorical shelters for women, and as promoters of women's rights. Yet, just as no two feminists are alike, neither are their organizations or relationships. Using the theoretical lens of Foucauldian post-structuralism, this chapter discusses some of the more relevant findings from interviews with 16 women in ten feminist organizations. Emphasis falls on the dimensions of power and leadership.

Theoretical framework

Foucauldian post-structuralism is concerned with the shifting, fluid, and political ways in which power is operative in all relationships and social spheres.[1,2,3,4] Rather than a sovereign power (the boss, God, king) Foucauldian post-structuralism offers a notion of power as exercised (used) rather than held (owned) by all people. Foucault develops the concept of disciplinary power, which is power embedded in the complex web of relationships and discourses that surround us. Self-discipline, or the ways in which we control ourselves in response to perceived power, is of particular interest to Foucault. In feminist organizations this self-discipline may be reflected in acquiescence to funding priorities of governments, silence when listening to less-than-competent directors, and not answering back when being spoken to in ways we do not like. Disciplinary power is a Foucauldian concept that challenges the notion that feminist organizers can empower anyone – since participants, board members and directors all exercise power in different ways; that is, they use technologies or micro-practices of power, such as the circle formation, group work, participatory learning, and personal storytelling. These micro-practices embody a capillary-like power that works its way through systems of human interaction and language, producing regimes of truth (fictions): we tell all to other feminists and we 'act' cooperatively at board meetings so others will like us. This may result in confessional activity such as inappropriately dis-closing personal information to please the group. Or, it could produce resistance, such as inventing stories to subvert the exercise.[5] Resistance to a technology of power[6] such as the circle, or to the implicit rule to be 'nice', is key to Foucauldian post-structuralism. In recognizing the resistances we see the power that everyone exercises, regardless of organizational position.

Research methodology

Research participants included eight directors and (minimally paid) assistant directors, and eight volunteer board members of ten feminist organizations in 2005. These included resource centres, transition houses for victims of violence, and pre-employment and counselling centres. The staffs and boards were female, and all saw themselves as having at least an advocacy role for women. None exist to make money and all ten depend, at least to some extent, on government funding. They are situated in eastern and rural Canada, an area known for chronic unemployment. Semi-structured interviews were conducted with the 16 female participants, ranging in age from 25 to 60 years, who have been involved from a minimum of one year to a maximum of 25 years (median involvement was five years). Four of the participants were no longer serving their organizations in an official capacity but still maintained some form of relationship. Of the 16 interviews, four were carried out by e-mail, four in person, and eight by telephone. These 16 participants' responses are reported selectively below, and analysed using a Foucauldian post-structuralist discourse analysis.

Consensus – when the director resists

One of the technologies of power operative in these rural feminist organizations is the use of consensus to make decisions. As feminists, the participants in this study worked toward flattening their organization's structure, and making decisions by consensus rather than by voting. As a decision-making structure, consensus purports to create conditions where there is considerable inclusion and safety in speaking. Yet, in many ways, consensus is a fiction that works to produce a regime of truth: that good feminists decide things together and generate no conflict.

This regime of truth does indeed produce effects – a loyalty is created. It was indeed observed that almost all of the women interviewed indicated that consensus and voice were used positively to deal with conflict. Only those outside the feminist organizations (board members who had left the organization, silently resisting by leaving) would say anything contrary to this. An executive director of a shelter for women who are victims of domestic violence referred to the board's inability to come to agreement on a trivial issue. The need for consensus, and the belief in it, resulted in stalling and frustration on the part of the board. This is her account:

> The first several weeks that I was on the job … I'd go home with all this reading … books of staff meeting minutes and, you know, log notes and stuff, just trying to figure out what was going on…. And in the staff meeting minutes, the subject of a clothesline kept coming up over and over and I was really puzzled. So I went to work one morning and said, 'Tell me, what is it with this clothesline?' And they said, 'Well, we need one.' And I said, 'Well, put one up. What's the problem?' And the staff person said, 'Well, the board hasn't approved it,' and I said, 'What?' 'Well, you know, we have to get approval from the board [and they couldn't agree]'…. So they just thought I was quite ballsy when I just went out and got some Ready Mix concrete and got a kid to put up a fuckin' clothes line, excuse my mouth.[7]

The resistance here is to extremes of consensus. The resistance of this director was to make a direct decision, circumvent the board, and resist its power of governance. This narrative points to the ways in which power was exercised: by the board members in refusing to come to agreement on a seemingly insignificant issue, and by the director when she usurped the board's authority and produced a tale or fiction of how she saved the day. In analysing these seemingly innocuous stories, we see how all participants, regardless of rank, exercise power. Their technologies of power are different, however. The good feminist organization used consensus; the board resisted the consensus by stalling; the director resisted consensus and the board by making the decision. All were playing with power, albeit in different ways. In telling the story the director was able to break down the fictions of unity, and to see her organization as much like other community organizations. Breaking silence was a way of resisting the fiction of unity.

Feminist pay – when money talks

Another technology of power within a feminist organizational framework is for leaders, board members and staff, to use a flat pay structure whereby all employees, regardless of position or role, are paid the same. This technology produces a regime of truth that all service is equal. While equal pay may produce the effect of everyone feeling valued, it also glosses over differences in responsibility, and can produce resentment and factions. One director talked about her response to the 'equal' pay structure. Her resistance was to change the structure, but not without careful consideration:

> I said we are a collective and we still use that word collective … so it's only recently that, you know, we look at my job description and look at what my responsibilities are and say, why would somebody who is coming in on a project start the same? They're not carrying the same responsibilities that an Executive Director needs to…. So we've changed the pay scale to acknowledge that.

So, feminism, which for that woman and that particular organization once meant equal pay, has changed to reflect varying weights of responsibility. The feminist principles, when taken to include pay, produce resistance, in this case in the director of the organization. She and the board members who came to agree with her, recognize the different work responsibilities held by each member of staff, and the need for a pay structure to reflect this. The resistance in this instance was to the seemingly innocuous power of the money – a technology of power – and the equalization of pay. With a change in pay structures the meaning of 'collective' was stretched to recognize that the effects of power were already coursing through the organization. The equal-pay structure produced a kind of self-surveillance, in this case in the director, who agreed to the equal-pay situation for several years prior to changing it. The self-surveillance is seen in her initial compliance for fear that others would think her a bad feminist. Her resistance involved remaining silent for some time and then, after a few years, overtly seeking change in the pay scale, though not without continued questioning of whether the decision had been 'collective' or not.

Some of the women used the interviews as a means to 'return the surveillant gaze'[8] and break the silence; to speak, if not directly to the person they had a problem with, to the world. By talking back, they became radicalized agents. The interview became a gaze turned to the gaze. In a Foucauldian sense, they were able to negotiate the conflicted terrain by illuminating the hidden ways that the others (in some cases, non-feminists) resisted them. Once we understand the different ways in which all feminists exercise power, and their reasons for doing so, we are more inclined to accept a variety of ways of participating in feminism.

Inclusion: when a warm climate excludes

One of the technologies of power that was observed in these feminist organizations – in part because of adherence to feminist principles – was the deliberate creation of an inviting climate that included only women and that tried to be diverse in terms of race, class and ability. Attempts were made to 'talk things through', as one director described her leadership style. This climate resulted in several effects, the first being the feeling of safety. One former board member of an organization observed that 'It is a good idea to have all women; women are less inclined to "grandstand".'[9] In this comment, she acknowledged that the climate supports equal voice and respect. Yet this too produced effects. Inclusion had the effect of self-surveillance, people (board members, leaders, participants) thinking they had to say nice things to one another and about the feminist organization. They would be careful not to say the wrong thing when talking to people 'outside'. One former board member requested an advance copy of the transcript of the interview so she could remove anything that might suggest her organization was engaging in 'cat fights'.

A 25-year veteran of a women's centre talked of her shock when a staff member had a very public altercation at a community function. The staff member had shouted at a former board member, attacking her over an old incident. The veteran feminist expressed disappointment with the staff member's behaviour and noted that feminists do not often model their beliefs in civility and unity. The concern, in this instance, appeared to be the airing of the organization's dirty laundry in public rather than the behaviour itself. The fiction this veteran feminist had come to believe was that good feminists are warm and friendly both within the organization and in public; and she wanted them to model or practise a more inclusive type of behaviour. The fiction of inclusion had produced in her the fear of truth, fear of conflict, and an investment in silence. Power had produced in her a fear of exposure. In recounting these stories we are able to come closer to understanding and working against these fictions.

However, in other cases warmth and safety had a different kind of effect. One woman, who had spent three years as a board member, pointed out that she could no longer be part of an organization that was so cliquish. It was recognized that her resistance involved leaving her local organization as she did not feel welcome. She identified a core group of members who had been there for a long time as 'the true decision makers'. When the effect of the power is to produce self-surveillance and to create fictions of a happy family, then factions are the result, even if these are created on the periphery by those who leave. As significant as factions are the fictions of warmth, and these also need to be addressed. When it appears that the board of any feminist organization is functioning well, and that the director is doing a good job, this may in fact be a good time to trace the power relationships. In such circumstances participants are likely to have more time and commitment to invest in renewal and development. Inclusion is a disciplinary technology that produces effects such as a tenuous sense of security, but it does not minimize resistance. In realizing and critiquing practices, even the 'good ones', feminists can work toward the inclusion of difference(s).

Setting agendas and priorities: when order produces disorder

Our study revealed that feminist organizations, such as the ten in this study, were perpetually short of funds and bound to government purse strings for operational funding. This state of financial precariousness was complicated by the rural and economically disadvantaged context in which they operated. Although the organizations operated essential services for the government – protecting women and children, and providing literacy and pre-employment training – they were always in need of funds and therefore beholden to government bureaucrats. Being on the permanent look-out for funds, each organization had to ensure its house was seen to be in order, that it had regular meetings, that it appointed an executive (creating hierarchies), and, of course, that it followed government rules for funding. In other words, they became bureaucracies.

Government power appeared to course through the organizations and was omnipresent in conversations with the participants. One woman, who had been a board member for ten years, commented that the government funding structure (on a project-by-project basis) contributes to internal conflict. In describing this particular centre, the interviewee told of how there was little 'room for overtime pay. Women put in too much [time] and sometimes don't get paid.... This causes some friction in that they expect others to do the same.'

Although the government has succeeded in producing feminist subjects who appear compliant and work hard for little remuneration, some feminists resist by speaking out as this woman did, or by working collectively to resist the government. Participants told how they resisted by applying for one project and being 'creative in how funds were used' and also indicated that they usually complied by setting up the necessary organizational executive framework and then operating through consensus. They 'mobilized' around election time 'offering' help to friendly candidates. They were effectively strategizing and lobbying.

This study also signalled the need to be alert to the ways that governmental and societal discourses affect or shape feminism. While these ten feminist organizations were supposedly autonomous, they had common goals, struggles and ways of resisting those who tried to affect them negatively. The interviews showed that they tried to resist the government casting them as beggars and victims, and the public labelling them as home wreckers (as in the case of shelters for abused women). As one executive director noted, 'It's been very convenient for politicians, and media and some bureaucrats, to paint us all as being a bunch of whacko, militant, man-hating, blah, blah, blah, to dismiss us.' This is a reminder that, while it is good for feminists to achieve justice, organize well, and effect change, and even be successful fundraisers, they do not want progress to be at the expense of their integrity and identity.

Discussion of the results

What can feminist organizers and organizations learn from this study that may be advantageous for an improved understanding of leadership and power? Feminists may recognize the commonality of their organizations with other community-based groups. They are affected by the power that is generated, as well as that wielded by funders and other external agents. As the stakes are high – caring for women and children – the organizations frequently resist these different forms of power while at the same time being affected by it. The challenge is to identify and understand the dynamics of power and how they use it to control themselves and others.

In looking at how the 16 feminists in this study operate at the micro-level, and how they build their organizations, we are able to come to terms with the fact that fictional and stereotypical readings of feminist organizations exist. While some of the women in this study wanted to perpetuate the fiction of warm and inclusive women's groups, others wanted to challenge such perceptions. In appreciating the diversity of views and perspectives it is possible to understand more fully how complicated the internal workings of feminist organizations are. It is also possible to resist the stereotypical readings – such as 'all feminists are crazy' – and increase integrity and purpose.

Post-structuralism helps us see how some of our foundational beliefs such as feminist unity, consensus, and public solidarity are only partially true and partially helpful.[10] Not all feminists are compliant, not all good decisions are made by consensus, and not all responsibility is equal. And, despite the fact that seemingly innocuous operating practices such as creating inclusive climates and flattening pay structures are good as ideas, in practice, they also have effects. These practices can also be examined and critiqued from time to time.

The study shows that directors of feminist organizations and board members may conduct themselves as if they are being observed, mentally putting themselves in a panopticon – a jail-like situation – where they always feel observed.[11] This perception of being watched may make us discipline ourselves so that others will think we are 'good or compliant feminists', and that we can get along with anyone, instead of being ourselves. In studying how we act and interact in such local situations we can undo fictions and heal factions among feminists, and encourage more truth telling.

This study of feminist leaders highlights the ways in which power can be both beneficial and problematic. It is beneficial for feminists when it helps them advance the cause of women in the local community by enabling them to access services, gain rights, or increase autonomy. But it can be negative when it stifles cooperation, makes people fearful of speaking out or produces inaction. In observing some of the ways in which we use power, we could become more attentive to its effects and work to increase our effectiveness and communication in our local organizations.

NOTES

1   Brookfield, S. D. (2005), *The Power of Critical Theory: Liberating Adult Learning and Teaching*, Jossey-Bass, San Francisco.
2   Chapman, V-L. (2003), 'On knowing one's self – selfwriting, power, and ethical practice: reflections from an adult educator', *Studies in the Education of Adults*, 35 (1): 35–53.
3   Dreyfus, H., and P. Rabinow (1982), *Michel Foucault: Beyond Structuralism and Hermeneutics*, with an afterword by Michel Foucault, University of Chicago Press, Chicago.
4   English, L. M. (2006), 'A Foucauldian reading of learning in feminist nonprofit organizations', *Adult Education Quarterly*, 56 (2): 85–101.
5   Hughes, C. (2000), 'Resistant adult learners: a contradiction in terms', *Studies in the Education of Adults*, 32 (1): 51–62.
6   A technology of power can be understood as any practice set to regulate society or a given space, such as, in this instance, an organization.
7   Name withheld to maintain anonymity.
8   Chapman, V-L. (2003), 'On knowing one's self – selfwriting, power, and ethical practice: reflections from an adult educator', *Studies in the Education of Adults*, 35 (1): 35–53.
9   A US term indicating a way of performing with a view to getting applause.
10 Tisdell, E. J. (2000), 'Feminist pedagogies', in E. Hayes, D. D. Flannery and A. Brooks (eds), *Women as Learners: the Significance of Gender in Adult Learning*, Jossey-Bass, San Francisco, pp. 155–83.
11 A panopticon is a circular prison with walls built round from which prisoners can be observed at all times. In Foucauldian theory this is considered to be an imaginary state.

Part 3

Building Organizational
Capacity and Resources

10

A Model for Social Change

15 Years Investing in Mexican Women

Emilienne de León, Amanda Mercedes Gigler,
Lucero González and Margaret Schellenberg

As Mexico's only women's fund, Semillas (Seeds) is breaking ground not only in gender-specific philanthropy in Mexico, but also in creating a model for Latin America that includes innovative donor strategies and results-oriented grant making. Semillas's mission is to empower women and girls through resource mobilization. In particular, it aims to support marginal and marginalized women's organizations[1] whose self-initiated projects are focused on the human rights of women and girls. It carries out its mission through grant making directed at women's non-governmental organizations (NGOs) and grassroots groups, and fundraising directed at both individual and corporate Mexican donors interested in investing in social change. Over the past 15 years, Semillas has created a fundraising model for social change that is unique in Latin America – one in which both donors and counterparts are recognized as partners in the feminist movement. Through grants and training, Semillas has helped to improve the quality of life of women, their families and their communities.

Semillas and grant making

Founded in 1990 by a group of prominent Mexican feminists, with encouragement and seed funds from the Global Fund for Women,[2] Semillas functioned as a funding channel for the first eight years of its existence and then became a women's fund.

Grant making has always been considered the 'heart' of Semillas. Today Semillas makes grants[3] to women's NGOs and grassroots groups for projects relating to women's human rights – especially those in which human rights, sexual and reproductive rights and health, prevention of violence against women, labour rights, rural and indigenous women's rights, and economic autonomy play an important part. Grants are made and administered by its Seed Grant Programme,[4] and projects focus on education, communication and strategies for sustainable development.

Semillas looks for projects that operate within a framework of human rights, recognizing that women's empowerment needs more than just economic stability, education and protection from violence. Semillas defines empowerment as a process that begins when a woman becomes aware that she is the subject of human rights; and that 'women's issues', such as sexual and reproductive health and domestic violence, are not 'private' but should and can be addressed as human rights issues. The second step in the empowerment process takes place when a woman appropriates her rights. This is an internal shift from understanding rights as an external, abstract concept to the assumption of a proactive attitude to women's rights as human rights. The third and final step in the empowerment process takes place once the woman has gained the skills and ability to transmit her understanding and knowledge of rights to other women, thus re-initiating the cycle of empowerment for the benefit of others.

Every project financed by Semillas in Mexico over the past 15 years has included a focus on women's empowerment and taken participants through these three steps. Examples of such projects include an indigenous artisan weavers' cooperative in the Sierra de Oaxaca, an advocacy organization in Mexico City, and a reproductive rights and violence prevention group in Guanajuato. Semillas respects the fact that Mexico is a highly diverse country with many distinct cultures, and that each organization has its own unique way of empowering women.

By 1997, Semillas had made grants to 39 projects for a total sum of US$175,000. Since then it has funded nearly 170 more women's projects, with individual grants ranging from US$5,000 to US$15,000. By the end of 2005, the organization's fifteenth anniversary, its grants had reached the US$2.2 million mark.

A new philanthropic model

During its first ten years Semillas focused on establishing itself as a viable funding option for international foundations interested in supporting human rights work in Mexico. Grants from the Global Fund for

Women, the MacArthur Foundation[5] and the Kellogg Foundation[6] were the primary sources of income for the first seven years of its existence. The support of international donors was important, not just because of the funding but also because it contributed to Semillas's growth, institutionalization, and maturity. The support of international agencies also contributed to its credibility and enabled the organization to position itself *vis-à-vis* the Mexican public, not just as Mexico's only women's fund, but also as an organization worthy of donor investment.

Crucial to the evolution of Semillas from an NGO that acted as a funding channel to a fully blown women's fund – a process that spanned the five-year period 1998–2003 – was a renewed focus on economic sustainability and organizational development. Internal restructuring and streamlining resulted in a clearer definition of staff profiles, and the recruitment of full-time and part-time staff with experience in fundraising and fund management (grant making, administration, and project monitoring and control). The most innovative aspect of this new focus was the idea that an organization based in the global South could raise and control funds from within its own country and align its grant-making objectives with its own mission and experience, rather than depending on and answering to international agencies. Until this internal restructuring took place, Semillas had been almost totally dependent on grants from US-based foundations. As the main objective of the organization's plan for economic sustainability was local resource mobilization, Semillas's strategic plan for 2001–6 included a plan for economic sustainability that was oriented toward developing a Mexican donor base. Semillas thus included in its mandate the recruitment of committed national investors who could identify with the organization's mission, and who valued the organization's track record as well as the credibility it had acquired among its stakeholders. The movement to fund women in Mexico would be precarious at best if Mexican donors were not able and willing to invest in it. By empowering Mexican donors through local philanthropy, Semillas began to shift away from the prevailing Latin American model of North/South dependency. In 2006, 70 per cent of Semillas's funds were coming from international foundations, 12 per cent from national corporations, and 13 per cent from individual donors.

Now, after fifteen years of experience, and with a philanthropic programme directed at building a Mexican donor base, the concept of philanthropy needs to be developed within Mexican culture. With so few national or Latin American models of progressive philanthropy that include social change, women as subjects of social investment (or philanthropy), and economic sustainability, Semillas has undertaken the enormous task of educating the public in the need for a new form of philanthropy. The organization refers to its new philanthropic model as *Mujeres Invirtiendo en Mujeres* (MIM – women investing in women) which involves strengthening and broadening Semillas's network of Mexican women donors (a first in Mexico and Latin America), the development of educational materials, exchange opportunities for stakeholders, training some of the donors, and workshops for counterparts to support the development of their own local donor bases.[7] Central to the programme is a public communications strategy that promotes to the general public Semillas's image as a women's fund. If successful, in the next few years Semillas will have developed an innovative philanthropic model based on parity among investors in social change (counterparts and donors) that is directed at Mexican women, and that could be replicated as appropriate among other Latin American women's funds and organizations.

Women investing in women

In 2001 Semillas organized a forum on women's philanthropy in Mexico. The idea of a network of women who invest in women was a product of the task force established to prepare the forum. Although 125 women attended the forum, and many were enthusiastic and wanted to volunteer for an MIM network, few were immediately ready to become donors. However, over the following months 25 women became donors and by the end of the year Semillas had 45 local women donors.

Following the forum Semillas's staff carried out a survey directed at women to establish a profile of Mexican women donors.[8] Of the 93 women interviewed, 75 described themselves as donors (to other organizations). Two essential points emerged from the survey. Firstly, there did not appear to be a single defining characteristic or pattern relating to women donors, as the 75 women were of varying ages, income groups, educational levels and civil status. Secondly, none of the women who identified themselves as donors had ever given to an organization working for women's rights, the prevention of violence against women, or women's health. The main conclusions that Semillas was able to draw from the study were that all women are potential donors, and that major efforts would be needed to promote Semillas and make it visible as a women's fund.

Broadening the MIM network

Between 2001 and 2003 Semillas tested several strategies for broadening the MIM network. These included a newsletter, house parties, large breakfast events, and even a second-hand clothing shop, 'Madame MIM', that used the slogan 'style with experience.' By 2003 Semillas had received donations from close to 200 women, and of these, 40 were committed monthly donors. By the end of 2004, after three years of operation, the MIM network had received almost US$90,000. However, the difficulty of retaining donors was becoming more and more apparent. The Semillas resource development programme now began to address this need by outlining systems for donor engagement and cultivation.

The modest success of the MIM network catalysed new thinking about fundraising and even about Semillas's mission. Grant making had always been Semillas's *raison d'être*, so fundraising was thus a task necessary for the accomplishment of its goals. Through the creation of the MIM network and the concept of women investing in women, the fundraising strategies that targeted Mexican donors started to be much more holistic and innovative. Semillas learned that fundraising is not only about money, but also resource development. It is about building partnerships that allow both donors and counterparts to contribute to Semillas's mission. It was found that this focus invited a relationship and recognized that donations follow engagement. Most importantly, it was established that these partnerships required nurturing, and that both donors and counterparts needed to participate in education processes, both together and individually, so they could better appreciate their respective roles. This peer relationship between donors and counterparts has become an essential element in Semillas grant making and in the development of activities, and represents a direct challenge to Mexico's highly stratified class structure.

Fundraising for social change

For many years Semillas described its work as 'philanthropy with a gender perspective', meaning grant making directed at improving women's social conditions in Mexico, and especially the human rights of women. When Semillas began its 2001–6 sustainability plan, it began using the term 'social investment in women' to promote the idea of long-term investment as a means to achieve social change. Semillas includes both donors and counterparts as partners in the investment process, in a relationship of equals. This concept also allows Semillas to position itself as an ally, rather than a beneficiary, when negotiating grants from large foundations. The organization is more frequently considered as a partner on an equal footing, with a say in how money for social change should be allocated to each project. Women investing in women means women sharing a commitment and the resources (human, financial, organizational, leadership) at their disposal to improve other women's lives and change the inequality status that exists between women and men in Mexican society today.

In preparation for Semillas's fifteenth anniversary celebrations, several donors and counterparts were interviewed. Wendy Salas, a young woman who coordinated a counterpart organization that trains and promotes young activists for sexual and reproductive rights, commented:

> It's like investing in yourself, but through and supported by someone else. One group of women dares to contribute their money, and another group of women dares to use that money for their own benefit, for the benefit of those who gave the money … and even for the benefit of those who are never going to find out that someone gave money and someone else carried out a project.[9]

From this perspective, money becomes a tool for social change by supporting and fuelling activism. Semillas also believes that in order for money to make a difference, two essential elements are required. Social change for women begins with 'women's rights as human rights'. That is why Semillas's grant-making priority is always women's human rights. The second requirement is that women's organizations have access to the funds and resources that they require to carry out projects that are designed by themselves so that they will have a positive effect on their lives. As a women's fund, Semillas ensures these processes by acting as a bridge between donors and women's groups.

Sustainability and the survival of NGOs

In order to further fine-tune its strategic planning and long-term grant-making capacity, in 2004 Semillas undertook a feasibility study to determine this capacity[10] as the evidence that it needed to demonstrate to donors that there is a critical and permanent need for grants, and that the funds obtained by Semillas will continue to play a crucial role in the development of women's NGOs. This information has been essential in making a case to donors (both national and international) for their ongoing support of Semillas's work and for the development of an endowment fund.

The hypothesis established for the feasibility study was that there is a flight of international donors from Mexico, leaving a vacuum or a gap in the support for women's NGOs that cannot be filled by Semillas alone. From a survey in which 58 women's rights organizations participated (35 counterparts, 23 non-counterparts), it was learned that:

- international funds are the primary source of income for 29 NGOs, with 13 reporting that those funds represent more than 70 per cent of total current income;

- 32 NGOs (63 per cent) reported that if they did not receive inter-national funds within the next year they would have to reduce services, programmes or staff, or not be able to grow as planned;

- five NGOs said they would face a severe crisis or have to close;

- at least six former counterpart projects had closed in recent years;

- only eight respondents (14 per cent) indicated that they would be unaffected by a lack of international funds; and

- 83 per cent (or 46 of the 56 NGOs that responded) named fund-raising as their top priority, while 8 per cent named it as their second priority.

The survey and other sources (consultations with international donors and leaders in women's NGOs) provided crucial evidence that women's NGOs in Mexico are facing a funding crisis. It was established that urgent measures needed to be taken not only to ensure the survival of the organizations themselves, but also to avoid jeopardizing the many advances in the feminist agenda and the women's movement that had been made over the past two decades. If organizations do not quickly begin to develop and implement long-term strategies to ensure their sustainability, many will disappear or become so marginal that their projects will cease to have any impact. Most certainly they will not be able to defend themselves against the onslaught of Mexico's expanding right wing. Another major concern is where the new generation of leaders will come from, and how will it be nurtured to identify with and defend achievements to date.

Without a strategic and successful funding plan that addresses these crises, Semillas will have neither viable counterparts nor the NGO substructure that it has depended on as a grant maker, making the case for the development of an endowment fund untenable. The crisis appears to be widespread and affects feminist and women's NGOs in all parts of the country.

Semillas is not proposing to rescue or save organizations whose survival is in jeopardy. However, it does recognize its responsibility to its stakeholders as a women's fund. Its role is to create awareness, raise money, lobby international donors on behalf of women's organizations, develop networking structures, build support for a movement, and train individual women from organizations in building local donor bases. Semillas's resource development programme is creating viable models for greater social investment in women over the next decade. This programme needs to continue to be strengthened within Semillas – with staff, board and donor training in fundraising for social change – and it needs to continue to be presented to counterpart organizations as an important and viable long-term strategy for sustainability.

As Mexico's only women's fund, Semillas is a key player in addressing the funding crisis and for generating new ideas regarding grant making for women's NGOs. Semillas alone cannot rescue any organization. However, it has its fundraising experience, and the MIM network is a unique model and a valuable resource for the building of local donor bases to be shared with women's NGOs in supporting a shift towards other funding strategies. It also has valuable expertise and tools to contribute to the sustainability of non-governmental organizations. Feminist NGOs share a wealth of experience in working with grassroots communities and urban/popular sector women, in developing innovative strategies that empower women, and in leadership development. At the intersection between women's rights and development with a gender perspective, Semillas as a fund is an essential link between women's NGOs and international donors. As such, it has had to make the case to international donors for their participation in a strategic funding plan to guarantee the survival of a feminist agenda and move Semillas and other targeted NGOs to a new level of sustainability.

In addition to Semillas's general grant making to women's NGOs and grassroots groups for human rights projects, fundraising training among counterparts became a priority in 2005. In one training session a young woman remarked that 'This workshop has changed my life. I want to be a social change fundraiser! I want this to be my work as an activist.'

Semillas is currently creating a network of expert fundraiser–activists in Mexico through a training programme for young women working in women's NGOs. The Kellogg Foundation has been a key ally in developing Semillas's local philanthropy programme, and was the first to support the fundraising training programme. The Global Fund for Women and the Open Society Institute have also contributed to funding this programme, and participants from the first (2005–6) generation have already begun to increase their organizations' incomes. Las Libres (the free ones), a feminist NGO in Guanajuato, is creating alliances with local businesses and organizing fundraising tours in the United States seeking individual donors. In Jalisco, a rural women's organization called CAMPO created the Red MIM del Campo (MIM rural network) to attract women donors from Guadalajara, Mexico's second largest city. And a group of young activists from Elige, the Youth Network for Reproductive and Sexual Rights based in Mexico City, successfully and confidently approached more funding institutions during their first three months in the training programme than they had in the previous eighteen! These are real, tangible advances within the feminist movement, and represent a fundamental shift among activists as to how money is viewed. Is money talked about? Is it dirty? Is it an embarrassment? Or is it, as Semillas has learned the hard way, an essential part of planning: a tool for social change that will allow the movement not only to grow but to become economically sustainable?

NOTES

1   Semillas identifies marginal women and girls as those whose basic needs (food, education, housing) are not met, such as the poor, indigenous/rural people, and domestic workers; and marginalized groups of women and girls whose rights are not recognized by society, such as sex workers, lesbians, and, again, domestic workers.

2   See <http://www.globalfundforwomen.org> (last accessed 13 September 2006).

3 The selection process consists of a call for proposals that address women's human rights issues. Depending on funds available, specific areas are usually highlighted as when, for example, Semillas received a large grant from the David and Lucile Packard Foundation (see <http://www.packard.org>) for health, sexual and reproductive rights. Grants are only accepted if the conditions are aligned with the Semillas mission.

4 Programa Donativos Semilla (PDS).

5 See <http://www.macfound.org> (last accessed 13 September 2006).

6 See <http://www.wkkf.org> (last accessed 13 September 2006).

7 One of the most important benefits of the MIM network is that these funds are unrestricted. Semillas pools the money annually, and 85 per cent is granted to projects through its Seed Grant Programme; 15 per cent is retained by Semillas to cover administrative costs. The MIM network funds enable Semillas to finance projects in which no foundation or corporation is interested, as is often the case with, for example, lesbian and bisexual women's rights, domestic workers and advocacy.

8 'A Study of Mexican Women Donors', Semillas internal document, 2002.

9 Quote from the 2005 Semillas document *Mujeres Invirtiendo en Mujeres*, presented at the organization's fifteenth anniversary.

10 Schellenberg, M. (2004), *A Feasibility Study to Determine Semillas Future Grant-making Capacity and Strategies*.

11

Reflections on Strengthening Leadership in Community-based Organizations in India

Pramada Menon

When a new organization comes into being, there is always the pressure to do things differently, to make sure that mistakes are not repeated. Sometimes, because one is so conscious of wanting to be different, there is an effort to reinvent the wheel. And yes, there are ways in which the wheel can be reinvented! Companies exhort us to buy their tyres because they are different from others. We know that they are round, are made of rubber, and move in a circular motion, and that the only difference may be the marketing strategy employed, and perhaps some new technology that ensures a 'different' product. Similarly, when one creates a new organization, there is the temptation to say one is different from the rest. It requires tremendous self-control to say, 'We are not different. We owe a lot to what went on before we came into existence and to the movements and organizations that preceded us. All we are doing is finding new ways of addressing old challenges.'

Creating Resources for Empowerment in Action (CREA), a women's human rights organization,[1] began in the following way. A group of us who had been working in organizations in India and abroad felt a little less challenged and mildly disillusioned with the work that we had been doing previously. We felt a need to comple-ment what was already being done; most importantly, we wanted to create spaces for learning and putting theory into practice in a way that was at once exciting and beneficial. We wanted to have fun doing our work and to infect the people with whom we worked with that same enthusiasm. This was a formidable task for a young organization, but we felt that unless we dreamt and learnt to push ourselves beyond our own boundaries, we would not achieve change in the world.

What did we want to change and achieve? We wanted to develop innovative ways to address issues of gender discrimination, social injustice suffered by particular groups and communities, peace and conflict, the imbalance of power relations in societies, and the lack of access to information and services for poor and marginalized people. We wanted to create networks for social change that would strengthen civil society organizations, build leadership capacities in a new generation of development professionals and empower individuals to defend their own rights. Above all, perhaps, we aimed to be a catalyst for learning. We realized that the process of empowering articulate leaders would require a focus on issues of sexuality, violence against women, sexual and reproductive rights, women's rights and social justice. We would have to create programmes that would bring together people and ideas, start conversations, open horizons, make people ask questions, and introduce new perspectives. This was an ambitious wish list! But we knew that a great deal was possible if we set our hearts and minds to it.

The work we have carried out to date in India has shown us that women, like other groups and communities of underprivileged and marginalized people, face an encompassing poverty of resources, education, health and information. This poverty denies sustainable livelihoods and limits personal growth. It is the result of a complex interplay of variables ranging from socio-economic conditions to cultural, political and historical factors. In a society where a woman's needs are systematically placed at the bottom of the pile, her capacity to take decisions for herself is always severely limited.

In India, most grassroots interventions and development strategies have so far failed to improve women's lot in society. We felt that to foster any real change in the lives of women, CREA's interventions should address issues that affect both their material conditions and their social status. We also realized that in order for women to improve their own personal situations it is necessary for them to develop their own understandings of the complex socio-political, legal, cultural and economic structures that shape their lives. Out of this came CREA's Community-Based Leadership Programme.

The beginning

Sixteen Indian community-based organizations (CBOs) from Bihar, Jharkhand, Uttar Pradesh, New Delhi and the north-eastern states[2] partner CREA in this programme. Its long-term goal is to strengthen the leadership capacities of the women associated with the CBOs and enhance their use of formal and informal human rights mechanisms to address development and women's rights' issues.

CREA visualizes leadership as a dynamic quality that is present and could be enhanced in most individuals: the ability to deconstruct existing notions and norms of society, to develop her own understanding of what is appropriate, and then to take decisions that will improve well-being. Leadership is thus a quality that enables people to live their lives as they choose, with dignity and with sensitivity to other people's choices and decisions. The leadership programme works on the assumption that leadership is not a fixed state of being but a process through which women assert their rights by continually evaluating relevant experiences, questioning their roles in society, challenging power structures and effectively catalysing social change.

The process

We identified who would be part of the Community-Based Leadership Programme by travelling to different states in India and meeting with organizations and activists. These meetings enabled us to identify the issues facing grassroots organizations. Those that surfaced most regularly included the lack of women in leadership positions within organizations (a phenomenon not limited to rural India); the lack of information in Hindi (the local language) on women's human rights issues; and, perhaps most importantly, the lack of understanding of the interrelatedness of issues that affect women. The organizations with which we met raised issues of women's rights, livelihoods, natural resource management and local self-governance. However, very few of them focused on the issues of violence against women, sexuality and sexual rights, or reproductive health. And a question often raised by these groups was why organizations interested in social justice and poverty alleviation should concern themselves with the status and health of women.

At that stage we realized the importance of working to ensure that organizations saw their work as part of a larger human rights framework in which issues were not put in convenient little boxes but were interrelated and interdependent. For example, making the right to education a reality for adolescent girls requires addressing issues of sexuality. Girls are frequently not sent to school when this is far from the village, as families fear their daughters might bring shame and dishonour on them as the result of an inappropriate relationship. Many people at the grassroots believe that human rights have nothing to do with them and that they are solely the concern of international bodies such as the United Nations.

Spreading awareness of the relevance of human rights to all concerned, especially women, has proved to be quite difficult. Although it is understood that the status of women affects the general well-being of local communities, states and the world community, at the grassroots it is often not clear why improvements in women's health, including sexual and reproductive health, and freedom from violence, have anything to do with poverty alleviation.

It is in situations such as these that we have to wonder how the human rights of women can be explained, let alone understood, by those who have never stepped out of their villages — although the international community, meanwhile, considers the human rights of the woman and the girl-child to be

> an inalienable, integral and indivisible part of universal human rights. The full and equal participation of women in political, civil, economic, social and cultural life, at the national, regional and international levels, and the eradication of all forms of discrimination on grounds of sex are priority objectives.[3]

Although significant progress has been made in integrating women's rights as part of human rights discourse, for the majority of women in India, and in many other parts of the world, the exercise of these rights remains more of an aspiration than a reality. Conversations with grassroots organizations and activists revealed that there are three important areas of women's lives in which discrepancies exists between the acknowledgement and exercise of their rights. These are sexuality, reproductive and sexual health, and violence.

Having identified these as the issues on which CREA would need to focus, the critical question remained of how to engage with geographically distant organizations. Traditionally, urban-based NGOs working on women's rights have field offices, which legitimizes their claim to working with local women. Battles often ensue over territory and 'ownership', and smaller NGOs and networks, desperate for resources, frequently get caught in the middle. We were clear that by being based in Delhi we could only provide support in the form of training and the development of resource materials in Hindi. It appeared unfair of us to train women on how to confront domestic violence and then, when they needed support to follow cases through, fail to offer a physical presence. Training is relatively easy, but the real test comes when people, trained in exercizing their rights, need support in doing just that. Fortunately, the CBOs who were part of the leadership programme expressed great interest in learning more about women's human rights, issues of sexuality, and violence against women. Nonetheless, these were unfamiliar issues to them, on which they had no previous experience. We thus decided to provide information and focus on the training of women working within these CBOs, who would then be well placed to decide on the type of support needed by the communities in which they worked.

Deciding on the strategy to be adopted by the programme was difficult. It was tempting to see CREA as an organization that would respond to all the needs of the CBOs, but we were also clear that we had limited resources. Many internal discussions, and those held on an individual basis with CBOs, resulted in the decision that CREA would work as a support organization. The organizations identified were small women's groups working on women's issues without too much exposure to the world of human rights. They would be provided with training on issues identified by them at a time and a pace most suitable to them. It was also decided that CREA would not provide any financial support except for travel to attend CREA training sessions and workshops. The training and capacity-building initiatives within the leadership programme could best be characterized as building a bridge between formal human rights treaties and the realization of human rights at the organizational and individual level.

Until this point, partner organizations had been identified but they had not come together to discuss the Community-Based Leadership Programme or their roles within it. A meeting was convened at the project site of Vanangana, a feminist organization working on issues of violence against women in the Karvi Chitrakoot district of Uttar

Pradesh, a partner in this programme. Each partner organization was asked to nominate two staff members who would take part. The only condition we made, to ensure continuity of the process on which the organizations were about to embark, was that once a decision had been taken on participation, the organization in question had to ensure that the same representatives followed through with the whole process.

Prior discussion and transparency about membership were considered important: it had to be clear that only training and information were to be offered, and that no financial resources would be provided. Under these conditions, and considering the programme's fairly loose structure, we expected some organizations to lose interest. However, what ensued made it amply clear that there was indeed a great need for different kinds of programmes, as people were dissatisfied with what was currently on offer.

The meeting was a great success. All the women present were excited; for many, it was a unique opportunity to participate as, for once, the heads of organizations were not the only ones involved. Every woman present was able to make her own decisions. It was also unique in that it did not promise funds; perhaps most importantly, the objective of the meeting was to enhance the individual learning of the participants. They were not expected to return home and immediately establish a training programme on which they would be evaluated. They were, however, expected to come, learn, meet with each other, share life experiences and develop strategies that would help them decide for themselves on what and when they wanted to share when they returned to their respective organizations. The very essence of this programme was to enhance skills and understanding of issues related to women's rights. We considered it important to begin with the individuals and then move on to the organizational level.

This meeting also saw the development of a core set of beliefs and convictions[4] to guide the leadership programme, rules of engagement for members, and an outline of what the individual organizations could contribute to the programme.

During the training process itself we realized that we needed to pay special attention to creating spaces that allowed women to reflect, share and decide for themselves. Being frequently caught up in the 'numbers game', and the need to promise donors deliverable end products, we had constantly to remind ourselves of the importance of facilitating the organic growth of the process. Despite the stipulated time periods in which we were often obliged to reach our goals, we could not pretend to force the issue and 'drive' everybody towards our established goals, as we considered this to be inherently counterproductive.

Four years of training

The leadership programme is developed around the needs of the partner organizations. Each year a list of issues on which each partner CBO would like to focus has been drawn up, and on the basis of these training and workshops have been planned. This planning has always been mindful that the ultimate goal of the programme is to enhance the leadership capacities of women, and to ensure their access to information so they are able to exercise their rights and improve their economic, political and social positions.

Over the last four years, a number of leadership programme workshops have been held on issues of women's leadership, violence against women, gender and patriarchy, sexuality and reproductive health, sexuality and sexual rights, human rights, communalism and legal rights. However, it was also discovered that quite a few of the organizations lacked the knowledge needed to plan an advocacy campaign; they also needed help in documenting the work and the processes they were promoting to alter power structures within their respective villages. These needs were incorporated in workshop programmes.

Partner organizations have also been active participants in other CREA programmes such as the Institute for Rights, Activism and Development, a human rights institute for women working in the development sector in India, and exchange programmes. Some members also participated in meetings of the Indian Association of Women's Studies, the 2004 World Social Forum held in Mumbai, and the 10th International Women and Health Meeting held in Delhi in September 2005. Reshma from Sangatin in Sitapur, Uttar Pradesh, said after attending the World Social Forum:

> It was at the World Social Forum that I realized that violence against women or the negative impact of globalization is a worldwide phenomenon. Violations exist whether the women live in Burundi, Colombia or India. It was amazing to meet with so many people and learn so much.

In February 2004 and December 2005, partners in the leadership programme carried out a self-evaluation of the process using a participatory methodology that enabled them to discuss the changes individuals had seen within themselves since 2002. All of them agreed that their training had contributed to increased understanding of women's issues and enhanced their skills in negotiating women's human rights with local governments and the communities in which they work. The legal training enabled them to frame their human rights violations within the provisions of the Indian criminal code and address power inequities resulting from gender discrimination. Most of them also found themselves addressing gender inequities within the family and at a community and organizational level. This evaluation process high-lighted that the individuals who had received training on sexuality, and the organizations in which they worked, felt they were better able to address issues of sexuality and sexual rights within the communities in which they worked. However, and most importantly, the training on sexuality seemed to have helped individuals in their relationships with their partners.

The representatives of the partner organizations participating in the leadership programme have indicated their desire to continue with the leadership enhancing process; they also feel the need to expand the programme to include other CBOs so that more organizations can benefit from the programme. The range of resource materials created in Hindi through this programme has been accessed by partner organizations as well as others working in the field on issues of women's human rights. There are regular requests for the training manuals on gender and violence against women by organizations in India, which appear to indicate that grassroots organizations find the manuals useful.

The leadership programme and the CBOs involved have taught CREA many interesting lessons. The successful work of partner CBOs and their interactions with CREA have convinced us of the need to create more programmes in Hindi so that other CBOs can gain access to information and resources on issues of women's human rights. Other facets of CREA's work – such as the training undertaken in English by the Sexuality and Rights Institute in collaboration with TARSHI (Talking About Reproductive and Sexual Health Issues) and The Institute for Rights, Activism and Development – provide valuable experiences and materials (now to be translated into Hindi) for use by partner and other community-based organizations.

The challenges continue

The leadership programme has been very exciting, and the increased understanding of issues relating to women's human rights amongst the representatives of the CBOs has inspired CREA in its work. We have a number of requests from other organizations working in the Hindi-speaking regions of India who would like to participate in the programme. However, with the increasing demand for resource materials the question of sustainability arises.

Most donors are interested in the leadership programme having a larger and wider geographic focus. It currently counts only sixteen partner CBOs, but increasing demand from other CBOs means we need to face the question of how to include other organizations within this programme without becoming unwieldy. Partner CBOs who have been with the programme for a period of four years are at a conceptually different level. So how are we to balance the levels of understanding without being condescending to the new partners?

How sustainable is a programme such as this? In present-day terms, 'large is beautiful' in the language of development and rights advocacy, yet the leadership programme will always have to remain small if we wish to address the needs of the partners adequately. We realize that 'small' is also relative, however, and wonder for how long donors will continue supporting successful but small interventions without insisting on larger, replicable projects.

Although this Community-Based Leadership Programme has initiated a process of questioning within its partner organizations of social, cultural, economic and political power structures that have an impact on women's lives, it is clear that it may never lead to radical social change. Nevertheless, it will continue to do what it does best: enhancing the understanding of women's human rights amongst partner organizations and providing them with the convictions to question and challenge the discrimination and violations of human rights faced by women.

NOTES

1   Further information on CREA and its activities may be found at
    <http://www.creaworld.org/about_us.htm> (last accessed 9 September 2006).

2   Mahila Bal Jyoti Kendra and Mahila Jagran Kendra from Bihar; Damodar
    Mahila Mandal; Prerana Bharti, Prerana Niketan, Samarth Mahila Sanghatan
    from Jharkhand; Association for Advocacy and Legal Initiatives, Sangatin,
    Vanangana, Tehreek, Astitva, Gram Unnati Sansthan, Social Action Research
    Centre and Sahjani Shiksha Kendra from Uttar Pradesh; North-East Network
    from the north-eastern states and Action India in New Delhi.

3   Clause 18 of the Vienna Declaration and Programme of Action, adopted by
    the United Nations World Conference on Human Rights, 14–25 June 1993.
    See <http://www.unhchr.ch/huridocda/huridoca.nsf/(Symbol)/
    A.CONF.157.23.En?OpenDocument> (last accessed 9 September 2006).

4   Some of the core convictions were: women's rights are human rights; all work
    should be guided by feminist principles; and no individual or group will be
    discriminated against on the basis of actual or perceived age, marital status,
    disability, language, nationality, caste, class, religion, education, ethnicity, sexual
    orientation, profession, dress or appearance.

12

Virtual Seminar on Gender and Trade

An Innovative Process

Verónica Baracat, Phyllida Cox
and Norma Sanchís[1]

The complexity of trade as a platform for carrying out feminist analysis and advocacy strategies represents enormous challenges for the women's movement, as does access to the relevant institutional interfaces, since these pay scant attention to the demands of civil society. Ignorance and resistance to integrating gender perspectives in the trade may compound these problems.

The women's movement in Latin America has extensive experience in promoting gender equality through campaigns and in monitoring public policy on emblematic issues such as domestic violence, sexual and reproductive health, sexual exploitation and others. While macroeconomics and international trade have not yet been included as priorities on the movement's advocacy agendas at decision-making levels, a growing number of women are becoming involved in mixed organizations and social movements seeking to counter some of the negative effects of trade and globalization. The strengthening of the feminist perspective in decision making, and integrating a gender-oriented analysis of developments in this area are considered vital to the movement.

The objective of this chapter is to reflect on the training of trainers in gender and trade initiated by the Latin American chapter of the Gender and Trade Network (LAGTN),[2] and to present its most recent and pioneering experience: the Virtual Seminar on Gender and Trade.[3] Its innovative process contributes to the strengthening of the women's movement in Latin America in three different ways: by dealing with the issue of the relationship between international trade and gender;

through the training of trainers, with a focus on popular education; and by integrating conceptual contents by offering a virtual seminar that takes advantage of new information technologies. The virtual seminar was designed to encourage and facilitate the building of networks, strengthen existing ones, and optimize their influence on gender and trade issues, within the broader context of improving technologies for democratic participation.

Training trainers in gender and trade – the process

Created in 1999, the International Gender and Trade Network[4] is a network of gender-specialist feminists who provide support and tools to women's groups, NGOs, social movements and governments. It also helps to evaluate the impact on women of free trade treaties, and to formulate policies that promote social justice and gender-sensitive economic development. As one of its objectives, the network's Latin American chapter[5] proposes to strengthen the capacity of the regional women's movement to influence national and international mechanisms for economic integration.

Two main problems were identified within the economic integration process. First, the narrow representation of the women's movement signalled the need to broaden the involvement not only of women but also of civil society as a whole in the dynamics of international trade. The other problem is the lack of gender perspective that needs to be addressed through its integration in the mechanisms of international trade. Over recent years the women's movement has increasingly worked towards incorporating non-traditional themes into the economic integration processes and linking its actions with other sectors of the social movement. At the same time, some economic justice organizations are also trying to influence the inclusion of gender-sensitive procedures on the agendas of institutions involved in trade. Both of these processes need to be strengthened.

Countries of the region are simultaneously engaged in a wide variety of trade negotiations, ranging from bilateral and multilateral trade agreements to common market negotiations. The highly technical nature and lack of transparency of negotiations severely hamper a clear understanding of the aspects under negotiation and the vested interests of the most powerful stakeholders. While on the one hand these factors curb and limit the participation of certain sectors of civil society, their lack of understanding and information also result in an inability to satisfactorily and effectively defend their positions and statements with the clear concepts, empirical data and statistics that would legitimize and add credibility to their claims. Awareness raising and training on issues of gender, economics and trade agreements thus become imperative for increasing the participation of civil society in general and the women's movement in particular, so as to optimize capacity to influence decision-making processes. The training needs to enable different civil society groups to become empowered and share power among other like-minded stakeholders. This requires building capacity and commitment among civil society's weakest sectors through increased awareness, organization and participation.[6]

In 2002, LAGTN launched a process to train trainers on issues of gender, globalization and economic integration so as to generate a critical mass of women in the region who are able to mobilize resources and efforts, thus creating a ripple effect within civil society. The objective was to generate a nucleus of trained women who could provide momentum in broadening the circles of debate and in involving other sectors of the women's movement in monitoring the impacts of governments' decisions in the region.

The experience of the virtual seminar

Virtual education uses new technologies to deploy alternative learning methodologies for people otherwise limited by geographical location, teaching quality and time. While it is true that not everyone in Latin America has access to information technologies or telecommunications, it is also true that distance education is a means to optimize available resources, widen the geographical scope and increase the number and variety of students.

Virtual education is a particularly valuable tool for the inclusion of women, with potential to provide them with improved opportunities and access to education and training. Distance education is often the only way some women can obtain accreditation for new knowledge due to their productive and reproductive loads. It also facilitates networking by connecting stakeholders who share interests but are geographically distanced.

The Gender and Trade Virtual Seminar was held between October 2004 and April 2005 as part of the project 'Gender and Trade Training and Information Networks in Latin America', funded by the United Nations Development Fund for Women (UNIFEM).[7] The project also involved the consolidation of networks so they could share experiences and monitor activity throughout the region. Its objectives were to contribute technological and methodological knowledge of gender, international trade and regional agreements; update participants on the advances of regional multilateral and bilateral negotiations and civil society positions on them; link Latin American organizations working in gender, economics and trade; and, finally, to generate a network of women, enabling the exchange of knowledge and experiences in gender and trade issues.

The project generated a surprising level of interest from the very beginning of the dissemination and registration process. Although the original goal was 50 participants, 170 people applied and 120 were accepted. Applicants were asked to complete a form and send it in by e-mail as part of a selection process based on experience in gender, economics and training, and institutional affiliation.

The selected seminar participants – 110 women and ten men from 15 countries of the region – were representatives of women's movements, social and grassroots organizations, union members, academics and people interested in issues relating to gender, economics and trade. Of this group, 60 per cent participated actively in the programmed activities.

The methodological challenge of this virtual training on gender, economic and trade agreements was to integrate a highly heterogeneous group of people representing a variety of organizations, countries of origin, and, of course, levels of experience on these issues. Some were very involved in both gender and trade issues, others in one or the other, while a third group had little background in either area. A conceptual introduction on gender and development was provided as a common denominator for initiating work, and instructors and specialists were asked to prepare intermediate-level texts, with triggers[8] for those interested in more in-depth information.

The methodology also included readings prepared especially for the seminar with inputs from regional specialists, discussion forums, practical exercises and the preparation of monographs on selected themes. In all cases participants were encouraged to reflect on the concepts introduced in the light of personal experiences in each country, and to undertake group work to facilitate exchange and networking. The seminar was carried out in both the Spanish and Portuguese languages.

The meticulous planning of the seminar provided excellent results. The efforts of the e-learning and informatics specialists in setting up the discussion forums and designing the website were fundamental in generating clear and accessible products that were highly valued by the participants. Marco from Ecuador expressed his satisfaction with the seminar:

> Thanks for the material and for all the work of those who facilitated this space. It's always important for the person or persons who make development and learning possible for others to receive recognition.... I also hope there will be some type of continuity for this space and that we take advantage of it to do something together, although I'm aware this doesn't depend on the facilitators but on each of us.[9]

Likewise, the topics selected, the length of texts, the trigger questions for discussion forums, and the exercises and tasks prepared by the teaching team were also considered effective. Facilitation proved to be a key component, supporting convergence with the technology and methodology proposed, as well as permanent accompaniment to maintain momentum.

The first stage of the seminar included three conceptual modules: international trade from a gender perspective; the multilateral trading system and its risks and potential; and social mobilization in response to economic policies in Latin America. Questions formulated by the coordination staff for each of these modules stimulated rich discussions through which collective knowledge was constructed as a result of many high-quality interventions. Of the 57 people who participated in at least one of the forums, 40 per cent also took part in two or more.

The number and quality of the exercises submitted was encouraging and the level of participation, considered by experts to be more than satisfactory with 44 people submitting at least one exercise, was surprising considering group diversity and the fact that enrolment was free of charge.

In the first module the forum topics and exercises were designed to explore and systematize knowledge of individual national economies and identify the main policies and trends affecting the situation of women, examining the interdependencies of globalization and free trade. The aim of the second module, on the multilateral trading system and its risks and potential, aimed to apply gender concepts in analysing international trade instruments and to explore similarities and differences among the various trade agreements of the Latin American countries. Finally, the third module analysed expressions of social protest tied to economic or trade policies in Latin America and types of women's participation within them.

The second stage of the seminar took place in January 2005: it included the writing of a monograph and a final discussion forum in April, in which the monographs submitted were examined and advocacy experiences shared. A tutor assigned to each participant or team provided ongoing guidance. The most representative exercises and monographs were published on the seminar website[10] and dealt with themes ranging from the impacts of globalization and free trade treaties to microbusinesswomen or social mobilization in the region. All analyses included a gender perspective.

Questionnaires were used to evaluate results after the first stage of the seminar (December 2004) and at the end (April 2005). The forums for debate and exchange via e-mail provided valuable input for the monitoring and evaluation processes. The evaluations received were very positive and in the final evaluation participants rated the seminar as 'very good' to 'excellent', with similar results for the degree to which expectations were satisfied. Every one of the participants requested continuity for the seminar. The topics of greatest interest during the second stage were social mobilization around trade agreements; advances in and the implications of trade negotiations and agreements; paid and volunteer work; and power relations between countries. The feedback of Julia from Peru reflects the general sentiment of seminar participants:

> I want to congratulate you for this valuable contribution and also thank you for giving me the opportunity to participate.... I have to tell you that thanks to you I have developed new outlooks and new employment possibilities at both the union and grassroots levels.[11]

Even though the project has now concluded, the seminar network is still intact and we continue to share information from the entire region. While it is still too early to evaluate the impact of this effort, participants from MERCOSUR countries, the Andean region, Mexico and Central America have already been getting more involved in influencing trade negotiations in their respective countries or regions, and in training on issues relating to gender and trade.

Conclusions and lessons learned

The main strength of the seminar, of course, was the distance-learning opportunity it provided to a relatively large number of people from a wide geographical area. However, we encountered several difficulties, of which the following are the most significant. Not all the people who might be interested were able to participate because Internet access is still limited in the region; certain technical limitations discouraged participation, such as disconnections, and lengthy downloading times for documents; and 40 per cent of participants were unable to continue mainly due to conflicts with their regular activities and schedules, technical problems on their side, or because they did not read the entire proposal before registering for the seminar. Another strength is that information technology is a potent mechanism for inclusion once the initial trepidation is overcome. Although its use is already common within the women's movement, it is important to highlight that virtual training allows women in different parts of the region (who otherwise might not be able to access forums of this type) to work together, and, as we saw from Julia's testimony, the experience often optimizes pro-fessional opportunities.[12]

A third aspect or strength, when comparing virtual education with more traditional methods, is that although the former requires much more rigorous planning, clarity and visual consistency in the texts and other teaching materials, and attentive monitoring and follow-up regarding instructions and timetables, there is a much wider outreach and a more efficient use of available resources. The high quality and quantity of the exercises demonstrated the value of diversity and the wealth of insights.

Another strength was the considerable interest in the concept of the virtual seminar itself. Despite the brief period of dissemination (less than three weeks), which was mostly carried out by e-mail through different networks and the LAGTN web page and bulletins, the seminar had a broad impact and extended beyond the usual channels of the feminist NGOs and networks. This demonstrates the potential of electronic networking throughout Latin America, and the possibility of building on this specific experience through similar projects.

The project also demonstrated that a useful, democratically available tool can strengthen ties between organizations and networks working in seemingly incompatible areas and competing for funds, and that it is possible to coordinate and harmonize efforts. The fact that other networks in the region responded to the virtual seminar proposal by sending the invitation out to their members is an indication of the synergy created.

Finally, the forum, although temporary, generated opportunities for meetings between and exchanges among diverse civil society stakeholders. This, as we have demonstrated, has wholly positive repercussions for the construction and strengthening of a movement around the issues of gender and trade. The result is a waiting list of over 50 people for future similar seminars. There is thus no doubt in our minds that virtual exchanges are useful and valuable instruments in building networks for sharing and cooperation and in strengthening the women's movement.

NOTES

1   Latin America Gender and Trade Network, Training Area, Argentina.
2   Information on the Latin America Gender and Trade Network can be found at <http://www.igtn.org/page/533> (last accessed 10 September 2006).
3   The Virtual Gender and Trade Seminar was organized by the coordination personnel of the LATGN training area, headquartered in Argentina. It was held from 9 October 2004 to 30 April 2005 at the regional level and in virtual form. The technical team comprised: Norma Sanchís (coordinator), Verónica Baracat (deputy coordinator), Nora Lizenberg (e-learning advisor), Eberhard Kaul and Roxana Ullianow (informatics assistance) and Lucía Santalices (translator). The teaching team included: Norma Sanchís, Alma Espino and Graciela Rodríguez (instructors), Verónica Baracat (facilitator), Patricia Jaramillo, Rebeca Salazar and Carolina Villarroel (tutors).
4   See <http://www.igtn.org> (last accessed 10 September 2006).
5   See <http://www.generoycomercio.org> in Spanish (last accessed 10 September 2006).
6   Sanchís, N., V. Baracat, and C. Jiménez, (2004), *El comercio internacional en la agenda de las mujeres*, ITGN–UNIFEM, also available at <http://www.generoycomercio.org/docs/Comercio_Mujer_final.pdf> (last accessed 10 September 2006).
7   See: <http://www.unifem.org> (last accessed 10 September 2006).
8   In information technology, a button that automatically activates a programme or a link directing the Internet user to further information.

9   Marco V. Bombón, seminar participant from Ecuador.
10 The seminar does not have a permanent website. However, some documents can be found at <http://www.generoycomercio.org/docs/publicaciones/matcap/Publicacion-Seminario-Virtual.pdf> (last accessed 11 September 2006).
11 Julia Petronila Cabello Acevedo, seminar participant from Peru.
12 Lizenberg, N., V. Ginocchio, and N. Graciano (2005), 'La formación docente a distancia: una cuestión de mujeres?', unpublished paper presented (in Spanish) at the Fifth International Congress on Distance Education.

Part 4

Broadening the Support Base
of Movements

13

Zimbabwe Women Writers

1990–2004

Mary O. Tandon

When Zimbabwe achieved independence in 1980 the few women's organizations that existed were generally focused on improving the economic situation of women. Teaching them to set up and run income-generating projects – to help reduce poverty and enhance their economic and social status – was the general practice. After several years, however, it became clear that the income generated was minimal, and that attempting to run such projects only increased the already heavy burden on women.

In the mid-1980s women's organizations in Zimbabwe changed their emphasis from income generation to women's empowerment through education aimed at raising awareness of their political, economic, human and legal rights. As a result, a number of organizations focused on advocacy for women's rights and equality, violence against women, legal services, health issues and women's role in politics, micro-finance, and the media. Little importance was given to writing as a means of promoting gender equality. Zimbabwe Women Writers (ZWW), which was established in 1990, is the first women's organization in Zimbabwe and in Southern Africa to address gender imbalance through writing and publishing.

This chapter focuses on the internal dynamics and strategies used to develop, strengthen, and sustain the ZWW organization, which rests on the broad participation of women in the region. It covers the mechanisms for inclusion of both literate and illiterate women from all walks of life; the building of alliances and partnerships within the region; and the problems of fundraising, resource mobilization and sustainability. The conclusion considers the problem of raising finance to sustain the organization.

A brief history of writing and publishing

Prior to 1990, the year in which Zimbabwe Women Writers (ZWW) was formed, the state and civil society, in the name of tradition, culture and religious norms, silenced women and denied them the right to freedom of expression. Those who dared go against cultural norms were frequently labelled as 'unfeminine' or 'Westernized'. Women usually had no formal education, and, if they did, it was very limited. Furthermore the multiple tasks they had in the home left them with little time to read or write, even if they had access to books and writing implements. However, this does not mean that there were no women writers before ZWW was created. There were a few fortunate ones, although their writings were not as visible as those of men. The publishing industry was also male-dominated, which meant that female authors had difficulty in getting their works published. It was not until around the 1990s that there was a notable growth of books by African women.

The publishing industry in Zimbabwe can be traced back to 1954, the opening of what was then the University of Salisbury and the establishment of the Rhodesian Literature Bureau, a government body that promoted vernacular publications. The Literature Bureau had total control of the publishing sector and, although writing workshops were held, these were only for male writers.

The birth of Zimbabwe Women Writers

In 1989, nine years after Zimbabwe's independence, a series of discussions were held at the University of Zimbabwe concerning the gender imbalance in literature and publishing. These meetings resulted in a workshop for women writers the following year, during which it was concluded that a women's organization would be necessary to provide the appropriate environment for women writers to join forces, build confidence, and begin to express their ideas and their problems through writing. This gave rise to a small coordinating committee and the subsequent creation of ZWW a year later.

Like most beginnings, the process of building ZWW was a long and uphill battle. We believed in the value of women's writing and the contribution it could make in offering a totally different perspective on society. But there were no resources, and as we had not yet established our identity, we could not get financial assistance. But we did have women members, a vision, determination and the courage to face the many challenges ahead, and we relied on our own resources to tackle these. We first needed to establish a legal identity and be registered under what we thought would be Zimbabwe's Social Welfare Act. The organization's constitution was drawn up by one of its members and submitted for registration of ZWW as a non-profit organization. Although this was initially refused due to a technicality, after nearly two years of research and administrative procedures ZWW was finally registered as a trust.

The dynamics of reaching out for membership was our second challenge. While literacy would seem to be a self-evident prerequisite for writing, ZWW still faced the dilemma of whether membership should be limited to literate women in mainly urban areas or include women from rural areas where illiteracy is rife. We had to consider how to help women to put their stories on paper; and whether we could justify the creation of a women's writing organization and exclude the 60 per cent of women who lived in rural areas. In the end ZWW decided to extend its membership to all women in Zimbabwe who aspire to write, or at least communicate their stories.

The decision was based on ZWW's mission to empower women through reading and writing and the publication of their works, expressed in its main objectives: to develop writing skills; to promote literacy among women; to advance women's writing and the appreciation of literature; to encourage the reading of women's writings; and to celebrate positive images of women in writing.

The organization is conscious that literacy and writing cannot be limited to academic renderings and that narrative skills must also be embraced. Even though a large proportion of ZWW members are unable to read and write, they have important life stories to tell and the organization provides the space where women are able to break away from daily chores, meet and tell their stories, share problems and solutions, and voice opinions and ideas. We value these opportunities and ensure that stories can later be transcribed in the most appropriate manner. Women are encouraged to tell their stories in the language in which they feel most comfortable, in the presence of another ZWW member or a family member or friend who is able to transcribe the story. In this way we have received manuscripts from schoolchildren who have recorded the stories of illiterate family members. This effectively reduces the generational gap, and builds bridges between those who are illiterate and those who are not, as well as between rural and urban women.

The membership challenge

Membership is open to all women in Zimbabwe who aspire to write. An annual membership fee for rural members is half that for those in urban areas.[1] It was not difficult to recruit members in the city and urban areas, as communication was easier and educational levels higher. Women already had more exposure to and experience of issues of gender imbalance, and faced fewer impediments when it came to writing their stories. It proved more difficult to convince women in rural areas to join the organization, and so our early efforts concentrated on urban recruitment. Two-day writing-skills workshops were held among members who then helped promote ZWW among a wider public. Gradually, writing-skills workshops spread out from the urban areas into districts and provinces. Workshop participants were provided with food, accommodation, transport and a small allowance to compensate for time usually spent in the field or on household duties. This system also provided an incentive for husbands to allow their wives to attend workshops. Between 1994 and 1998 membership grew from 18 branches throughout Zimbabwe to 88 branches. With each branch having at least 15 participants, this represents a growth of at least 1,320 participants over those four years.

The challenge of broad and inclusive participation

Its broad participation base soon challenged ZWW to respond effectively to this rapid growth in membership. A fund-raising process was initiated to strengthen its secretariat and resulted in assistance from the Norwegian Agency for Development Cooperation[2] in 1992. This paid for a one-room office with basic office equipment, a coordinator and skeleton staff. The following year Hivos[3] provided ZWW with institutional support for specific writing-skills workshops. During its early life ZWW was called upon to hold many such workshops, and in the face of this demand sought help from experienced women writers such as Norma Kitson.[4] However, as the number of branches increased, it became difficult to carry out skills workshops in individual branches. Branch leaders were thus trained so that they, in turn, could train branch members. Members submit their writings to ZWW office for constructive feedback from reviewers. Works are then returned to the authors for editing and re-submission for possible publication.

Progress in the world of publishing

ZWW had to build its capacity to work with publishers. Most publishers will only accept books that meet specific criteria, and commercial publishing houses only accept texts that are economically viable. In 1992, ZWW printed its first, 86-page anthology of short stories and poetry, simply typed and stapled together. Although we were unable to find a publisher, a thousand copies were produced and sold to Zimbabwean women. This was a great boost for the confidence of women who saw their work 'published' for the first time.

The first official publication was the *Anthology of Zimbabwe Women Writers* in 1994.[5] Over 100 authors contributed their stories and poems. The foreword by the then Minister of Information, Post and Telecommunications, David Karimanzira, commented that 'The diversity of the material is one of its delights. The writing is from women throughout Zimbabwe, from the urban centres to the rural lands, from professional and academic women to land-workers, housewives and domestics. All of them have something important to say.'

We made a considerable effort to promote writings that project positive images of women, legitimizing their struggle for fundamental rights and freedom. In 1995 ZWW was commissioned by the United Nations Children's Fund (UNICEF) to write a series of five booklets for primary schools entitled *There's Room at the Top*.[6] The aim was to provide positive career role models for children, especially girls.

In 1997 ZWW ventured into the two major local languages, Ndebele and Shona, publishing a selection of short stories and poetry in these languages as well as in English. Zimbabwe Women Writers' *Selections: English Poetry and Short Stories*[7] had a second reprint in 2001; its title is *Inkondlo*[8] in Ndebele, and *Nhetembo*[9] in Shona. In 2004 *Nhetembo* was selected by the Zimbabwe School Education Council for use in secondary schools, and was reprinted after some stories were rewritten to the Council's specifications.

Over the years ZWW improved the quality and content of its publications. For example, *Women of Resilience*,[10] published in 2000, is a book based on interviews conducted by ZWW members with women freedom fighters in the liberation of Zimbabwe. It reminds readers of the role women played in the liberation war and enhances the image of women in society.

Perhaps the most notable ZWW publication appeared in 2003. *A Tragedy of Lives*[11] was based on interviews by ZWW members with women prisoners and ex-prisoners. This important book raised issues that could influence positive change – especially for women prisoners – in the judicial and prison systems in Zimbabwe, and it strengthened ZWW as an advocacy organization. Themes addressed included the degrading living conditions of women prisoners, their social conditions when they are released, and, more importantly, how innocent children are obliged to stay with their mothers in prison in the absence of someone to care for them. *A Tragedy of Lives* won the National Arts Merit Award the year following its publication.

The marketing challenge

Zimbabwe Women Writers usually markets its own publications. It is in this area that we need to increase our capacity and collaborate more closely with publishers. The Ministry of Education was also approached with a proposal to incorporate some publications in school curricula. Although the initial reaction was not encouraging, our persistence paid off, as mentioned above with the adoption of *Nhetembo*.

Writing beyond borders

Besides publishing, ZWW also promotes the power of writing beyond national boundaries. After seeing ZWW's publications, some South African women approached ZWW to share experiences on how to begin a writing group. As a result of this contact, South Africa now has Women in Writing, a flourishing women writers' organization based in Johannesburg. Zimbabwe Women Writers also collaborates with the Ugandan women's writers organization, Femrite,[12] through the exchange of publications, joint workshops and other cultural and literary events.

The organization tries hard to engage its members in literary activities such as public readings of members' writings, writing competitions, art and writers' festivals such as international book fairs.

Our weaknesses and limitations

Zimbabwe Women Writers has a small secretariat: the director, an assistant who is also responsible for organizing programmes and workshops, a bookkeeper, a part-time accountant, and a general clerk. Funding limits the size of the team, and the heavy workload means that it has sometimes been necessary for members of the board of trustees to assist the secretariat in the carrying out its programme of activities.

We have always been heavily dependent on donor funds, and the situation has been particularly difficult since the beginning of the millennium. There are many contributory factors. Some donors pulled out of Zimbabwe in protest against the Land Reform Policy instigated by President Robert Mugabe in the year 2000: although these donors concede that the land reform was justified, they believe its implementation created instability not only for the white farmers but also for the general population. Other donors were not convinced that literature, art and culture contribute to strengthening civil society, and prefer to fund more visible social issues such as HIV/AIDS and human rights.

For the past decade ZWW has been sustained by one major donor, Hivos,[13] and has also received funds from the Canadian International Development Agency, the Global Fund for Women and the Norwegian Agency for Development Cooperation. These funds were for specific projects and not administrative upkeep. However, the running of the organization involves a variety of fixed costs, such as telephone charges and salaries for programme officers, that are additional to specific project costs and for which funding is required.

The economic sustainability of ZWW is the permanent challenge, especially since the turn of the century. The current inflation rate[14] makes it especially difficult. The short-term, project-specific funding does not allow ZWW to establish a permanent base, and this makes for insecurity and anxiety regarding the organization's development.

The way forward

The major impediment to growth is clearly funding, and there is a need to undertake some strategic planning that will guide ZWW toward greater financial independence and economic sustainability.

One way forward is to strengthen our links with commercial publishers, such as Weaver Press, so that ZWW's works can be made available in the national and international marketplaces. The printing of *A Tragedy of Lives* was a start; meanwhile, until we manage to publish more books, ZWW will continue with the in-house publication of members' works.

To date, ZWW has been writing and publishing first, and only then assessing the market. Another strategy would be to write to market demand, after research to determine what books are likely to sell. Although ZWW did not benefit financially from the adoption of the five *There's Room at the Top* booklets in public schools, and the current administration has not show much enthusiasm for including more of our materials,[15] a more systematic cooperation with the Ministry of Education could be envisaged in the future: there is a general consensus on the need for appropriate reading and teaching materials in local languages. We have already set a precedent with the publication of *Inkondlo* and *Nhetembo* in the Ndebele and Shona languages respectively. The organization also has the advantage of members who speak and write both languages, and who could, with appropriate funding and guidance, develop valuable teaching materials.

Conclusion

Since 1990 ZWW has focused on urging women to take a stand against discrimination, deprivation, and oppression; we have promoted women's development by providing members with tools for empowerment; and we have enabled them to gain confidence as writers whose works are published. These three facets of the organization's work are mutually reinforcing and thus help in its strengthening. However, ZWW's future is threatened and quite unpredictable in the current unstable political and economic environment. I would like to use the analogy of the baobab tree that is extremely drought-resistant and is known to survive for thousands of years. Just as a seed takes root, grows up and develops into a healthy tree, so ZWW has flourished since its planting. Now it has been struck by a period of drought and, like the baobab, it is losing all its leaves; it might even appear to be dead. But there's life below the soil and, when the conditions are right, it will spring to life again.

NOTES

1   Editor's note: although the figures of ZW$5 and ZW$10 were cited by the author as membership fees in rural and urban areas respectively, these can only be indicative as Zimbabwe's current annual inflation rate is at 1,184 per cent, according to online figures of the Reserve Bank of Zimbabwe (last accessed June 2006).

2   See <http://www.norad.no> (last accessed 11 September 2006).

3   The Dutch Humanist Institute for Co-operation with Developing Countries. See <http://www.hivos.nl> (last accessed 11 September 2006).

4   For more about Norma Kitson see:
    http://www.revolutionarycommunistgroup.com/frfi/168/168_nki.html
    (last accessed 15 October 2006).

5   Kitson, N. (ed.) (1994), *Anthology of Zimbabwe Women Writers*, ZWW, Zimbabwe.

6   This is a series of five booklets published between 1995 and 1999. All the stories were researched and written by members of ZWW. The Canadian International Development Agency provided financial support in the development, printing and distribution of the booklets. Booklets 1 and 2 (1995), booklet 3 (1996), and booklets 4 and 5 (1999) were edited by the Curriculum Development Unit (CDU) of the Ministry of Education, Sport and Culture, and published in Harare by the Ministry of Education in Association with UNICEF.

7   ZWW (2001), *Selections: English Poetry and Short Stories*, Zimbabwe Women Writers, Harare.

8   ZWW (1998), *Inkondlo*, Harare, Zimbabwe.

9   ZWW (1998), *Nhetembo*, Harare, Zimbabwe.

10 ZWW (ed.) (2000), *Women of Resilience*, Harare, Zimbabwe.

11 Musengezi, C. and I. Staunton (eds.) (2003), *A Tragedy of Lives: Women in Prison in Zimbabwe*, Weaver Press, Harare.

12 See: <http://www.wworld.org/about/affiliates/femrite.htm>.

13 ZWW became a Hivos partner in 1997. Over the years, Hivos has provided the organization with financial support for various aspects, including institutional support, capacity building and networking, staff development, programme development and gender mainstreaming. This support was in the form of 2–3-year contracts during consecutive years. The current contract, which will be the last one, started in 2006 and will end in 2008, bringing the total period of support to 10 years.

14 See Note 1.

15 There are two further booklets in *There's Room at the Top*.

14

Amnesty for Women

Building Mechanisms to Integrate and Empower Migrant Women in Hamburg, Germany

Sol Viviana Rojas and Raquel Aviles Caminero

> The women who leave are daring to seek success. Leaving is already a success.[1]

When many Latin American women decide to migrate, they embark not only on a journey to another country, but also on an odyssey toward deep change. Both the possibilities and the challenges they face are determined by gender. They initiate separations of time and space from their communities of origin, their homes, their children, and sometimes even from their partners. They leave the familiar behind to face new challenges so as to improve their lives and those of their families – to 'get ahead'.

Unlike migrant men, who generally find employment in agriculture, industry, construction or manufacturing, most of the work available to migrant[2] women is in traditionally 'feminine', socially devalued service areas: caring for the elderly, the sick and children; domestic work; and the sex industry. And this work, as it usually takes place outside the formal economy, is poorly paid. Moreover, it tends to fall outside the scope of labour legislation and instruments regulating international migration, thus exacerbating the vulnerability of women.

In Hamburg, Germany, there is a significant presence of Latin American women migrants who often travel alone to seek employment. These women face unknown scenarios where their precarious grasp of the language becomes a barrier to accessing legal aid and protection. They are frequently 'invisible', and programmes and services for migrants are rarely gender-sensitive: they are therefore oblivious to the impact migration has on the lives of the women who arrive in Germany.

This case study offers reflections on the work of a group made up both *of* and *for* migrant women who form part of the Latin American section of Amnesty for Women *(AfW)* Hamburg. The group provides support to women migrants who are in the process of integration by assisting them in the development of their employment and life prospects. The specific proposal of the Latin American group (AfW-LA) is to widen the horizons and opportunities of migrant women who have had different migratory experiences and whose backgrounds demonstrate a great diversity with respect to legal status, origin, age, educational and cultural level, and command of the German language. Their prospects are expanded by providing them with opportunities to share and learn from life-enriching experiences, and by helping them adapt to their new country and gain control over their own lives. The first part of the chapter provides an overview of AfW-LA and the psychological counselling it offers, and then describes how the group developed, outlines its objectives, and explains how it operates through its facilitators. It also deals with some of the challenges being faced. Finally, it analyses results, sums up the lessons learned, and proposes strategies for future action.

Amnesty for Women

Amnesty for Women (AfW) promotes self-help through a wide range of advisory services, accompaniment, legal aid, psycho-social counselling and training, as well as through a public awareness campaign. Its objective is to strengthen the social and legal status of women migrants and thus facilitate their long-term integration in Germany.

Created in 1986, this non-governmental organization has three sections: Eastern Europe, Asia and Latin America. There is one full-time, salaried person responsible for each section, and interns and volunteers are in charge of a variety of activities: language courses in German, English and Spanish; dance, cooking and sewing classes; and the TAMPEP[3] and FENARETE[4] projects sponsored by the European Union. From the outset, AfW has worked actively to prevent violations of migrant women's human rights and to combat any type of violence or oppression that may be inflicted upon this vulnerable group.

Those who collaborate with AfW are also usually migrants themselves and speak German, English, Polish, Portuguese, Russian, Spanish, Thai and Czech; in most cases, they are able to help women who come for counselling in their own languages.

Funding from government institutions such as the Department of Social and Family Affairs (BSF),[5] and the Department of Support for Family, Youth and Social Order[6] is used to cover AfW fixed costs, professional fees and other expenses. However, these 'full-time' posts are often underfunded and depend on professionals who are committed to the cause and frequently offer their services on a voluntary basis.

The Latin American section (AfW–LA) is coordinated by a part-time social worker. In 2005 a total of 1,015[7] counselling sessions took place. These provide information on a wide range of issues.[8]

Psychological counselling

The following observation is typical of many immigrants: 'The first time I heard the word "depression" was here in Germany ... where I come from it doesn't exist. [There] you might be sad, but I think "depressed" is something from here.'[9] AfW–LA was inspired by the perception of a need for a more comprehensive approach to the problems faced by migrant women. The psychological counselling service provided by two psychologists[10] working at AfW–LA is anonymous, free and in Spanish. The isolation and loneliness of many women are frequently revealed in these counselling sessions, together with the anguish and insecurity they suffer as a result of the language barrier and the need for socialization. While psychological counselling helps a great deal, it is not always enough.

The Latin American section

The main goal of AfW–LA is to provide a support network with which Latin American women can identify through discussions, the sharing of experiences, frustrations and insights, and by seeing themselves as protagonists capable of changing their own personal situations. It is thus a group made up *of* and *for* those who decide to participate in its activities.

The group is flexible in the development of activities that respond specifically to the needs of participants, and which are aligned with three main objectives: to generate tools and strategies contributing to the integration process of women by broadening their social networks and empowering their symbolic and social capital; to encourage discussion on how to tackle the obstacles and challenges of migration, and generate alternatives of knowledge, self-knowledge and power; and to explore possibilities for the development of personal potential and skills in, for example, decision making, teamwork, conflict resolution, problem solving and communication, negotiation and participation.

As the great majority of potential group members do not speak German, it was decided that the language spoken in the Latin American group would be Spanish. Outreach is by word of mouth and by simple flyers (when funding permits) that announce specific activities or special topics to be addressed in group sessions. These might be as varied as migration and arrival in a new country, recognizing and expressing feelings, talking about difficult things, 'what I will do to reach my goals', how to fill out a job application in Germany, problem solving and positive thinking, or the Christmas party. Some special sessions have a limited number of participants due to their nature. However, there are regular AfW-LA meetings on the last Tuesday of each month at the AfW hall. Colleagues also hand out flyers during formal legal advisory sessions or psycho-social counselling. Although flyers are distributed on the street, most women learn of the group through word of mouth: people attending the group tell their friends and acquaintances.

As migrants themselves, the two psychologists facilitating the group (the authors of this case study) have a particular interest in the issue of migrant women. As they themselves left their countries of origin and have experienced the sorrows and challenges of migration it is relatively easy for them to relate to the situations in which migrant women find themselves. In addition, their command of Spanish and German and familiarity with institutions working in health and education in Germany make them conduits of information.

On arrival in Germany a typical migrant has five basic needs: to interact and communicate within the new environment; to secure a means of economic subsistence; to create a social network with affective content; to find or create a space that allows her to rebuild and/or give new meaning to her identity; and to reconstruct her life project.

Two tools have been particularly useful for the group: the Pan American Health Organization manual developed to promote life skills among Latin American children and youth,[11] and *Tales of Coming and*

Going and Mental Health,[12] which addresses the relation between migration and stress, and the consequent impacts on the mental health of migrants.

Every six months a list is prepared with themes of interest to group members, and a vote is taken to select just six topics. A record is also kept of each group meeting in order to follow up on what was discussed and analyse results, if time and resources permit. However, it is often difficult to follow up on the women participating in the group, since participation fluctuates so greatly. Many women stop attending the meetings for a lengthy period of time and then may occasionally return. Others take on new commitments and responsibilities and do not come back, although thanks to friendships with women in the group we frequently hear of their progress and difficulties.

Some results: empowerment, friendship and independence

In order to ensure ongoing support and continuity in the group's more informal social activities, some adaptations have been necessary. These include holding meetings later so those who work can attend, and in the case of mothers with small children, activities with games are organized while the group is meeting. Some participants have also started to organize and lead some activities such as the Christmas party, and in giving tips on finding work and living in Germany. When possible, participants with experience or stories to tell are called upon to share these and speak before AfW–LA groups. This, of course, contributes to self-esteem and a sense of empowerment of the women within the group, demonstrating that they are indeed a vital part of the group and are expected to participate. The group thus provides a variety of opportunities for women to get together, to share and learn from each other's experiences, and to freely express their feelings in a secure environment under the supervision of professionals and, most importantly, without the impediment of language barriers. Esther, one of the participants, commented on the strain of not understanding anything.

> I knew I was going to have to learn German and get a job where I could earn money. Earn money and save up to bring my son over. But, yes, at the beginning one is very surprised. I can't forget the smell of toasted almonds at Christmas ... and the snow. Things I had never seen before.[13]

Another work group contributes to strengthening the independence and organizational skills of participants. It enables women to work towards developing their full potential on a variety of different levels, and to re-evaluate men's and women's roles and responsibilities, as well as analysing and reflecting on migration and biculturalism. According to María, who participated in this group:

> It seems to me that when you start to earn money like [husbands and sons] do, they treat you with more respect. Since I've been here I have my sons make their own beds and help with the household chores. I'm not there all the time anymore to go running around after them.[14]

While one group might serve as a bridge between the country of origin and the 'adopted' country, where friendships are made and information exchanged – on employment possibilities, day nurseries, secondary schools, German language classes – another group receives information about their rights as women and migrants, and develops the skills and abilities to identify and prevent situations of violence and oppression. Eliza's contribution is a reflection on general sentiments regarding such situations:

It's good to talk about issues of violence against women, because that way you can tell a friend in need that there are houses (*Frauenhäuser*) where she can go for shelter and that the police protect her. Sometimes it seems that as a woman you have more rights here than back home. Although as a migrant you have fewer, of course.[15]

It is, of course, through all these activities that valuable support networks are created, confidence is gained, and lives are rebuilt, and the facilitators themselves benefit as professionals from the abundance of rich experiences and the challenges of group activities.

Some lessons learned by the group

Migration is a traumatic personal experience that involves numerous changes in external realities, with consequent impacts on internal realities.[16] Nevertheless, with a suitable support network, migration can be an enriching experience that allows people to develop hitherto undiscovered capacities and potentials.

The great fluctuation in group attendance was initially a matter of reflection and concern for the facilitators, who were uncertain about what to expect: one day no one might come to the meeting and the following day there would be more women than anticipated. From the outset, AfW-LA characterized itself as offering free and voluntary participation, and has therefore accepted and adapted to these fluctuations. It has, for example, taken steps to accommodate women with children, which includes most of those attending. While this was considered a problem at the beginning, it has created a sense of solidarity among the women: as one of the mothers commented, 'My daughter can finally talk to other children in Spanish and hear that it's not just me who speaks to her in my language.'[17]

Some women emotionally affected by homesickness and longing for what they left behind find the group to be a place where they can work out their sorrow. At the meetings participants face up to what they have lost and what they have gained in the new country. This helps them let go of idealized attachments, so their emotional energy can be invested in new relationships.

The group has indeed underscored the complexity and subtlety of each step of the integration process, but at the same time has been an instrument of empowerment and support for its members. At one of the sessions, Auria[18] arrived with Ana[19] and her two children. Ana told the group she had been in Germany for three months and had just lost her German husband. It made her feel quite 'desperate' not to understand the language, know her way around or understand how 'the country worked'. A support network was created within the group and four members offered to accompany her to an appointment with the lawyer and show her how the public transport works in Hamburg (the city map, trains and buses, ticket prices, timetables, etc.), take her to the kindergarten where one of them had her children, and bring her to the institute where another had learned to speak German. This experience led the women in the group to reflect on the changes they had made in their own lives, their achievements, and what they had learned since arriving in Germany. Narcisa from Ecuador commented to Ana: 'Look at me; I was just like you when I came. I can understand you. But this passes, I assure you. You learn the language and find work and get your children ahead. It's hard at first, but you keep on going.'[20]

It has been very important for women like Narcisa to participate in the group by sharing their own experiences, knowledge and skills, with no one's contribution having any greater or lesser value than anyone else's. Because there is no judgement, feelings of guilt and defensiveness subside, as do tendencies to justify actions. It is easier to arrive at an understanding of oneself, identify feelings, rescue values and reconstruct an identity chosen with greater freedom.

To summarize, we feel that the work of AfW-LA includes four specific positive elements for migrant women. It provides a healthy environment in which women are able to develop a sense of worth independently from that assigned by society at large. It also offers valuable examples of other women who have survived and indeed succeeded in overcoming similar situations. Another vital facet of AfW-LA's services is that it provides a framework for communication, a network of friends and a support group, all of which facilitate integration. Finally, the group also helps to detect and change erroneous attitudes.

Strategies for future action

Our experience has confirmed the scarcity of national and international migratory policies aimed at women, despite evidence showing that current regulations have a gender-differentiated impact.[21] Migrant women suffer multiple forms of discrimination since factors of class, ethnicity and legal status overlap with their gender condition. They move between two cultures, that of their country of origin and that of their place of destination. Different values, norms, customs and even languages tend to exert psycho-social pressures that are not easy for them to manage, and the consequences are often marginalization and discrimination within their new society. Providing migrant women with their own exclusive space allows them not only to reposition themselves in their adopted society, but also to reflect on their identities and – often for the first time – their rights as women.

Our strategy for integration is based on the precept that migrants are expected to play an active, participatory role in fostering self-help, self-confidence and, above all, independence within the group, as the basis for their integration in society. They are therefore an integral part of the AfW-LA group. Each woman is expected to become a protagonist both within and subsequently outside the group, in her new-found home. She finds the liberty to express her ideas without fear, with the facilitator of group sessions yielding centre stage to participants and limiting her interventions to ensuring that meetings run in an orderly and respectful manner: every opinion counts and there is mutual respect for individual decisions, beliefs, values, style and personal orientation.

There is a clear need to network with organizations for migrants in order to join forces, diversify tasks and responsibilities, and make efforts more efficient and effective. Equally evident is the need for support and the sharing of experiences, successes and failures with organizations working in the same area.

NOTES

1   Interview with Sonia Hurtado, Chilean psychotherapist practising in Hamburg.
2   We use the term 'migrant' in this chapter to refer to all the women who benefit from AfW's services. Their legal statuses vary: for some participants, Hamburg is just a staging post; others are legally established in the country; others again have no legal status. Some also have temporary residence permits; some travel between Spain, Germany and their countries of origin; others are already permanent residents in Germany.
3   European Network for Transnational HIV/STI Prevention among Migrant Sex Workers.
4   Professional Training for Peer Educators in Prostitution.
5   Behörde für Soziales und Familie.
6   Amt für Familie, and Jugend und Sozialordnung Unterstütz.
7   According to figures in the AfW 2005 annual report, 55 per cent of the women were from Ecuador, 19 per cent from Colombia, 16 per cent from Brazil, 8 per cent from Peru, 4 per cent from Chile, and 12 [sic] per cent from other Latin American countries. One woman can have several counselling sessions over the course of a year.
8   AfW counselling sessions are held on the following issues: separation, *parens patrie*, and child support; residency permits; domestic violence; naturalization; marriage by proxy, marriage contracts; paternity recognition; pregnancy, childbirth, and abortion; information about studying and training; employment counselling and labour rights; psycho-social issues; kindergartens; economic problems; and housing.
9   Vilma from Venezuela, December 2003, during a group activity.
10 The work is for two people, only one of whom receives a token salary, while the other's 'part-time' post is partially subsidized by another project.
11 Pan American Health Organization (2001), *Enfoque de habilidades para la vida para un desarrollo saludable de niños y adolescentes*. Available only in Spanish at: www.paho.org/Spanish/HPP/ADOL.
12   California–Mexico Health Inititiative (2004), *Tales of Coming and Going and Mental Health: Manual for Health 'Promotores/as'* (manual), see:

<http://www.ucop.edu/ cprc/prmtrsmn.html>.

13 Esther from Venezuela, November 2004, during a group activity.

14 María from the Dominican Republic, October 2005, during a group activity.

15 Eliza from Chile, February 2005, during a group activity.

16 Grinberg, R. and Leon Grinberg (1984), *Psicoanálisis de la migración y del exilio.* Ed. Alianza, Madrid.

17 Ana from Costa Rica, December 2005, during a group activity.

18 Auria from Colombia, September 2005. One of the group's regular participants.

19 Ana from Costa Rica, September 2005, during a group activity.

20 Narcisa from Ecuador, September 2005, during a group activity.

21 UN Division of Population (2001), *World Population Monitoring 2000: Population, Gender and Development,* United Nations, New York.

15

The Korean Women's Trade Union

A Foothold for Women Workers' Rights

Jinnock Lee

This chapter examines the Korean Women's Trade Union (KWTU) as a new model for organizing women workers in South Korea. The KWTU was formed in response to deteriorating conditions of employment for women workers in 1999, in the aftermath of the 1997 East Asian economic crisis. This crisis had a disproportionate impact on female workers. Women were the first to be dismissed, and regular, salaried workers were replaced by part-time workers, particularly in female-dominated sectors.[1] As a women-only trade union, KWTU was established in an attempt to remedy this situation. Its aim was to organize women workers who were scattered in different types of employment which neither acknowledged their status nor gave them access to existing trade unions. Although there are two other women-only unions, the Seoul Women's Trade Union and the Korean Confederation of Women's Trade Unions (affiliated to the Korean Confederation of Trade Unions) I focus here on the work of the KWTU as a union that serves a wide range of industries and jobs not covered by the other women-only unions. The chapter also explains how the KWTU has attempted to overcome some of the barriers to organizing this new group of women workers.

The KWTU was founded in 1999 with eight regional branches (Seoul, Incheon, Busan, Gwangju-Chunnam, Gyungnam, Gyunggi, Chungbuk, and Daegu) by members of the Korean Women Workers Associations United (KWWAU), itself founded in 1987 as a spearhead organization in the women's labour movement. Its establishment was considered necessary to overcome the lack of bargaining power and an organizational base in KWWAU workplaces.[2] While working closely with the KWWAU, the KWTU has taken the form of a nation-wide, regionally based union, which is recognized as having a significant organizational framework capable of unionizing employees in small and medium-sized enterprises, irregular workers and the unemployed. One of the most serious obstacles confronting a regional union attempting to unionize workers and retain members is distance: there are often considerable distances both between union offices and shop floors, and between officials and union members. The unstable status of women workers and high job volatility also lead to fluctuating membership. The development of programmes and organizational tools not only for recruitment of new members but also to retain old ones thus became crucial.

Despite these obstacles, the KWTU has generated tangible outcomes by organizing numerous sectors of the workforce, such as irregular school staff (nutritionists, librarians, laboratory assistants, cooks, and after-school teachers); special-category employees (such as golf caddies or scriptwriters); and subcontracted workers (who might include cleaners, hotel maids, clerical workers, and workers in manufacturing industry). Membership of the union has grown steadily from 380 in 1999 to approximately 5,000 in 2004, and the issues of women workers have drawn wide public attention. This is a great achievement when it is considered that the majority of members are individuals geographically scattered in small- to medium-sized workplaces with fewer than ten employees.

Organizational strategies

The organizational strategies adopted by KWTU are threefold and are an integral part of its operations. Its first and most distinctive feature is that it has taken the form of a union, while maintaining an intimate relationship with the KWWAU. Cooperation with an established civil organization has enabled KWTU to use a variety of methods that have provided the basis for the organization of workers. The second aspect of its strategy is the gender perspective that provides tools by which those who have hitherto been unable to unionize are given a voice. The KWTU has been attempting to unionize unorganized workers by providing outreach services in communities and researching working conditions – as in the cases of home managers' cooperatives and cleaning workers in universities.[3] Finally, KWTU has designed a variety of activities to be carried out among small groups to overcome difficulties associated with sustaining membership, and to empower women at a personal level. This approach involves a 'women–friendly' organizational model that strengthens leadership and women's collective caring attitude and responsibility so as to encourage participation in union activities.

The KWTU has been developing diverse strategies to help attract and educate members, such as public campaigning, counselling, surveys and the provision of welfare programmes. These have all been made possible through cooperation and assistance from KWWAU, which is renowned for its expert knowledge of women's labour issues and wide experience in human resources. The Equality Line service is an important example of a tool that has played a key role in organizing women workers into unions. This is a telephone counselling service on women's employment issues run by the KWWAU in eight regions since 1995, and is partially sponsored by the government. Phone counselling is a primary route for women workers to obtain information about labour laws and the KWTU, and represents a first step in resolving their problems. Although most telephone counselling does not result in any specific action, the service has resulted in numerous examples of successful unionization: the recruitment of 88 CC golf caddies[4] and school irregular workers[5] into the KWTU are prime examples. Equality Line demonstrates that the organization of women workers is dependent on who is available to listen to workers with immediate needs. KWWAU's resources and its network thus provided the basis on which KWTU was able to develop and establish its own action programme.

It is important to recognize that collaboration with KWAAU has moved women's labour issues – which tend to be confined to workplaces – into the social arena. It has also enabled collaboration with existing unions and other women's groups, increasing public awareness of women's labour issues and of taking collective action, as in the case of special employees. The 'special employee' category is a discrete group of people – 90 per cent are women – within the 'irregular workers' category who do not fit conveniently into other legally recognized categories. They include the golf caddies, insurance workers, irregular school workers, and domestic workers, and it was the union that first raised the question of a minimum wage for all of them. KWTU's actions have resulted in the formation of committees involving a wide range of organizations such as the Korean Confederation of Trade Unions (KCTU), the Federation of Korean Trade Unions (FKTU), Women's Link, Korean Women's Associations United and the Korean National Confederation of Women. The creation of KWTU has also been crucial in setting up the Commission for Women's Labour that includes representatives of nine organizations (including some of those mentioned above) and holds regular meetings in an attempt to organize collective action for the protection of women workers' labour rights.[6]

Reaching out to women workers

While the above examples of the unionization of special employees demonstrate that the KWTU, in cooperation with the KWWAU, has opened the door to many workers who approached KWTU of their own volition, the KWTU has also attempted to reach out and find workers in need by identifying specific problems from a gender perspective. University cleaning workers, who had their workplaces evaluated first-hand, are a good example. A survey carried out in 2001 by KWTU involving a sample of 528 cleaning workers subcontracted by 107 companies revealed that 22.9 per cent of respondents were paid less than the minimum monthly wage, equivalent to approximately US$360 (or 421,490 won) in 2001.[7] The KWTU embarked on a campaign to establish a minimum wage based on subsistence requirements with the KCTU and the FKTU, and succeeded in drawing widespread public attention; although the law has yet to be changed, this intervention did result in a steady increase in the minimum wage to the equivalent of US$540 (or 630,000 won) in 2004, and the announcement by the Ministry of Labour of the plan to carry out the 'General Inspection of the Minimum Wage' in October and November each year.

Another example of successful organization on the basis of the gendered division of labour in society is the cooperative of home managers, formed in November 2004. This initiative was promoted by KWWAU in 1998 with the establishment of a Headquarters for Unemployed Women. It also acquired a certain official status as it was sponsored by the government, which needed a proxy organization to deal with the appalling living conditions of women after the economic crisis in 1997. It organized a mutual aid society focusing on middle-aged female heads of households in eight regions: this society provided income support, after a means assessment, and medical assistance. The majority of the members of the mutual aid society joined the KWTU and provided the basis of the home managers' cooperative with a mandate to create jobs and facilitate the long-term economic independence of middle-aged women employed as housework assistants, midwives, babysitters and nurses in the housework service industry. Although there were only 200 members in the union's division of domestic services in the regional branch in Busan in 2004, there is considerable potential for growth as it responds to the need for an organizational tool that allows for the unionization of the increasing numbers of domestic workers who find themselves geographically dispersed and in a legal vacuum.

A women-friendly organizational model

The goal of KWTU is to overcome the limits of the existing union movements in which the rate of female membership has been in constant decline as the focus is on full-time, male employees in large enterprises.[8] The women's union is also attempting to embrace women through *meaningful* unionization: it 'eschews the organizational model which regards women as a primary target of unionization as in existing unions'[9] which are targeting women workers simply to boost dwindling numbers. This strategy is referred to in all KWTU documents as a means to promote the idea of its 'women-friendly' organizational model.

The union's organizational model is designed to respond to women's needs to unionize and takes into consideration their double workload of domestic and paid work. Married women make up 71.3 per cent of KWTU's membership.[10] Childcare was selected as one of the key issues in increasing the union membership of women. As a result, each branch of the KWTU has been developing diverse childcare systems. For example, should all members need to take part in a particular activity, a nursery teacher is called in to take care of the children, or else union members themselves rotate childcaring responsibilities. Similarly, the KWTU facilitates the participation of full-time union officials through gender-sensitive working conditions that take life cycles such as marriage, birth and childcare into account.

The KWTU is also aware of the differences involved in organizing women and men. For example, the majority of KWTU members tend to lack confidence and have difficulty leading and participating in conferences and formal meetings where they are unfamiliar with procedures.[11] Emphasis has thus been placed on activities in small groups of union members, where they become familiar with the rules and procedures of unions operating in a public sphere and enhance their organizational skills. The majority of current members gain proficiency, self-confidence and leadership skills by holding positions – heads, managers, accountants, and public relations officers – within small groups that provide them with opportunities to build on these skills.

The KWTU manuals such as *How to Run Small Groups*, *Basic Programmes of Small Groups for Union Members*, and the *Guidebook for Union Supporters*[12] stress the importance of listening and speaking as means of enhancing the union's integrity. For instance, one of the programmes for small groups is 'discovering and opening oneself up': this involves telling stories, an activity through which women are able to overcome both powerlessness and lack of confidence while working towards self-transformation.[13] The sharing of stories helps alter the tendency to perceive employment relations as personal problems and also creates an affinity with and empathy for other union members who are employed in different sectors and occupations. Storytelling also represents a first step in developing a discipline in the formalities of working in the public sphere and ensuring the women are better equipped to defend their rights and improve their chances of becoming effective members of the movement.

Small-group activities are also recognized as helping union members develop fully fledged relationships with other members, making the union a welcoming and intimate place. Commenting on and sharing experiences of the daily routines of the workplace and the home facilitates bonding and solidarity within the union; in turn, this leads to the spontaneous development of support mechanisms such as childcare facilities. It is in such circumstances that the principles of 'let them talk' and 'listen' assume particular relevance, as the context provides ways and means to approach and involve women in the union, and to further reflect on gender identities, creating a bridge between the public and the private lives of the women.

By encouraging all members to speak out freely, KWTU contributes to non-hierarchical communication between members and officials and thus helps promote union democracy. Furthermore, the democratic management of the union boosts the unity of union members, especially when it comes to collective action in workplaces. For instance, the KWTU 88 CC Division of golf caddies was successful in collective bargaining through delicate strategies using the women-friendly model of organization. The small groups established in the initial stages of union formation are where they discuss strategies and the direction their struggles are taking. The experience gained in the democratic decision-making processes provides them with a strength that contributes to the integrity of union members. The success of this process can be measured by the fact that only one member out of more than 200 in the KWTU Division of 88 CC Golf Caddies left the union while they went on a strike that lasted for 43 days, including an all-out strike lasting 27 days in October 2000.

Conclusions

In this brief chapter I have been able to focus solely on KWTU's organizational strategies. I believe that a women-only union is a striking example of a means to remedy a situation in which women's work tends to be informal and fragmented; it vividly demonstrates a way to empower women and achieve democracy through a women-friendly approach. However, the growth of the KWTU is an ongoing story. The shortage of funding and trained union officials is still an unresolved issue. New strategies to maintain union members also need to be developed continuously. These issues notwithstanding, the KWTU's vigorous initiatives are writing a new chapter of South Korean labour history from a women worker's perspective.

NOTES

1 Deregulation in the labour market has affected both men and women. However, according to national statistics (2003) the impact of flexible employment patterns has been more severe on women workers, with 70.7 per cent of the female workforce categorized as temporary daily employees compared to 46.7 per cent of their male counterparts.
2 Choi, Sang-Rim (1999), 'Presentation at the Conference for the Formation of the Korean Women's Trade Union', unpublished document of the Preparatory Committee for the Korean Women's Trade Union and the Korean Women Workers Associations United (in Korean), p. 26.

3   Information on these outreach programmes is not yet available in English.

4   The Union of 88 CC Golf Caddies, KWTU Division, established in October 1999 as a result of the counselling services, is South Korea's first trade union of golf caddies. As golf caddies' legal status as workers was contested, no previous attempts had been made to form a union until the 88 CC golf caddies were unionized through the KWTU. Golf caddies were not legally considered workers as they are paid by their customers, and are therefore categorized as 'special employees' – 90 per cent of whom are women, including cleaners, hotel maids, clerical workers and insurance agents.

5   Irregular school workers attempted to organize themselves in the form of occupational associations. They include part-time teachers, lecturers, IT assistants, nutritionists, librarians, cooks and their assistants, laboratory assistants, touring professional coaches and administrative assistants, and number approximately 100,000 people. They are classified as sundry labourers and have no holiday pay, rights to holidays or annual leave, even after having worked for the same school for extended periods. This case has drawn wide public attention since it demonstrates that flexible employment with few social benefits has been reinforced by the government through the Ministry of Education.

6   Although this commission experienced severe internal conflicts due to differences of opinion on the reform of maternity protection in 2001, it still holds regular monthly meetings.

7   Choi, Sang-Rim (2004), 'Analysing women's labour movements for empowering and organizing women workers' (in Korean), discussion paper for the Fifth Anniversary of the Korean Women's Trade Union, 21 August, 2004, p. 27.

8   The current rate of unionization of the female workforce is 6.2 per cent, dropping from 11.1 per cent in 1987, while it is 14.9 per cent for men, with a decrease of one third over the same period. This contrasts with a 200 per cent increase in the number of women employed. It is alarming to note that female unionization peaked in 1989 with 13.4 per cent unionization, and plunged to just 5.6 per cent after the 1997 economic crisis. See Kwon, Hye Ja (1999), *The Crisis of Women's Employment and the Expansion of Atypical Labourers* (in Korean), Federation of Korean Trade Unions, Seoul.

9   Korean Women's Trade Union (2000), *Strategies for Organizing Women Workers in the 21st Century: the Experiences of the Women's Trade Union and its Future Tasks* (in Korean), papers for an International Workshop on the First Anniversary of the Korean Women's Trade Union, 28 August–1 September 2000, Korea Women's Trade Union and Korean Women Workers' Associations United, Seoul.

10 Han, Sung-Hee, Myung-Sook Kim, Joo-Hwan Lee and Jin-Young Park (2001), *Women-Friendly Organizing Scheme for the Empowerment of Women* (in Korean), report for the Second Anniversary Symposium of the Formation of the Korean Women's Trade Union, 29 August 2001, p. 35.

11 *Ibid.*

12   Internal KWTU documents published in 1999, 1999, and 2001 respectively.
13   Oppenheim, L. (1991), 'Women's ways of organizing: a conversation with an AFSCME organizer', *Labour Research Review*, No. 18, pp. 45–59.

16

Power in Bridges

A Romanian Story about Spreading Feminist Values

Camelia Blaga

The purpose of my case study is to share the experience of the Association for Gender Equality and Liberty (ALEG), a young Romanian organization that seeks to integrate the feminist legacy into today's youth culture and incorporate feminist principles and values into its own development as an organization. The study shows how a small, young organization with very limited funding can make a significant contribution to building feminist values despite the hostile environment in which it works. I use the example of our annual awareness campaign – the Gender Equality Festival – to demonstrate the effectiveness of the mechanisms of inclusion we use to broaden participation, how resources are mobilized and our search for economic sustainability. Finally, mention is made of why we consider the integration of feminist principles in our operations to be so important and one of the keys to our success to date.

The social context

During a training session on feminism, Irina, one of our teenage members, remembered the day 'My Romanian teacher explained that "misogynists are men who hate women, and feminists are women who hate men"'! This is, in fact, a true reflection of what many members of Romanian society feel: that feminists are usually frustrated women who oppose (traditional) family values. After the 1989 revolution there was a great urge to revert to the patriarchal values that obtained before communism took hold forty years previously. Although a few clear feminist voices had spoken out in the early twentieth century before communist rule, and spoken strongly enough to win Romanian women a partial right to vote as early as 1929, there has been no reinstatement of these values in recent years.

The gender-blind equality forced on society by the communist régime made the feminist movement appear superfluous, as the 1948 Constitution gave women full political and labour rights. Although 'equality', like the economy and the 'happiness' of the nation, had a prominent place in propaganda, today we realize that the patriarchal system remained well entrenched in both the public and private spheres.

A recent incident revealed that young people in Romania today are still strongly influenced by tradition when it comes to gender issues, and that gender education for youth is a problem that needs urgent attention. An essay contest for teenage girls organized by ALEG on Women's Day, on the theme 'Eight reasons why I'm happy to be a woman', had a disappointing response, and what we did receive was profoundly disturbing. One essay happily cited the Romanian dictionary's definition for 'woman' as a 'married female being'. The author made no attempt to challenge this definition and went on to celebrate 'indescribable female beauty' and the advantages of being able to deploy high heels and make-up to hide physical shortcomings.

This teenage messenger provided us with a perfect and sad example of the stereotypes with which Romanian girls are confronted from the moment they are born. Femininity continues to be associated mainly with beauty, with marrying 'the prince', attending to his needs and looking sexy. A change in political régime is not enough to free minds from gender stereotypes. So what is to be done in a country in which patriarchy lives on but 47 per cent of women are under the impression that there is real equality?[1] Where the major national religion[2] forbids women to set foot on the altar? Where women who appear on television are 'high-life VIPs, prostitutes or irresponsible mothers'?[3] Or where an employer tells his young female employee, concerned about her low pay, 'Cheer up miss, you'll get married soon and then your husband can give you some money!'?[4]

There have to be alternatives that will allow us to escape from such stereotypes. But how can the limitations of stereotypes be recognized if everyone tows the same line?

The birth of ALEG

The Association for Gender Equality and Liberty (ALEG) is the first and so far the only non-governmental organization (NGO) set up in Sibiu County – one of Romania's most dynamic counties in the centre of the country – with the aim of promoting gender equality and fighting gender-based discrimination and violence. The idea of ALEG was born in the spring of 2002 while two of its current members were working with a Peace Corps volunteer on a project that introduced gender awareness sessions in five schools in Sibiu. The students were thrilled to discuss gender relationships in a school setting, and some even suggested that such discussions should be included in the curriculum. The evaluation of the project prompted the idea: why not create an NGO with a focus on gender equality and youth? Two years later, in 2004, ALEG was legally constituted with a mission to challenge gender stereotypes, expose sexism and build feminist values, particularly among young people. ALEG's work began at the local level in 2004, relying on a small team of twelve members, both women and men, working as volunteers.

We believe ALEG's focus on young people to be critical as we are dealing with great potential for personal growth and also vulnerability. It is recognized that people form patterns of socialization in early life, and that once attitudes and behaviours are established they are very difficult to change. As the adage goes, prevention is always better than cure.

The fact that young Romanian people have virtually no access to information, let alone educational materials on feminism and gender equality, is the other reason we decided to work with them. The media are infused with portrayals of women as sex objects, while 'serious' matters tend to feature men. So while young people are free from the token feminism of communism, they are also deprived of any feminist influences whatsoever. This is jeopardizing the vestiges of the feminist legacy and allowing sexism and homophobia to flourish.

The Gender Equality Festival kicks off

The organization's main project in 2004 was the Gender Equality Festival – a successful awareness campaign organized for young people in Sibiu.[5] We knew our campaign had to start by challenging stereotypes and presenting alternatives based on gender equality. Most importantly, we recognized the importance of addressing both women and men in order to make a real difference in human relationships. These principles guided us throughout our work. Although we started off with empty coffers, we had plenty of enthusiasm, some great ideas, and quite a bit of experience in community projects. We knew that a key to our success would be to involve our target group at all stages, especially in the planning. Empowering young people by involving them in decision-making processes is one of the feminist principles we have incorporated in our organizational values and it has proved an effective mechanism for inclusion.

A core group of five young people brainstormed to dream up festival events that would convey our message against gender discrimination, sexism and stereotypes. Form and content had to blend well. In the end we settled for activities that were innovative but not too costly. The president of ALEG coordinated both the planning and implementation of the campaign with a core team and 42 volunteers recruited from local schools.

The journalist in the team came up with the idea of the street event 'The Human Puzzle', where volunteers carrying big letters would line up in the main square of the town to spell out our organization's vision: 'I choose equality'; 'I choose diversity'; 'I choose not to be a victim'; 'I choose a life without violence'. The idea of choice is also a key element in our philosophy and is reflected in the acronym ALEG which, in Romanian, means 'I choose'.

We also decided to hold a workshop for young journalists to address the unfair representation of women in the media. Another proposed activity was the 'Gender Surgery Show', which aimed to clarify the difference between sex and gender and challenge gender stereotypes through entertainment. A fourth activity entitled 'Portrait of Your Thoughts' was chosen. This was an interactive and creative display through which girls and boys could express their personal beliefs and wishes and be photographed with their 'Piece of Mind'.

We thus had a plan, but in order to carry it out we needed two basic ingredients: community support and good publicity. We therefore needed to build bridges, reaching out to different local stakeholders as well as internationally. The innovative nature of the proposed activities helped us further in raising funds, recruiting volunteers, finding local partners and triggering media attention. Two young Peace Corps volunteers who were teaching English at the local secondary schools helped us get a small project grant of US$3,000 from Peace Corps Romania and to recruit 42 of their students as volunteers. The Peace

Corps volunteers were extremely supportive of our ideas and managed to inspire enthusiasm for the festival in their students. The fact that we incorporated the principles of empowerment, team spirit, celebration of diversity and solidarity throughout our work also kept up the volunteers' excitement and engagement.

We were also successful in establishing local partnerships that enabled us to turn the festival into a large community event while keeping costs low. For example, when we approached the Gong Theatre for Children and Youth with our proposal, the theatre manager was so enamoured of our idea that she not only agreed to host our event without any charge but also offered to sponsor our posters and the costumes for the theatre parodies. Another important partner was the 'Lucian Blaga' University's Faculty of Journalism, which offered us the workshop room and facilities for the media seminar, as well as the services of Brânduşa Armanca, one of the few feminist editors-in-chief of a national media organization, who agreed to participate as guest speaker. And finally, with the agreement of Sibiu City Hall, we were able to organize our street event, 'The Human Puzzle', in the main city square.

The media campaign

ALEG also produced a TV and radio public awareness advertisement against domestic violence as part of the festival. This was aired at prime time for six days by Antena 1, the main local TV station, and also on two radio stations. Four local newspapers covered the festival itself.

The Gender Equality Festival proved to be an excellent way of bringing young people into the feminist movement. The medium, with the support of the press, the youth theatre and our own innovative ideas, and with its message of fun, friendliness, interaction and creativity, captivated many people.

Many of the participants decided to join the organization after this campaign. There is no doubt in our minds that awareness-raising activities can indeed represent a mechanism for inclusion if these speak the language of, and are attractive to, potential stakeholders.

The challenge of sustainability

While the first festival had been funded by a small Peace Corps grant, the second one held in October 2005 had to be self-funded. We therefore decided to optimize the chances of a successful second event by strengthening the bridges we had built and the networks we had created the first time around. In doing this we kept our bridges open to all those who had supported us the previous year, and all our collaborators received a copy of the report on the first festival in which plans for the second festival were laid out. We also worked to convince new sponsors of the benefits of helping us to extend the project. By keeping costs to a minimum, we were successful in finding sponsorship for the entire second festival from local companies.

Another important decision of the campaign organizers was to increase the level of responsibility and involvement of young people in the campaign, and thus apply the principle of empowerment within our own team. The volunteers and group members of the first festival were more than happy to have a say in the organization and development of the second event. They organized themselves into a youth club within the organization, and with some support and guidance they worked on creating the theatrical events as well as other aspects of the festival. Although it was on a smaller scale, we consider the second festival as significant an experience as the first: it really put to the test our capacity to stay focused and committed to our values of equality and empowerment. We were able to demonstrate within our own team that feminism is about sharing power and making everyone feel included, whether they be women or men.

The final good news on which I can report in this case study is that, after presenting our project to the local authorities, the County Council agreed to help fund our third festival (October 2006). Sustainability has been ensured thus far and we believe that it is a direct result of our commitment to building feminist values first and foremost within our organization. This is particularly important in a country where few people understand what feminism is about, thus, the best way to teach its values is by putting them into practice.

On the importance of bridges

One of the important lessons we learned while working on building partnerships was the power of effective networking – a feminist principle that facilitates success when effectively applied. Frequently NGOs are concerned about sharing projects with partners for fear of losing control. We managed to find a balance between including others in the project and not compromising our purpose; we selected partners who shared our values, and we also worked at strengthening the valuable relationships that had been created. These relationships also involved building permanent bridges with other important stakeholders – the local theatre, private enterprise, the media and local authorities – who are key to ensuring ALEG's long-term sustainability. This is part of our commitment to sustainability and our strategy to ensure support for further festivals.

The Gender Equality Festival was not the creation of a sophisticated group of people with an established reputation and ample funding. The association was, in fact, a newborn organization when we started working on this project. Success depended on our determination to make a difference in spreading feminist values using innovative means, and to start practising these values within our own team. Some of the main principles that guided us were networking, power sharing, thinking outside the box, and reaching out. Today these principles are taught in any organizational development course but we have come to embrace them naturally via feminism, as none of these progressive principles would have made it into mainstream organizational culture without the women's movement. That does not mean that all feminist organizations are democratic. I believe the challenge is to fight the insidious patriarchal mindset not only on the banners and posters but in the office too.

At the end of the first festival we produced a 'good practice' guide-book to help other Romanian groups organize similar events. In the short time since its founding in April 2004, ALEG has taken advantage of many opportunities to partner with and join national networks of NGOs working against gender-based discrimination and abuse, such as the Gender and Development Peace Corps committee[6] and the VIF Coalition.[7]

The success of this first project has been a stepping stone for the development of our small organization, which has now started women's rights work in rural communities around Sibiu and is building one of the few feminist resource centres in Romania. Another lucky coincidence – that the city of Sibiu, where we are based, has been selected by the European Union as the cultural capital of Europe for 2007 – will create further opportunities for our development and the success of our planned activities.

So do not ever feel powerless if you are a small grassroots group facing what seems to be a hostile environment for your work. Try to step out of the unfriendly conditions and rise towards your vision. Achievement comes from great vision and good strategy. Your reach will be as high as you dare to aim and as long-lasting as the network that supports it.

NOTES

1   According to the 2000 Gender Barometer, 53 per cent of Romanian women consider there is no real equality between women and men. The Gender Barometer formed part of 'Research on Domestic Violence and Violence in the Workplace', a study undertaken by Romania's Centre for Partnership and Equality. Further information available at <http://www.cpe.ro/english/> (last accessed 9 September 2006).

2   In the late 1980s, the Romanian Orthodox Church, by far the largest denomination, claimed some 16 million members, roughly 80 per cent of the country's total population.

3   According to the study 'Aspects Regarding Gender Stereotypes in the Romanian Media' published in January 2005 by the Society for Feminist Analyses – AnA in Bucharest.

4   Incident recalled by Liliana Popescu (2004) in her book *Gender Politics*, Maiko, Bucharest.

5   This festival was so successful that it was held on a smaller scale in three other cities in 2005, with the support of the Gender and Development Committee (GAD), a national network of Romanian activists, and US Peace Corps volunteers.

6   The GAD committee is a group of ten Peace Corps Volunteers and ten Romanian counterparts networking on projects that promote gender equality at the national level.

7   The VIF Coalition refers to the Coalition of NGOs Working in the Area of Violence Against Women that was founded on 1 February 2003, during the Conference for the Prevention and Elimination of Domestic Violence organized by the Centre Partnership for Equality (CPE) and the Initiative for Family Health in Romania, part of a USAID-funded programme. More details can be found at <http://www.stopvaw.org/2005_Report_to_UN_Division_for_Advancement_of_Women6.html> (last accessed 10 September 2006).

17

Widening the Base of
the Feminist Movement in Pakistan

Shahnaz Iqbal

This case study reviews the crucial role played by the Women Law and Status (WLS) programme of Shirkat Gah' – also known as the Women's Resource Centre – in expanding the feminist movement, especially in rural Pakistan. It also reviews the programme's evolution, strategies and challenges, and summarizes the lessons learned.

The WLS programme evolved at a particular time in history: a few years after the most retrogressive decade of military rule in Pakistan, led by General Zia-ul Haq between 1977 and 1988, left in its wake a series of draconian laws introducing brutal punishments in the name of Islam and reinforcing already pernicious customs that affected women in often barbaric ways. Support for negative customs and the reduction in the legal status of women and minority groups created a severely depoliticized country and a disheartened civil society.

Days under the Zia regime were completely different from those during which Shirkat Gah was established in 1975 – the International Women's Year – when we had a democratic government supportive of women. But it was under the harsh rule of Zia that we learned an important lesson: the fewer the number of women willing to fight for their rights, the easier it is for rulers to suppress them.

So it was that in 1981 Shirkat Gah became the catalyst for the Women's Action Forum, a platform of action that led the resistance against negative changes proposed or passed by the Zia regime. In the mid 1980s, Shirkat Gah decided that its effectiveness as a resource centre for women depended on expanding its network from community to national and international levels. Operating from the homes of Shirkat Gah members, in no more than a decade the organization managed to reach out to women in four provinces of Pakistan and set up offices in Karachi, Lahore and Peshawar, while at the same time lobbying policy makers, mobilizing women and building capacities at the grassroots in selected areas of work.

The Women Law and Status programme reaches out

The rigid patriarchal society, combined with an appalling 36 per cent female literacy rate, convinced Shirkat Gah that transforming realities at the grassroots demanded wide-ranging activism and linkage between pertinent actors. It was thus that the Women Law and Status (WLS) programme was established in 1994.[2] Shirkat Gah devised its 'Outreach' component to work closely with community-based organizations (CBOs), the actors best positioned to understand the needs of the community; this reaching out was intended to help the programme achieve its long-term goal of catalysing and facilitating women's empowerment. In the medium term, Shirkat Gah's goal is to improve women's access to rights; to promote democratic norms and better governance; and, finally, to strengthen initiatives challenging the use of culture/religion to deny rights and those promoting women's human rights internationally.

Outreach operates on the premise that women rarely know the difference between customs practised in their communities and statutory legal provisions, and that one of the biggest hurdles for Pakistani women seeking to challenge existing norms is their legal illiteracy, compounded by isolation from support groups and state institutions. Outreach therefore aims to empower women by informing them of existing laws, providing information on how to seek legal redress, and creating linkages within a support system. This supporting network is intended to help them interpret the myriad forces affecting women's life choices and thus to clarify the options open to them.

To address the high level of ignorance of existing laws and the prevalent sense of helplessness, WLS created the concept of 'legal consciousness' as part of a legal demystification process that helped people distinguish between customs and the state's legal provisions, develop an understanding of how state laws are formulated, and explore the relationship between the law and human rights. This process was facilitated through the provision of information and the carrying out of legal awareness sessions.

Without trumpeting itself as a feminist project, this legal conscious-ness work creates awareness of patriarchal structures, strengthens norms of social justice and facilitates people's participation in building a democratic society. It encourages actions directed at amending laws and customs that jeopardize the exercise of human rights in general and women's rights in particular.

The strategy: working with womens' groups and CBOs

By the mid-1990s grassroots organizations were tending to concentrate on the formation of small groups and on institution building in a development context. At that time none of the local groups focused on – or indeed understood – women's human rights or the violations that were commonplace. Seeing its role as a catalyst and facilitator, the Out-reach programme decided to identify and work with groups, and an input strategy was adopted. The widest Outreach circle consisted of groups, usually comprising CBOs that regularly received information and were invited to special events such as the 8 March (International Women's Day) activities. From these groups, a selected number of people were included in the 'capacity-building' category as beneficiaries of training in legal awareness and other themes such as gender aware-ness, advocacy skills, planning, and report writing. Within this capacity-building category, two or three groups, identified in each province as 'core groups', would become actively engaged in advocacy campaigns on local, national and international issues.[3]

Legal awareness sessions focus on family law, fundamental rights, police procedures and aspects of criminal law, and particularly laws that relate to sexual violence. Some CBO members attending training sessions are then selected to receive an intensive paralegal[4] course that includes the concept of fundamental human rights (from the perspec-tives of the UN and the Pakistani constitution) and the crucial role of the women's movement and its fight for women's rights. Core groups and a few other Outreach groups (ORGs) also receive training in UN and national mechanisms relating to women's development and rights, and in advocacy techniques. This combination enables ORGs to partici-pate in broader advocacy campaigns as well as initiating their own.

The Outreach programme has two cardinal rules. The first is never to indicate that customs practised by any community are wrong or bad – no matter how inappropriate we personally feel them to be. Instead, we help women understand their own situation by informing them of how other villages, provinces and societies deal with the same issue and by highlighting the content of the legal statutory provisions. The second rule involves never deciding for the group or community what their agenda should be. Hence, if local groups tell us, 'We want to learn about the laws on divorce or domestic violence but we cannot speak of these issues in our communities,' we never question their decision.

These rules have been key in changing the perception people have of our programme. Instead of being seen as an outside intervention – one therefore presumed to have ulterior motives – our programme has been appropriated by the ORGs, to the extent that they indeed feel it is their programme. The outcome is that frequently groups, within months of starting to work with us, will address not only the issue of divorce in their communities, but also the more complicated, taboo issue of domestic violence.

In keeping with Shirkat Gah's emphasis on participatory approaches, Outreach faced and addressed challenges as they arose, assisted by a constant process of interaction and assessment of past work and future needs with ORGs, and periodic in-depth independent evaluations.[5]

The challenge of increasing legal awareness

Unlike other development interventions focused on the grassroots, we do not offer any concrete services or financial benefits. Instead, through our actions we speak of working together for changing society. The ORGs took longer to understand this new approach and the value of our work. To introduce a human rights perspective in phase one, Outreach focused on the needs of CBOs – such as preventive health, solid waste management, adult literacy and theatre for development – to initiate activities and establish linkages with them. But as a result of growing awareness and interest in women/human rights issues, WLS was able to greatly reduce this type of input in phase two (1996–8), and discontinue it completely thereafter, concentrating exclusively on legal consciousness. Today, WLS receives far more requests for legal assistance sessions than we can accommodate, as our resources only allow us to work with some 45 ORGs annually.

Another challenge was how best to train local paralegals. The first paralegal training organized in Sindh in 1994 was a learning experience in more ways than one. Apart from major logistical disasters, the external resource persons from the lawyers' community were inexperienced in transferring knowledge to grassroots women with rather basic education, and concentrated on lectures on various aspects of law with little scope for participatory learning. As a result, when the WLS team ran a successful follow-up session it went on to develop its own paralegal training course (1994–6) and its own capacity to run the course, complemented by a few lawyers as subject specialists.

Yet another issue was the propensity of lawyers to view any issue on the basis of whether the case could be won in court, with no consideration given to the sustainability of dispute resolution processes in the community. Shirkat Gah encourages and trains paralegals to mediate and negotiate disputes without going to court in the first instance. Only when this is not desirable or possible do they facilitate court cases.

We learnt that providing awareness of legal redress in the formal system could be counter-productive in the absence of access to that legal system. Consequently, in 1996 we introduced a small legal assistance component and started exploring how to institutionalize legal aid and assistance on a wider scale, by initiating a lawyers' network with selected groups.

The impact of Outreach

We learnt as we worked. When we initiated Outreach, we presumed that the role of traditional practices, commonly justified on religious grounds, in denying women rights would make the *maulvis* (Muslim clerics) the focal point of resistance to change. Instead, we quickly learnt that the real source of resistance was local power structures and elites. Take the case of Latifan, a woman in a remote village of Sindh who was constrained by an unhappy marriage contracted in childhood. On discovering in a paralegal training course that marriage was not necessarily a lifetime sentence, Latifan wanted a divorce but was unwilling to approach the court because she felt a court decision would be unacceptable to her husband and both their families. Her husband, already married a second time, was only willing to divorce Latifan if she paid him Rs10,000 (approximately US$175) as compensation. This sum was beyond her means.

Latifan gained enough family support and self-confidence to approach the court after two years: the very first time that the centuries-old stricture on dissolving marriage was being challenged in her area.

Meanwhile Latifan's husband approached the local landlord (who traditionally adjudicates such disputes) to resolve the matter. Offended that someone in his area 'of jurisdiction' dared think of approaching the formal legal system, the landlord instantly imposed a fine of Rs30,000 (US$525) on the girl and threatened the Outreach team with dire consequences if they ever visited the village again.

This first case taught us several lessons. Taking a case to court is not simply a matter of providing legal assistance; women need significant support to even arrive at the decision, and also need help in mobilizing family members. The selection of a qualified and experienced lawyer for a case is vital, as few lawyers in remote areas have experience with family law. We also learnt how necessary it is to constantly shift attention – and intervention – from the legal system to the informal system, and to cope with both simultaneously.

Within six months of us starting the Outreach activities, two women cancelled their arranged marriages. This had us jumping for joy. Many more such cases followed.[6] The focus on family-related laws helped women negotiate their rights within the family, whether opposing forced or child marriages, opting out of abusive marriages, or insisting on the right to work or to be mobile. During our legal awareness sessions in a Punjab village women learnt that dower – often denied women through customary practices – should technically be fixed in keeping with the economic status of the husband. When one woman who had been married for over 30 years shared this information with her husband, it started a family discussion. The husband promptly gave a buffalo and a calf to his wife as belated dower, and announced that his two daughter-in-laws would also (retrospectively) receive dower according to the newly learned concept.

Since 1994, Outreach has built legal consciousness among some 7,000 people from 285 organizations and 795 geographical areas through the legal awareness sessions (30 to 40 each year) and between two and four major trainings in a variety of subjects (such as human rights, legal rights, violence against women, gender awareness and advocacy). Events aimed at raising awareness of violence against women have involved some 4,000 individuals and 180 organizations and colleges. Outreach groups, many supported by the 78 paralegals trained by WLS, have widened the pool of women's rights awareness and activism through their own legal orientation meetings, reaching over 1,800 persons, and also through events organized by them in their respective areas to celebrate International Women's Day or World AIDS Day, or to highlight the issue of violence against women.

An important part of advocacy is community mobilization on policies, and the number of persons reached through advocacy campaigns is beyond calculation. Together with guidance on the human rights instruments of the United Nations, government policy documents and international commitments, taking policy initiatives to the grassroots, and bringing their issues to the national and international levels, creates a broader base for the women's movement.

Mediation and dispute resolution

In using their knowledge of legal provisions outside the court system, an increasing number of ORGs have successfully carried out mediation, which is a new phenomenon in local dispute resolution forums.[7]

Parallel to this, WLS has made some inroads in the *jirga* (tribal council), the local non-formal system of dispute resolution in the conservative North-West Frontier Province, a traditionally all-male forum where women are represented by their male relatives. *Jirgas* in WLS Outreach areas now recognize the provisions of statutory laws and adjudicate women's issues. In one case, for instance, a woman's abusive husband sent her back to her parents, with a newly born daughter. The *jirga* first consulted the Outreach team and later ordered the husband to agree to his wife's demand for dower and divorce. Further, in a truly radical departure from accepted norms, the *jirga* ruled that the woman was free to remarry whom she pleased. The most unexpected progress is that a local woman (trained by WLS) was invited to join the *jirga* as a regular member.

Women Law and Status proactively ensures that linkages function in two directions: bringing the voices of women to the policy makers to broaden the national agenda, and linking the ORGs to issues being discussed or passed at the policy level (whether national or international). Thus, when the government established the Commission of Inquiry on Women in 1994, to formulate recommendations to improve the overall status of women, WLS distributed the Commission's questionnaire to ORGs. Most submitted their views on discriminatory laws, rules and procedures, maintenance and inheritance rights, women's political participation and violence against women.

The net result for the feminist movement has been the steady growth of ORGs and the active participation of grassroots groups in the Beijing 'plus five' and 'plus ten' review processes (facilitated by Shirkat Gha's WLS programme). Mobilization on women's rights has also led these groups to initiate their own events and campaigns: one example is the 16 Days of Activism Against Gender Violence (25 November–10 December) each year.

To highlight women's issues and promote discussion, WLS frequently uses a video cassette of the 1993 Vienna Tribunal (dubbed in Urdu). Initially, we were concerned about how women would respond to the diverse forms of violence covered in the Tribunal. In fact we found that not only were the video sessions well received, but women also spoke up about state and non-state actors as perpetrators of violence, linking this to an analysis of the overall socio-economic structures and systems that oppress women.

Today, our ORGs are well networked with like-minded civil society organizations and coalitions. On numerous occasions, most groups have joined events initiated or organized by the Joint Action Committee for People's Rights, a coalition of various civil society organizations and progressive individuals which was formed in 1990 to take action in the form of demonstrations, signature campaigns, seminars, and press conferences on issues of common concern.

When Pakistan and India came close to war in 1999, ORGs joined signature campaigns and rallies and discussed the importance of peace with people in their respective areas. In October 2004, 135 women from three groups crowded together on buses to join a national demonstration of a couple of thousand people in front of the national parliament in Islamabad to protest the issue of so-called 'honour killings'.

An unquestionable achievement of Outreach has been the consolidation of the movement's activists and the broadening of its base into rural areas. It has placed women's issues on the agendas of more than a hundred grassroots organizations that previously focused merely on service delivery of development work.

Conclusion

Looking back, we see that the women's movement in Pakistan was once confined to a few urban centres and mostly to middle-class women. It was therefore easy for those opposed to women's rights to dismiss the demands for women's rights as the voice of a few 'unIslamic', 'Westernized' and therefore 'alien' women, unrepresentative of the concerns of Pakistani women as a whole. The activism and engagement of the ORGs (and many others) invalidates this argument.

Outreach has learned some critical lessons from the movement. First and foremost, it now knows that community women are able to understand complicated power structures. We have proved that the common notion of local groups and community women being unable to understand complicated power structures is simply wrong. Instead of shying away from such discussion, we consciously include analyses of power – from the community to the global levels – in our interventions on legal consciousness.

We have found that a key ingredient in our work is to convey the universality of women's rights issues and women's struggles for rights. The use of the Vienna Tribunal video on violence against women helps break erstwhile silences and gives previously isolated women a sense of connectedness with women's struggles, inspiring them to act in their own contexts.

Citizens' actions for justice – for example, women's universal resistance to violence against women – also play a vital role in achieving positive change. This has been recognized in the widespread adoption of the 16 Days of Activism Against Gender Violence by ORGs, not forgetting that in order for women to take action in the defence of women's rights they must be informed of discussions at the provincial, national and international levels.

Presenting interventions 'on behalf' of 'poor women' is to be avoided at all costs. In sharing national plans, projects and proposals with women, we consistently emphasize that all issues are of equal concern to all of us. Similarly, it is equally vital to assure women that their voices, concerns and recommendations are being conveyed to decision makers at the policy level.

For women to challenge the *status quo* and power structures, they need to be assured of absolute support. Shirkat Gah has made itself available in all aspects and at all levels – including, if necessary, the provision of shelter to women survivors of violence in their own homes.

We have also found that women-specific groups do not always adopt the feminist agenda as their own. In order to encourage non-feminist groups to adopt a feminist perspective, we have always shown the interconnection between women's oppression, on the one hand, and injustice and underdevelopment on the other.

Finally, it is crucial to listen to women and support them in the decisions they take, even when these seem not radical enough or sometimes even inappropriate from our point of view. We must always trust them to act in their own best interests.

NOTES

1   Shirkat Gah, literally a place of participation, was formed as a non-hierarchical collective in 1975 by a group of women with a shared perspective on women's rights and development. The purpose of Shirkat Gah is to put women on the agenda through consciousness raising, lobbying of policy makers and initiating projects that translate advocacy into action. Shirkat Gah's main programmes include Women Law and Status, Women and Sustainable Development, Reproductive Health and Reproductive Rights, Women and Economic Autonomy and Green Economics and Globalization.
     See <www.sgah.org.pk> (last accessed 11 September 2006).

2   The Pakistan Women Law and Status (WLS) programme was part of the multi-country action research *Women and Law in the Muslim World* of the international solidarity network Women Living Under Muslim Laws (WLUML). WLS was preceded by legal, parliamentary archival research and field research – the latter being the first effort to document the varied customary practices prevalent across Pakistan and to gauge people's knowledge and influence of formal law. See <http://www.wluml.org/english/about.shtml> (last accessed 11 September 2006).

3   For further details read 'Reaching Out – Changing Our Lives' (1999), in *Outreach Strategies and Women Living Under Muslim Laws*, written and published by the Muslim Women's Research and Action Forum and WLUML.

4   WLS offers a paralegal training course every other year. This provides legal information and critically reviews the legal system from the perspectives of rights, social justice and development. Training involves two twenty-day sessions and topics include: conceptual framework and Pakistan's legislative system; basic constitutional rights and their enforcement; women and the United Nations; the Convention on the Elimination of All Forms of Discrimination Against Women (CEDAW) and other relevant international instruments; family laws, including Christian laws; the criminal justice system, including the Criminal Procedure Code and Pakistan's Penal Code; crimes against women; and fact finding. Trained paralegals conduct legal awareness sessions in their fields of expertise, establish links with practising lawyers, and assist people on legal matters and in fact finding when cases have to be referred

to lawyers. They also serve in liaising between the lawyer and the community.

5   External evaluations (1995, 1998, and 2004) confirm that WLS has indeed helped build women's self-confidence, increased their mobility and improved their understanding of and exercise of their rights.

6   Similar examples are reported in 'Creating Spaces: Shirkat Gah's Outreach Programme', in *Shaping Women's Lives – Laws, Practices and Strategies in Pakistan* (1998).

7   Concerned women prefer this type of intervention, as many do not want to approach the courts unless absolutely necessary because of the lengthy procedures and social stigma associated with these types of action. Organizations in the North-West Frontier, Sindh and Punjab provinces have successfully mediated family cases and provided legal help in numerous cases.

Part 5

Sustaining Work
in Situations of Conflict

18

The Women's Emancipatory Constituent Process for Peace in Colombia

Yusmidia Solano

Colombia's Iniciativa de Mujeres por la Paz (IMP – Women's Initiative for Peace) is an alliance of women's organizations, sectors and regional, departmental and local initiatives[1] that aims to position the women's movement as a political protagonist in negotiations related to the armed conflict in Colombia and in the subsequent reconstruction process. While establishing itself as an organization, it has also been participating in broader processes within the women's movement, and engaging in dialogue and negotiations with both civil society and the state.

This case study describes various parallel processes that have enabled us to sustain the work of women's organizations and movements in situations of conflict. Although the processes are ongoing, the period covered in this chapter runs from August 2001 to the most recent evaluation made in December 2004. A brief history of the IMP alliance is provided, together with the methodologies used to develop a common agenda for peace. Out of the common agenda came the Women's Emancipatory Constituent, an assembly held in November 2002 and organized on an annual basis ever since. The IMP agenda for peace is briefly discussed not only as the foundation for the movement in Colombia but also as an ongoing indicator of its health and thus its sustainability. The final section of this case study examines some of the most important lessons learned and describes the factors that, in our opinion, led to the success of our experience to date. We recognize that these are only preliminary reflections as it is still too early to evaluate the long-term impact the women's movement might have on other social movements, on changing public policy, or on the other profound transformations we are seeking.[2]

The emergence of the Women's Initiative for Peace

The Women's Initiative for Peace emerged as an alternative for peace built by women within an international context characterized by the acknowledgement of the importance of women's participation in processes of negotiation in conflict situations, and particularly after the approval of the United Nations Security Council Resolution 1325 on Women, Peace and Security, passed unanimously on 31 October 2000.[3] It was also a time during which negotiations in Colombia between the government of Andrés Pastrana (1998–2002) and the Revolutionary Armed Forces of Colombia (FARC) were taking place to come up with policies to deal with the internal armed conflict that had lasted more than 50 years. The process to create IMP started in May 2001 when women from different organizations had a meeting prior to attending the September 2001 Women's Peace Conference in Stockholm, Sweden.[4]

This conference was convened by leaders of the Swedish Federation of State Workers and the Women's Department of Colombia's syndicated unions,[5] with support from the Swedish International Development Cooperation Agency (SIDA) and the University of Uppsala through the Swedish embassy.

The organization of the conference was the result of arduous debates, with full participation by Swedish women. The initial document included the preliminary agreements on conceptual elements and political positions which guided the process of building the agenda the following year.[6]

Political action and construction of the agenda

Throughout 2002, IMP's coordinating team organized seven national seminars where decisions continued to be made on the nature of the agenda. At one of the seminars it was concluded that IMP is a process to articulate the political wills of women's organizations: as such it requires the strategic coordination of participants in order to strengthen the common understandings and enable us to move towards shared goals within a framework of ethnic diversity. We focus on two main objectives: political action to build the women's social movement as a collective force seeking the inclusive and representative fora of participation necessary for securing a lasting peace; and the construction of a women's social and political agenda as a platform for dialogue.

In working toward political action, the first of these objectives, IMP participated as one of the five major women's networks[7] that organized the National March of Women Against the War[8] in July 2002. This involved the participation of more than forty thousand women from all over Colombia, making it the most important citizen mobilization against war in recent decades: unquestionably, it contributed to the objective of building the peace agenda.

Regarding the second objective, building a woman's social and political agenda as a platform for dialogue, IMP decided to broaden the involvement of the women's movement that same year. Between July and August 2002 it organized seven national women's meetings or *encuentros* aimed at different sectors of women: small farmers, union members, Afro-Colombians, youth, women for peace and culture, indigenous peoples, and a seventh sector that included academics, public officials, politicians and representatives of feminist non-governmental organizations. Five regional *encuentros* were also held in September and October of the same year, in which 720 women from 272 organizations participated.

One of the most interesting and valuable aspects of the whole process was the use of a participatory methodology[9] that involved five complementary strategies: working together from the bottom up, changing power relations, recognizing different and diverse identities, prioritizing common needs, and ensuring that participants' opinions and contributions are registered and made visible. The last strategy was particularly important as participants' input provided raw material for the national seminars.

This participatory methodology generated six hundred proposals. These were reviewed by an IMP technical commission and sixty of them were finally presented at the Women's Emancipatory Constituent.

The Women's Emancipatory Constituent process

During the seminars that took place in 2002 it was determined that 'exclusion' was the condition that best described the situation of Colombian women. The seminar held in June resulted in a preliminary agreement on the twelve agenda 'items'[10] which were built around five forms of exclusion suffered by Colombian women. These were exclusion from the legal and safety perspectives, economic exclusion, social and cultural exclusion, exclusion as far as territorial, rural and environmental issues are concerned, and, finally, exclusion from involvement in the political sphere and in public life in general.[11] It was through the participatory methodology implemented at the sectoral and regional *encuentros* that consensus was finally reached on these exclusions and on the draft twelve-point agenda or action plan.[12]

It was in November 2002 that this agenda was finally discussed and approved in the plenary session of the first meeting of the Women's Emancipatory Constituent. This was held in Bogotá and was one of the most significant and inclusive political events in the history of the women's movement in Colombia.

The twelve-point action plan thus became the formal Agenda of Women for Peace, referred to as 'Our Pact for Peace', and was signed by approximately 300 women – although more than 900 were involved in the entire process – as well as by representatives of invited national and international organizations.

Due to the diversity and multiplicity of the constituents' interests, the dynamic for achieving final consensus on the agenda involved the successive and systematic construction of agreements. This involved, among other initiatives, a collective demonstration of women exercising their citizenship at the Colombian Congress. This important event at the beginning of the twenty-first century marked the entry of Colombian women as protagonists into the annals of national history, almost 50 years after having obtained the right to vote – a right they have continued to exercise in the midst of the war that is splintering the country.[13]

Our Pact for Peace: a wager for the future

The twelve items or action areas of the Agenda of Women for Peace, built around the five forms of exclusion, represent a considerable long-term challenge, and their advancement will require drawn-out processes involving pressure, mobilization and negotiation. It has thus been necessary to prioritize the plan of action and focus on concrete activities so that appropriate actions may be taken as political opportunities arise. Over the past two years activities have thus focused on agenda points one and twelve: these deal with the promotion of humanitarian agreements and guaranteeing women's participation in the peace processes, respectively.

The Women's Emancipatory Constituent is alive and well

The constituent processes that have taken place in various parts of the country[14] over the past five years, reflect a desire to exercise popular sovereignty in building the nation. They have been vital in articulating citizen rejection of the war and in the construction of alternative democracies. However, they reached their peak with the celebration of events and the definition of agendas for action. The Women's Emancipatory Constituent, however, is different in that it has maintained continuity by organizing plenary events in 2003 and 2004, and (at the time of writing) was preparing a fourth event for June 2006. The agenda has been negotiated with candidates for public office, and some of its points have been integrated in the local government development plans (for municipalities), and even in those of central government. However, IMP's intervention has had to respond to political changes at the national and international levels since the terrorist attacks that took place in the United States on 11 September 2001. This situation has resulted in the adoption of a war mentality and hegemonic conservative positions that brand any form of opposition as 'terrorism'. The agenda for negotiation with the Revolutionary Armed Forces of Colombia[15] (known by its Spanish acronym as FARC) thus met an impasse during the presidency of Alvaro Uribe (2002–6), who denied the existence of an internal armed conflict. The President makes reference to the 'band of terrorists' when speaking of the guerrilla movement, and therefore considers a military solution to be the only remedy. The government, nonetheless, has made advances in negotiations with the so-called Autodefensas Unidas de Colombia, an organization that represents paramilitary groups. It is within this new scenario that IMP has promoted high-visibility political actions in alliance with Ruta Pacifica de Mujeres,[16] a Colombian NGO, such as the National March to Putumayo, held in November 2003, in protest against the fumigation of coca fields with glyphosate[17] by the local government, and the International Meeting of Women Against War in August 2004. This latter event took place under the slogan 'No to a war that kills us or a peace that oppresses us': more than 30 international delegations, mainly from the Women in Black[18] movement, joined women from throughout the country, including participants from the first 2002 Emancipatory Constituent.

Other significant activities involved an alliance with the National Network of Women and the organization of two *agoras*[19] or assemblies. Both took place in Bogota in July 2003 and March 2004, with the slogans 'Voices and Thoughts of Women for Humanitarian Agreements' and 'Voices and Thoughts of Women on Truth, Justice and Reparation', respectively. The Women's Initiative for Peace has also joined forces with Mujeres en Alianza (Women in Alliance),[20] a lobbying group that was created to influence the government's legislative arm and has produced twenty draft laws. Operation Sirirí is another large campaign supported by IMP, based on a women's peaceful, non-violent strategy to bring about agreements of a humanitarian nature and changes in attitude among parties in conflict.

With the installation of the safe haven in Santa Fé de Ralito for the paramilitary forces and the establishment of a single negotiation team with the Autodefensas Unidas de Colombia on 1 July 2004, we were able to intercede in negotiations and propose the establishment of the 'National Advocacy Panel for the Right to Life, Truth, Justice and Reparation with a Gender Perspective'. This allowed us to monitor and denounce any irregularities in the peace negotiations as well as to lobby with Mujeres en Alianza for a draft law on justice and peace. Despite the introduction of some clauses to benefit victims, and further discussion of the draft law in Congress (at the time of writing), the legislation still does not entirely meet our demands – though it does, nonetheless, represent a step in the right direction.

At this point in our short but substantial history, we have come to realize that the armed conflict was far more entrenched than we originally imagined. We have also come to the conclusion that we need to use our resources in a more efficient manner so as to minimize the effect of conflict on women. As a result of these realizations, over the past year we have formulated our objectives in more concrete terms.

Lessons learned: a dialogue between different kinds of knowledge (with unity in diversity)

As part of IMP's growth process several lessons have been learned through self-evaluation. The first is the realization that an alliance such as ours requires a chain of resources that enables us to link efforts and talent at the international, national, regional and local levels. In addition to the financial and political assistance of SIDA, we have the permanent international solidarity, support and accompaniment of the Swedish Federation of State Workers, our partner in facilitating this funding, which has also shared valuable knowledge and experience in the field of negotiations. We also recognize that rights acquired through international processes should build on the experience and ancestral wisdom of Colombian women in their respective cultures and contexts.

We have learned of the importance of working with a diversity of interests, experiences and subjectivities of Colombian women, with particular consideration for those affected by the conflict and those who are fighting for peace. Debates and decision making should therefore benefit from participatory methodologies, in which we have acquired experience, and from the support team that has accompanied us for three years.

The empowerment of a collective work team has been key in our work, as it has provided vital support in the development of new ideas and the carrying out of new initiatives. This team includes the policy and methodology commission that provides guidance from a feminist perspective; the national team of 40 women representing different organizations, sectors and regions; and the team of facilitators who develop and apply the methodological tools and help weave the tapestry of IMP relations. The collective team also includes regional, departmental and local groups whose interventions on a daily basis, and frequently in heartrending scenarios of conflict, re-contextualize and contribute to the discourse to bring about the transformations we are all seeking.

There is a need for a bold, innovative and effective communications strategy. In this we have made progress, but not enough. It has included the preparation of 13 bulletins over three years, press conferences, interviews, posters, murals, leaflets, and videos on the history of IMP and the principles underlying its actions. We also succeeded in having the Women's Emancipatory Constituent broadcast on television.

We have also become aware over the years of the importance of maintaining an infrastructural base and a permanent administrative and logistical team.

Finally, we have learned that the capacity to generate agreements within the alliance has resulted in better conditions for promoting a policy of more extensive alliances with the rest of the women's movement in Colombia.

This brief synopsis has depicted the interplay at work in Iniciativa de Mujeres por la Paz: a dialogue between different types of knowledge and experience, one necessarily based on the pursuit of unity within a recognition of diversity.

NOTES

1   A complete list of organizations (272 in total) that are part of the Iniciativa de Mujeres Colombianas por la Paz (IMP – Colombian Women's Peace Initiative) can be found at <http://www.mujeresporlapaz.org/organisa.htm> (last accessed 13 September 2006).

2   For more comprehensive information on our work and related documents we invite readers to visit our website (in Spanish) at <http://www.mujeresporlapaz.org> (last accessed 13 September 2006).

3   The full text of the resolution can be found at <http://peacewomen.org/un/sc/1325.html> (last accessed 22 September 2006).

4   In addition to current members, IMP initially included Ruta Pacífica, Mujeres Actoras-Autoras de Paz, Mujeres de la Organización Nacional Indígena, Mesa Nacional de Concertación, and Proceso de Comunidades Negras, organizations that subsequently withdrew from the Alliance for different reasons.

5   Central Unitaria de Trabajadores (CUT).

6   The contribution of Irene Nillsson of the Swedish Federation of State Workers was particularly important during the conference.

7   These were: Iniciativa de Mujeres por la Paz, Ruta Pacífica de Mujeres, Mesa Nacional de Incidencia de Mujeres, Red Nacional de Mujeres, and Organización Feminina Popular. Of these, the first three also convened the Women's Emancipatory Constituent.

8   More information on the conditions that made this march possible can be found in Solano, S. Y. (2002), 'La situación actual del movimiento de mujeres en Colombia', *Programa Regional de Género y Políticas Públicas* (PRIGEPP), Facultad Latinoamericana de Estudios Sociales (FLACSO), Buenos Aires, Argentina. This essay was a contribution to FLACSO's PRIGEPP programme.

9   This was developed and supervised by Caroline Moser, with the support of Angélica Acosta and María Eugenia Vásquez.

10   The twelve points identified as agenda items are more along the lines of activity areas, as each has its respective strategies for implementation identified in the document, to be found (in Spanish) at <http://www.mujeresporlapaz.org/constitu02.htm>   (last   accessed   13 September 2006).

11 These five types of exclusion form the basis of the agenda, around which the twelve agenda items are built. These can be found at the site mentioned in the previous note.

12 Although the simpler term *agenda* is used, the document available (in Spanish) at <http://www.mujeresporlapaz.org/constitu02.htm> could also be considered an agenda for action or an action plan.

13 An account of milestones in the women's citizenship process and a profile of the armed conflict in Colombia can be found in Solano, Y. and E. Quiñonez, 'Cincuenta años de ciudadanía: cincuenta años de guerra', a paper presented at the International Meeting of Women Against War held in Bogotá in August 2004.

14 These have taken place in the municipalities of Mogotes (Santander) and Tarso (Antioquia), and the departments of Tolima and Antioquia.

15 The Fuerzas Armadas Revolucionarias de Colombia–Ejército del Pueblo or FARC-EP is Colombia's oldest and largest guerrilla group, established in 1964–6 as the military wing of the Colombian Communist Party. Source: Wikipedia 22 September 2006.

16 See <http://www.rutapacifica.org.co> a Spanish-language website (last accessed 13 September 2006).

17 See <http://www.narconews.com/Issue35/article1177.html> (last accessed 13 September 2006).

18 Women in Black is an international peace network that started in the Middle East and has spread to all regions of the world.
See <http://www.womeninblack.org/> (last accessed 20 September 2006).

19 An Ancient Greek word meaning public place, assembly, market. These *agoras* were thus modelled after the public events or fora held in ancient Greece.

20 Also participating in this alliance are Planeta Paz, Comisión Colombiana de Juristas, Red Nacional de Mujeres, and Confluencia de Redes.

19

From Individual Struggle to National Struggle

Palestinian Women in the State of Israel

Trees Zbidat-Kosterman

In this chapter I write of Palestinian women within Israel. We are of Druze[1], Bedouin,[2] Muslim and Christian origin, but not being recognized by Israel as having any nationality we are referred to as 'minorities', Israeli Arabs or non-Jews. As this community of women is part of the entire Palestinian people, I refer to them as Palestinians. The reader is given a brief overview of the history of this community, as well as a description of the impact on it of the establishment of the Jewish state in 1948: these are prerequisites for understanding the situation in which Palestinian women find themselves in Israel today. It is precisely this situation that created the environment for the establishment of the Palestinian women's organization Al-Zahraa, the strategies and achievements of which will be presented within this political historical context.

In 1969 Mrs Golda Meir declared that 'There is no such thing as a Palestinian people.... It is not as if we came and threw them out and took their country. They didn't exist.'[3] Palestinian women in Israel today are part of the Palestinian people who remained in their homeland that became the State of Israel after the 1948 war.

The historical context

The role and status of women within Palestinian society and within the family have undergone dramatic changes from the period of Ottoman rule (early sixteenth century to 1918) to the present. During that period Palestinian society was largely agricultural. Working the land was the basic means of subsistence and survival for the majority of the peasant population. Although women worked the land together with the men, they had no social standing or political power. However, within the extended family structure the wife of the chief of the *hamula*[4] assumed command over all other women in the family.

At the end of the Ottoman period, social, political, and economic developments led to the beginning of a structural change in the family. British rule over Palestine (1918–47) motivated many landowners to sell their properties to investors and thousands of landless peasants were forced to leave their homes and villages to seek work and shelter in the cities. This shift of power was further accompanied by an influx of European Jewish settlers, who had industrial and capitalist aspirations. Up until 1948, agriculture was the main source of income for 90 per cent of the Palestinian population.

These social and political changes, and fear for their country's future, motivated urban Palestinian women, especially from the upper and middle classes, to take action. It was mainly between 1904 and 1916 that Palestinian women engaged for the first time in social activism, organizing charitable societies in the major cities of Haifa, Akka, Jaffa, Nablus and Jerusalem. It was in Jerusalem in October 1929, after years of activism and work at the local level, that the first Palestinian women's conference was held.

The increasing participation of Palestinian women in public, social and political activities was terminated by the 1948 war, and especially among those who remained within the new State of Israel. With more than 480 out of a total of 573 Palestinian villages totally destroyed, the war eliminated the social, political, and economic infrastructure of Palestinian society. Eighty per cent of the Palestinian population – approximately 750,000 people – were forced to leave by Jewish forces (later the Israeli army), seeking refuge in neighbouring Arab countries, although many expected to return once the war was over. Only 150,000 Palestinians were able to stay within the new State of Israel, and of those who did, 40,000 found themselves refugees in their own homeland facing a shattered society and threats to cultural traditions.

Coupled with the Israeli government's policy of massive land expropriations, the effects of the war made it impossible to reclaim agriculture as the mainstay of Palestinian life. It was during this period that Palestinian society was also subjected to increased proletarianization and impoverishment, underdevelopment and even paralysis. Its people became a minority totally dependent on the Jewish-dominated economy.

Palestinians in Israel were isolated from other Arabs and segregated from Jews by military laws that controlled their daily lives; they could not leave their villages for work, for school or for any other reason without a permit from the military authorities. While the Israeli government granted citizenship to Palestinians in Israel, it never recognized them as a national group.

No Palestinian women's organization was established during this period except for the Democratic Women's Movement, a mixed Arab and Jewish women's organization.

The Israeli occupation of the West Bank, the Gaza Strip and the Syrian Golan Heights, after the 1967 war, came as a terrible shock to Palestinians who had lived for years under the illusion that the Arab countries would eventually liberate them. The war destroyed this illusion and a new political and economic situation emerged as demand for Israeli products increased employment opportunities for women and men. This process led to increased awareness among Palestinian women in Israel of discrimination against them based on their nationality and class. Increased political activism through demonstrations and other public activities became the norm as women entered the labour market and the educational system. Palestinian women joined with men in intensifying demands for full national and civil rights and for recognition as a national minority. Most importantly, the Israeli occupation of 1967 reunited Palestinians in Israel with Palestinians in the West Bank and Gaza, and dramatically encouraged the process of 're-Palestinization'.

It was at the beginning of 1980 that Palestinians inside Israel started to organize themselves nationally. Although equality and peace were the demands of several non-governmental organizations (NGOs) that emerged at that time, these were all established and run by men.

The establishment of Al-Zahraa

Palestinian women started to organize themselves in large cities such as Haifa and Nazareth, but the rural areas – home to 70 per cent of the Palestinian community – did not witness similar levels of activity.

In Israel, Palestinians live mostly in the North (the Galilee), and in the centre of the country – Al Mutalat – while Bedouins are based mainly in the Negev, in the south. The majority of Bedouins live in villages that are not officially recognized by the Israeli state and therefore have no infrastructure: no electricity or schools. The Bedouin still live in tents or iron shacks.

The women's organization Al–Zahraa[5] was established in the town of Sakhnin in December 1997. Sakhnin is a Palestinian town in the North (Lower Galilee) with 25,000 inhabitants. Although it started to receive basic services such as electricity at the end of the 1970s, today it remains a town with the infrastructure of a small underdeveloped village. Sakhnin still suffers from overcrowded classrooms, unpaved roads and a general lack of services.

With the expansion of Jewish settlements all around the town, built on land confiscated from Sakhnin, there is almost nowhere left to build. Sakhnin, like many other Palestinian villages, is now completely surrounded by these settlements.

Since the establishment of the State of Israel in 1948, no women's organizations have been established in rural areas and Palestinian women have had to stand by and watch the world change around them; a world in which other women have gained more rights.

In 1995, Wafaa Shaheen, the current director of Al-Zahraa, attended a course at Tel Aviv University on Jewish and Arab women and peacemaking. Participants included 31 Jewish and five Arab women. Wafaa felt that the content of the course did not include issues of relevance to her as a Palestinian woman. However, it did give her cause for reflection on her place as a Palestinian woman inside this Jewish state, and she was also able to appreciate how Jewish women were organized.

As a result of this experience Wafaa decided that Sakhnin needed an organization that worked on behalf of women, and she visited the Women's Council, a group affiliated to the local municipality, to see how they were organized and learn of its activities. However, she noted that these were of a non-political nature (cookery courses, embroidery, etc.) and quickly realized that this group was not the place where she could talk about changing the *status quo*, particularly as its members included women in positions of power such as the wives of the mayor, the local doctor and the headmaster. She thus called on nine women friends who were active in the Arab Democratic Party and together they drafted a declaration calling for the establishment of a women's committee that would focus on women's issues. This was signed by her friends and 400 other women in the town and sent to the town council.

However, the response was to dismiss Wafaa from her job as administrator within this council and a verbal admonition from the mayor (whose wife controlled the Women's Council committee). A campaign was promptly organized by Wafaa's friends and she was eventually reinstated.

It was at a conference in 1996 that these women met other Palestinian women from Nazareth and Haifa and learned how to establish an *amutah* or non-governmental organization; in December the following year Al-Zahraa, Sakhnin's own NGO, was formally constituted. Although during these first years, from 1997 to 1999, the founding members spent most of their time learning and gathering information both in the town and in surrounding villages, women from Sakhnin started to request courses on empowerment. In recognition of the importance of identifying and prioritizing needs, a needs assessment was carried out by Al-Zahraa. This enabled the organization to identify five priority issues that needed addressing.

The first of these issues was education among Palestinian Arab women. Girls attend school, but when they finish secondary school their families expect them to marry as soon as possible and start having a family.

Another issue of concern was the level of unemployment among Palestinian Arab women. A 2003 Ministry of Labour report indicated that while the unemployment rate within the Jewish community was just 6 per cent, it reached 15 per cent among 'non-Jews', or Palestinian Arabs. However, it is to be recognized that these figures only reflect the 'visible' cases of unemployment, as women do not usually register when they are without 'work'. Official figures for 1999 indicate that only 20 per cent of Arab women work outside the home.

The third priority issue identified was that of family honour. Girls carry the burden of family honour on their shoulders, and simply speaking to a strange man or an inappropriate form of dress are sufficient reasons for punishment. Stories abound of girls who are not allowed to study outside the village because of what the neighbours might think. The infamous honour killings, usually carried out by male members of the family when a girl or a young woman tarnishes her family 'honour', have gained notoriety throughout the world.

The fourth issue was the lack of women in decision-making positions. At the local level, for example, most teachers are women but headmasters are usually men; and in health clinics, while most nurses and ancillary workers are women, men always hold positions of authority. Even in parents' school committees, fathers rather than mothers participate, and outside the house it is the men who rule.

Finally, the fifth issue related to the question of identity, which has many repercussions for Palestinian women. This is related to their position within both the Arab and the Israeli communities: 'Who am I as a Palestinian woman inside Israel?' and 'Who am I as a woman in a patriarchal society?'

Getting down to work

The goals of Al-Zahraa are to improve the status of Arab women in their own society, raise awareness on women's issues among women themselves and in the Arab community as a whole, and support women's groups at the national level. The organization has two main objectives. The first is to develop and maintain a network of Palestinian Arab women and women's groups in Israel so as to enhance our work and serve as a type of umbrella organization for women's groups throughout the whole country. The second objective is to encourage women to pursue higher education and to empower them through a variety of means.

In August 1998 Al-Zahraa found a permanent location from which to organize activities. This served as a focal point for women eager to learn, seek new opportunities, and share experiences through a variety of activities that focused on the identified priority issues. Empowerment, which according to Al-Zahraa means allowing women to feel that they are not alone, was viewed as key to addressing these issues and was the subject of various courses. The empowerment process involved looking at the question of domestic violence, which is a serious issue among Palestinian women: many feel they are to blame for their situation; that they are alone in their suffering; and even that they have done something – such as being an inadequate housewife – to deserve such treatment. It was during emotional empowerment sessions that we experienced testimonies of many women who, for the very first time, were able to share their experiences of abuse over extended periods of time.

Al-Zahraa continues to be the focal point for activities, such as celebrating International Women's Day and training courses. Little by little, it has been making political statements with the support of up to 1,700 women: a clear sign that Palestinian women inside Israel want to change their lives. The organization has had an important ripple effect and its activities were later extended to eight other villages; it was not long before women from many other villages were asking us how we could support them in establishing their own women's organization. Al-Zahraa thus became a type of role model for them.

The Arab women's network

As a result of the overwhelming response from Palestinian women, Al-Zahraa started considering the establishment of a national network of Arab women, as a means to increase the organization's impact and to further its goals. It was in 2001, during the first national conference for Palestinian women in Israel organized by Al-Zahraa – to which we invited some Arab members of the Knesset (the legislative body or parliament of the modern state of Israel) – that the Palestinian Arab women's network was established.

This was a fairly informal grouping of 25 women's groups and organizations from all over the country who had participated in Al-Zahraa's courses on empowerment and leadership and who were keen to become more active in their own communities. However, there was a serious lack of organizational capacity.

The traditional *hamula* continued as the most important hierarchical structure in the villages, and we saw the same pattern of wives of powerful men organizing activities that did not threaten the *status quo*. By now we had accumulated sufficient experience to draw on the valuable results of workshops and courses developed for the women in Sakhnin and surrounding villages after the first conferences for Arab women in 2001.

In addition to skills training and capacity-building courses – on empowerment; on fundraising at the local, national and international levels; on recruitment strategies and motivational techniques – we made progress as an organization by becoming registered as a non-governmental organization. In December 2003 Al-Zahraa organized its second national women's conference, during which its present five-year programme was established.

Our five-year programme

The goal of Al-Zahraa's five-year (2005–9) programme is to improve the leadership skills of female activists and strengthen local women's organizational capabilities, with a focus on Palestinian Arabs inside Israel. The programme comprises four different types of activities: leadership courses for group coordinators at the village level; leadership courses in Arab villages throughout the country; study days and workshops throughout the country; and central conferences for Arab women drawn from throughout the country.

The programme's aim is to assist Arab women gain more influence in public institutions and in decision-making positions in Arab society and in Israeli Jewish society. We do this through the teaching of leadership skills that will serve in the establishment of groups and/or organizations at community level; in turn, these groups will have an impact on the broader economic, political and institutional spheres of their respective communities.

It is important to mention that all nine Al-Zahraa board members are also leaders in their respective villages. This ensures that we are permanently in contact with the grassroots and that the Arab women's network is in touch with the needs of women in their communities.

Training of Arab women trainers

We also encountered problems in finding Arab women trainers to carry out the leadership course in Arab villages throughout the country. We have women with academic backgrounds, but they all studied at Israeli institutions, in Hebrew, and in an academic context where Arabic studies are not a part of curricula. We therefore started our own course for trainers with an emphasis on the Arab community. At the beginning of 2006 four trainers started working in the villages, and another six will start in September and continue into 2007.

Learning from experience

Al-Zahraa started with nothing, and slowly became a well-known organization for Palestinian women inside Israel. Since we started activities in 1997 we have faced multiple problems and learned from them. One crucial lesson is that the outside world does not consider us as a community worthy of attention.

In 2001 Al-Zahraa sought the collaboration of the United Nations Development Fund For Women (UNIFEM), an international agency working throughout the Arab world as well as on the West Bank and in the Gaza Strip. We consider ourselves no different from Arab women in other parts of the world. However, the agency's response indicated that, like other UN agencies, it 'can support initiatives only in those countries with which the UN has a development assistance agreement (i.e. developing countries)' [6] and for this reason, they are not normally in a position to fund initiatives in Israel. The letter left us more than disappointed; it epitomizes the perception many people have of Palestinian women in Israel, and demonstrates one of the major constraints we face in accessing resources.

We, Palestinian women within Israel, consider ourselves Arab, and we face the same problems as Arab women in other Arab countries. Israel does not recognize us as Arabs, but as non-Jews, and it seems that the outside world also has problems with acknowledging our existence.

This lesson has taught us that putting Palestinian women inside Israel on the international map needs to be our top priority. We have contributed articles to many magazines and, of course, a variety of international organizations have helped us make our voices heard. We participated in international conferences; we have published a book in English and Arabic; articles have been written by Palestinian female writers from Israel – but there is still much we need to do to make ourselves visible.

Conclusion

After nine years of working with Palestinian women inside Israel, we see that slowly something positive has emerged. We receive more and more requests for courses from women who want to do 'something' in their communities. Our five-year programme gives us the capability to respond to some of their needs. It is a long struggle, but we see that in many cases its results are very positive. We see these positive results at the community level, where women have succeeded in establishing their own groups or organizations. But we also see very positive results for many women at a personal level. The task of Al-Zahraa is not to tell women how they should solve their problems; our responsibility as a women's organization is to give women the tools with which they can work towards finding their own personal solutions. We want women to organize themselves, to find common issues, to feel strong enough to raise their voices.

Looking at the new generation of Palestinian women, we can see that their future will be a better one. They already have higher expectations from life than their mothers. They are becoming more aware of their rights, and some of them are willing to fight for them. They are proud to be Palestinian, and refuse to consider themselves as second-class citizens. The struggle for women's rights progresses slowly but steadily.

ACKNOWLEDGEMENTS

Al-Zahraa would like to thank all those organizations who have believed in its work over the years; without them, I would not be here telling our story.
I would also like to thank the people from Shatil, Haifa who gave us advice when we needed it, and stood by us during the whole process. But most of all I would like to express my appreciation to all the women who continue to believe in us and our work.

New Israel Fund, Israel
Global Fund for Women, USA
Stichting Cordaid, the Netherlands
Stichting Mama Cash, the Netherlands
Zuster van Liefde, The Netherlands
Kerk in Aktie, The Netherlands
US/Israel women to women, USA
Christliche Friedensdienst (CFD),
   Switzerland

The Dutch embassy, Tel Aviv, Israel
The Embassy of Austria, Tel Aviv, Israel
Stichting Haella, The Netherlands
Kvinna till Kvinna, Sweden
Stichting Wilde Ganzen, the
   Netherlands

NOTES

1   Druze are a distinct religious community based mainly in the Middle East who are an offshoot of Islam and influenced by other religions and philosophies. Source: <http://www.wikipedia.org>.
2   Bedouins are Arab nomadic pastoralist groups found throughout most of the desert belt in Northern Africa and the Middle East.
     Source: <http://www.wikipedia.org>.
3   Statement to the *Sunday Times,* 15 June 1969.
4   The *hamula* is the bigger family structure (beyond the extended family), the ultimate body to which members of traditional Arab society owe their loyalty and functioning as a social reference group. Source: S. Nathan (2005), *The Other Side of Israel. My Journey across the Jewish/Arab Divide*, Nan A. Talese.
5   More information on the organization can be found at: <http://www.ittijah.org/member/alzahra.html>
6   Letter addressed to the author in July 2001 and signed by Ms Shoko Ishikawa, Officer in Charge, Asia/Pacific Section, UNIFEM.

20

Equal Representation in a Divided Society

The Feminist Experience in Israel

Dalia Sachs and Hannah Safran

During the 1990s it was a continuous struggle for the feminist movement in Israel to piece together the different groups and organizations working to promote women's rights from feminist perspectives. In order to enable collaboration between different groups of women who had not previously participated in feminist activities, a system of equal representation was introduced. It worked as a unifying system and had its merits and its faults. In this chapter we tell the story of the feminist attempt to create a new vision for activism in a multicultural society.

Living in a war zone and facing a globalized economy creates a difficult reality for women in Israel. As a result of the conflict between Israeli Jews and Palestinians we all live in fear and suffer the consequences of bloodshed. In this violent atmosphere women are excluded from public discourse while violence against all women is growing. The gap between affluence and poverty creates deep divisions between women from different ethnic, national, social and religious backgrounds. Under these circumstances tensions between women are difficult to bridge and working for change is harder than ever.

Despite these difficulties the feminist movement in Israel has been trying to develop a new agenda for action. A new idea, with the potential to open up common ground for action, was suggested by a group of Mizrahi[1] Jewish women. This was a system of 'equal representation' that ultimately evolved into what became known as the 'quarters policy'.[2] The idea resulted from an analysis of the main divisions and differences that have torn Israeli society apart, divisions that result in different life experiences of women from various socio-economic and national backgrounds. The feminist movement could not continue as a mainly middle-class Ashkenazi-Jewish[3] one. It had to embrace wider representation and a new platform of action so as to ensure its viability as a movement.

We are writing this chapter from our perspective as activists in both the feminist and the women's peace movements. We are lesbians; one of us is Ashkenazi and one of us is of mixed Jewish origin (Mizrahi and Ashkenazi); and we are both teaching at various higher education institutions, thus enjoying middle-class incomes. We are fully aware of the implications of our privileged backgrounds. Nevertheless, we are committed to social change and have been working together with women from other backgrounds and identities for the success of the vision of the feminist movement and for peace. We were both involved in promoting the process we are about to discuss.

The system of equal representation was first implemented in a national feminist conference that took place in 1992 in Israel, attended by more than 300 women. Since then and throughout the 1990s feminist conferences provided the principal meeting points for various groups of women and feminist organizations. This essay thus focuses on events surrounding those conferences that enabled cooperation between Palestinian women (inside Israel) and Jewish women, as well as between Ashkenazi and Mizrahi, and heterosexual and lesbian women. But this was a fragile and delicate cooperation. It also brought out tensions and bitterness that groups harboured against each other. In the process, each group and every woman had to confront and deal with their prejudices, learn to listen and be compassionate. Eventually each group became stronger and created its own agenda. New organizations were created; conferences based on the agenda of each group were organized; and coalitions provided an alternative way of working together.

In this chapter we discuss how the idea of equal representation was born, developed and implemented, and how it created a breakthrough in our thinking about women's strategies for action. We discuss the successes and the failures of our endeavours and the controversies they created. We also demonstrate how the collaboration between the Coalition of Women for Peace[4] and feminist groups, activated by the method of equal representation, brought about an understanding of the societal power structure; in so doing we address the interconnections between women, ethnic, and national oppressions.

Social divisions

Israel is a society divided by race, class, nationality, religion, ethnicity and different lifestyles. The pioneering Jews who started arriving in Palestine at the end of the nineteenth century were mainly of Ashkenazi origin. They are by and large still the ruling elite of Israel and form the hegemonic culture. The other large group in Israel comprises Mizrahi Jews, who migrated to Israel from Arab-speaking countries mainly after 1948 when the State of Israel was created. They spoke Arabic, were part of Arab culture, and were looked down upon by the early pioneers, who came mainly from Eastern Europe and aspired to create a new nation based on Western culture and ideals.

Another relevant social division in Israel exists between the privileged Jewish majority and the Palestinian minority. Palestinian women suffer from oppression due to their nationality – being Arabs in a Jewish state – as well as their gender in a traditionally patriarchal society. Lesbian women are also a particularly vulnerable group, suffering from a two-fold oppression as both women and lesbians. Over the last decade the impact of the struggle for lesbian and gay rights has gathered momentum. In most places in Israel women and men can now practise their chosen lifestyles, but total equality and societal acceptance are still a long way off, as Israel is a conservative society and many of its laws are based on religious traditions.

The feminist movement

The new feminist movement in Israel began in the early 1970s, placing in the public arena its critique of the place of women in society.[5] This movement raised issues such as violence against women, rape, unequal pay, sexual harassment and the inaccessibility of political participation for women. The movement achieved considerable successes in introducing shelters for battered women, and in creating hot-lines for women and rape crisis centres. Although women activists during that period exposed the Zionist myth that Israel promoted equality between men and women, they ignored the vast differences that existed between women. Nor were they united in their political positions against the oppression of Palestinians and the occupation of their territory, and this prevented Palestinian women in Israel from joining their struggles.

It was in the early 1990s that a distinct change started to take place within the feminist movement. The first Intifada[6] (uprising of Palestinians) created the possibility for joint activism between Jewish and Palestinian women in Israel.[7] This only became possible after a large number of Jewish feminist women began taking part in demonstrations opposing the Israeli occupation of the West Bank and the Gaza Strip. As a result, Palestinian women began to feel safe working with Jewish women and to organize activities and conferences. It was in this way that the women's peace movement grew in size and strength during the first Intifada. A series of four annual peace conferences were organized and held between 1988 and 1991, and as the Intifada was drawing to an end in 1991 and with the Oslo Agreement in sight[8] several women started working together on the idea of a feminist conference. This was when the late Vicky Shiran, a much-missed leader among Mizrahi women, proposed a new system of equal representation. The adoption in 1992 of this radical idea by the conference organizers ushered in a new era of feminist conferences.

Feminist conferences and the implementation of equal representation

The reality of most women under the hegemony of Israel was not having a voice of their own. It would usually be Ashkenazi women who spoke up in conferences, ran meetings and led the way. The proposed new conference structure involved the representation of four different groups. Mizrahi, Ashkenazi, Palestinians and lesbian women were to be represented on every panel and in every public event, and the number of workshops would be divided equally between women from these four groups. Preparations for the first feminist conference based on equal representation advanced with great anticipation. It was not an easy task for the organizers to find enough women from each group to volunteer to lead a workshop or take part in a panel discussion. Eventually, all these roles were allocated and the 1992 conference was considered a success.

However, not all the participants were happy with the idea of equal representation or with the assumption on which it was based. Many heterosexual Ashkenazi women, for example, could not understand the need for such a strategy; no doubt some feared, consciously or not, that equal representation could diminish their hegemony. Many also argued that they themselves had suffered underprivileged childhoods and discrimination, and that, as feminists, they were sensitive enough to the needs of other oppressed groups and did not require regulations to ensure space was given to Mizrahi, Palestinian or lesbian women. And although the conference allowed some of the tension between Mizrahi and Ashkenazi Jewish women to come out into the open and be discussed, many of the basic dividing issues were still invisible to participants. For example, coming from a more homophobic society, some women could not agree to the inclusion of lesbians as a distinct group. And although the pain and bitterness that some women shared publicly with other women was not easy, it was considered a necessary part of the healing process.

The second conference in 1993 generated an important debate between Mizrahi and Palestinian women on the different degrees of oppression from which each group suffered. Palestinian women found it difficult to distinguish between Mizrahi and Ashkenazi women, as for them both groups represented Jewish privileged women – as did lesbians, who at the time were also Jewish and mainly Askenazi. Another bone of contention for Palestinian women was that the Arabic language was not used at the conferences, with Hebrew being the only working language. They felt the need for a time and place for themselves.

It is important to stress that these conferences assumed considerable importance for the feminist movement as they served as an annual meeting place for feminists from a variety of religious, ethnic, cultural and socio-economic backgrounds. They were usually held in a central location somewhere in Israel, started on a Thursday afternoon and lasted until Saturday evening. These two full days of meetings usually involved ten discussion panels and approximately 70 different workshops attended by up to 600 women. In order to ensure the broadest possible participation, every attempt was made to keep costs down and to invite women from low-income neighbourhoods at subsidized rates. This enriched the experience and enabled some women to speak in public for the very first time. It also facilitated the identification of new leaders who were able to speak out on a variety of issues concerning women, and not just on topics related to their own groups.

In the absence of one strong feminist movement in Israel, this conference provided organizations with a venue and a powerful tool to give a voice to all women. The conferences were the place in which organizations and activists met, discussed, debated and practised the method of 'equal representation'. The planning of the conferences was a democratic and pluralistic process involving a large number of women's organizations from across a wide political and cultural spectrum. This joint process ensured ongoing dialogues throughout the year promoting inter-organizational cooperation. Between 1992 and 1999 six conferences were held, each one planned and prepared in collaboration with different feminist organizations.[9]

With the start of the second *Intifada* in 2000 many activists returned to work for the women's peace movement, dedicating all their time and energies to opposing Israeli government and military tactics involving the occupation of Palestinian territories and the oppression of its people. A split now grew between women who considered the national conflict as the focal point of oppression, and those who believed that class and ethnic oppression should be addressed first. There was no longer any energy to continue organizing feminist conferences. We have held only two national meetings since then. The first one was an emergency mini-conference in support of the struggle of Vicki Knafo, a single mother who ran a campaign against government cuts in social welfare; the second, in 2004, was an attempt to recreate the tradition of feminist conferences. We were unsuccessful in reorganizing the feminist movement, whose most active members continue to be engaged in the women's peace and anti-war movements.

Counting our successes and failures

Fifteen years later we can look back on the development of feminist activism in Israel and see that the 'quarters policy' resulted in heightened creativity and a process of empowerment. The conferences themselves had a ripple effect, creating synergies that resulted in the birth of new organizations and further conferences focused on the identities and needs of particular groups. Other organizations adopted the idea of equal representation in their daily activities. Coalitions were conceived between groups that would previously never have considered such joint ventures.

In 1996, when Mizrahi women felt that the feminist conference, for all the space it provided, was not broad enough to address issues and questions specific to their own realities, they decided to hold a confer-ence of their own. This resulted in a special and sometimes emotional encounter, as within a more favourable framework Mizrahi women felt more freedom to express themselves, and new important issues came to light. Some of these included the relevance of identity-based groups, making an impact on society, and working together or separately.

As a result Mizrahi women created Ahoti ('sister' in Hebrew), an organization devoted to representing underprivileged women, helping and aiding those who are deprived of their labour rights as well as those whose voices cannot be heard. Ahoti is dedicated to closing the economic, social and cultural gaps and works through projects, workshops and conferences that reach out to women outside the main big cities, in regions where access to information, good education and other resources is limited. The organization seeks to empower women personally, inform them of their rights as women and as workers, and help them develop alternative economic solutions.

Lesbian women also gained confidence and a strong voice in the public arena after setting up their own organization in 1992 and becoming more visible and vocal, demanding equal rights in society. The community of lesbians was always very active in the feminist movement and many lesbians took part in organizing the conferences. A strong group of activists was thus able to mobilize their community and their allies and achieve considerable gains within mainstream society. During this period other women were empowered to come out as lesbians in public while promoting their own Mizrahi women's community.

Palestinian women also started establishing new organizations and setting up projects while the feminist conferences were taking place. These tended to oscillate between working with Jewish women and the need to maintain their independence. Hot-lines and rape crisis centres that catered specifically for the Palestinian population were established, a shelter for battered Palestinian women was opened in 1992, and Kayan, a feminist organization for Arab women, was established in 1996 and became part of the Haifa women's coalition. Palestinian women organized meetings and conferences of their own, elaborating their own specific critiques and demands. Finally, in 2004, Aswat ('voices' in Arabic), a new group of Palestinian lesbians, was formed and included women who, for the very first time, were ready to talk publicly about their lifestyles. This represented an enormous act of courage by women who suffer acutely from oppression from three sides: as Palestinians in Israel, as women, and as lesbians within Palestinian society.

The creation of different interest groups and their ability to organize their own conferences raised new questions. There were many women who felt unsatisfied with the tendency to identify with one specific group, and women with 'hyphenated' identities such as Mizrahi-lesbian and Ashkenazi-Mizrahi began to make their appearance and have an impact on feminist thinking. It was no longer sufficient to embrace the quarters policy. Other identity groups – such as new immigrants, older women, and religious women – were now considered as 'equally important', alongside the original 'quarters'. Finally, it no longer sufficed to question who we were and into which family we were born. We learned that one's identity could also be a matter of choice: it was no longer considered a matter of destiny. We have learned that to identify with the oppression of others and fight together against social injustice is a choice we are able to make that is not necessarily solely based on or influenced by our original identity group.

Which way now?

In this chapter we have explored the complexities of the feminist movement in Israel and its endeavour to overcome divisions, racism and other forms of injustice. We were successful in creating the series of conferences and a synergy that broadened the involvement of women from different religious, cultural and socio-economic backgrounds. This synergy, that revealed some of the raw and painful conditions of many women prior to joining the movement for change, also infused the feminist movement with a new energy. The conferences and other initiatives provided the impetus to establish new forms of collaboration, joint ventures, and new perceptions of the feminist movement as a whole. Feminists are not one homogeneous group of people and feminism is no dogmatic doctrine, but rather a complex belief system that we women are all responsible for creating.

Israeli feminism has developed a unique awareness of the divergencies and interplays of race, ethnicity and national identities, socio-economic oppressions, oppressions based on sexual preference, multiple identities and issues. It has also affected the way women relate to society, insisting on the representation of all identity groups in other organizations, in workplaces, in panel discussions and elsewhere, thus infiltrating the Israeli social order.

We feel we are part of an international movement and would like to share our stories and ideas with feminist women worldwide, continuing this discussion by relating to each other globally in order to change our societies. We all understand that only together can we launch a new discourse, create alternative solutions, better women's lives, and open new paths to peace. The time has come for feminist women to create unity within diversity and proclaim our visions for a better world.

NOTES

1   *Mizrahi* Israelis are Jews whose families migrated to Israel from Arab countries. Although they make up more than half of Israel's population, they still suffer discrimination.

2   This was the popular name for the policy as four groups within the movement were represented: Ashkenazi and Mizrahi Jews, Palestinians who live inside Israel, and lesbian women.

3   Ashkenazi Jews are from middle, northern, or eastern Europe, or of such ancestry.

4   The Women's Coalition for Peace, comprising seven women's peace groups, was established in November 2000 to support the work of women's peace groups, to oppose the occupation of Palestinian territories by Israel, and to struggle for social justice and equality in Israeli society.

5   See Safran, H. (2006), *Don't Wanna Be Nice Girls: the Struggle for Suffrage and the New Feminism in Israel* (in Hebrew), Haifa.

6   Literally, 'shaking off' in Arabic.

7   Both Jewish and Palestinian women discussed here are citizens of Israel.

8   The Oslo agreement between Israel and the Palestine Liberation Organization was signed in 1993. This period came to an abrupt end in October 2000 with the outbreak of the second Intifada.

9   The feminist non-governmental organizations were: Claf, the Community of Feminist Lesbians; Isha l'isha – The Haifa Feminist Center; The Israeli Women's Network; Kol Ha'isha – a feminist centre, rape crisis centres (of which there are twelve around the country); *Noga* – a feminist magazine; Shin – Equal Representation for Women; Tandy – a movement of democratic women.

21

The 'Motherhood' Strategy of Indonesia's Suara Ibu Peduli

Monika S. W. Doxey

May 1998 marked the end of Suharto's 30-year authoritarian government in Indonesia. During this time of political upheaval, feminist activist members of Suara Ibu Peduli (SIP) – The Voice of Concerned Mothers – used the valued identity of *Ibu*[1] (motherhood) strategically to unify and empower women, and to give them a political voice. After 1998, in the post-Suharto reform era, feminist activists had to deal with the challenge of moving beyond the essentialist identity of motherhood that had been a core value of activism previously. They needed to build an inclusive vision that could represent the complex heterogeneity or diversity of Indonesian women, while continuing the initial work of repoliticizing the women's movement.

This case study focuses specifically on how grassroots SIP activists were able to help reconstruct women's *Ibu* identity when the political opportunity arose in 1998. It was then that they empowered women to break out of the confines of domesticity under state Ibuism[2] and gradually reconstruct a new identity while moving into the political sphere. The case study also shows how feminist activists were able to generate discussions that challenged the gender ideology[3] of *Ibu* and its unifying aspects by critically analysing or deconstructing its disregard for the complex heterogeneity and diverse identities of Indonesian women.

Strategic use of state Ibuism's essentialist identity

Prior to 1998 Indonesian feminists argued that the gender ideology known as state Ibuism or state motherhood marked clear limits to women's identity for the purpose of depoliticizing them.[4] It was in this way that the government was able to control women as a collective and limit women's empowerment to the domestic realm. One form of women's depoliticization was promoted through the Suharto New Order state gender ideology enshrined in the official paradigm of women's roles, the *Panca Darma Wanita* (five basic obligations of women). This stated that the woman's role is to be a wife at her husband's side, the nation's procreator, a mother and an educator of children, a housekeeper, and an Indonesian citizen – in that order.[5] This official paradigm was responsible for constructing a unified hegemonic and dominant identity for women centred in the domestic sphere of *Ibu*, whether within the nucleus of the biological family or as a mother and wife in the macro sense of the national family. The woman who performs biological, social and cultural duties within the biological family also carries out her state duties for the national family in a controlled and depoliticized environment. In constructing state Ibuism the Suharto government also reaffirmed the national discourse of *unity in diversity*.[6] *Ibu* as a mother and wife became a static female identity unified across ethnic, religious and class boundaries.

Political activists realized that they could build on and use state Ibuism to their advantage even before the fall of Suharto. However, new political opportunities[7] for feminists appeared during the economic crisis in 1998 that eventually brought Suharto and the New Order government down, and it was after its downfall that feminists discovered even greater opportunities to reformulate state Ibuism. By reconstructing women's identities they were able to endow *Ibu* with new, empowering meaning.

State Ibuism's rationale that a hegemonic or dominant identity was needed to unify the women of Indonesia as a political force was turned to SIP's advantage. It became an integral part of the organization's strategy, not for the purpose of controlling the population or depoliticizing women, but to empower them by giving them a political voice. Under the banner of the Voice of Concerned Mothers activists were able to appeal to and mobilize women from many different ethnicities, religions and classes who could relate to the *Ibu* identity. This strategy has been used successfully by many groups of mothers around the world to oppose state or military atrocities.[8]

The SIP strategy involved using *Ibu* to overcome ethnic, religious and class differences. In other words they essentialized the mother's identity *strategically*. Strategic essentialism is derived from the post-colonial theorist Gayatri Spivak's concept of the practice of essential-izing or using a fundamental, easily understood and unifying identity (motherhood in this case), at particular historical moments such as during political upheavals.[9]

Motherhood or *Ibu* as an identity promoted by SIP thus became a unifying and empowering political identity. Women were initially attracted to the seemingly apolitical identity of motherhood. However, the addition of the word 'concern' in the group's name indicates an *active* subject in that it not only implies a need for change but also suggests a concern to find an empowering political voice.[10] Finally, it implied a concern for children's welfare as well as that of the nation.

Enacting the *Ibu* Identity

From the beginning of 1998 events in Indonesia were to create three important political opportunities. These were the economic crisis, the rise of the movement that demanded the disbanding of Suharto's New Order government, and, finally, the government's violent reaction to the uprising. The activities through which SIP was able to take advantage of these political opportunities are described below.

The first activity, carried out in response to the economic crisis, was the organization of a street rally to demand government action on the rising price of baby formula milk and basic commodities. A collective grassroots women's organization was then formed, and thereafter SIP began to reconstruct *Ibu*'s position in the domestic sphere by bringing the demands of women – the concern for household economics and feeding the family as a mother, wife and housekeeper – from the private into the political domain. In this process it was necessary to emphasize the gentle qualities of motherhood in order to tone down the radical and transgressive nature of the street demonstration, as taking to the streets was considered beyond the sphere of respectable women.[11]

Then, on 23 February 1998 a peaceful demonstration took place. The women chanted, carried banners and handed flowers to passers-by and the police who came to disband the rally; they also led non-denominational prayers and sang the patriotic song 'I Saw our Mother-land'. This song symbolized their position as the mothers of the nation and the valued role of mothers throughout the ages, evoking feelings from the struggle for nationhood in colonial times. The song equated motherhood to the nation and alluded to the need to rally youth so as to free and rescue the motherland from her deepest sufferings caused by the colonial power that took her dignity and dispossessed her of her wealth.[12] In this way SIP linked motherhood with the national struggle.

The state was unable to dismiss these actions as carried out by a deviant political group and representative of the antithesis of civilized womanliness[13] because of SIP's focus on the moral dimension of the theme of motherhood. In the trials of three of the women involved in the law-breaking demonstrations, the defence case was that the women's concerns were not political – and when evidence was produced to this effect, their political cause and moral stature gained a wider appeal. The state attempted to define the women's activities as treacherous and subversive but was unable to press home its case as the women concerned did not challenge state Ibuism's construction of them as wives, mothers and housewives. The media depicted them as *Ibu* with symbolic flowers, mother's milk, songs and prayers against the state's aggressive symbols of tanks, guns, soldiers and teargas.[14] The state was not able to implicate them in subversion as they neither belonged to a political party nor ascribed to any ideology other than that imposed by the state.

Unlike hierarchical, state-sponsored women's organizations, SIP became a grassroots movement that spread to most areas of Indonesia, providing basic food to alleviate the impact of the economic crisis on poor women who were unable to feed their children. It acted as a mother to the nation by helping to feed the poor and, in this manner, showed women throughout the country – and especially the poorest – that empowerment was possible by working as a collective independent of state control.

The second political opportunity seized by SIP was the rise of the student movement to disband the Suharto New Order government.[15] On this occasion SIP moved from voicing demands to opposition – not overtly, but as a mother of the nation supporting its 'children', who, in this case, were university students. It assumed its 'maternal' role by mobilizing logistical and collective support for student demonstrators in the form of rice packets, water, medicines and clothes, and carried out other domestic chores such as cooking and taking care of the students' basic needs. In return, the students acted as human shields for their 'mothers' during subsequent SIP-organized demonstrations. Despite claims during a trial of several activists that their actions during the student uprising were apolitical, their supportive action, newsletters and rhetoric were considered openly critical of the New Order government and thus political.[16] It was in this manner that SIP started empowering women to voice political opposition.

The final political opportunity seized by SIP resulted from the state's violent reaction to the uprising. This provided activists with the opportunity to raise the issue of violence against women in society, and to draw attention to the fact that the female victims were mothers.

One of the results of this process was SIP's establishment of the first women's crisis centre. Then, after Suharto's resignation in May 1998, SIP went on to lobby the new government to investigate violence against women by the military and the state. More specifically, SIP reacted to the fact that Chinese Indonesian women were raped as part of the *modus operandi*[17] of military special forces and that incited violent mass riots in May 1998.[18] Women from SIP and other NGOs worked together as '*Ibus*', despite official sanctions, to support the female victims of violence by attending and protecting them; through their activism SIP and its allies aimed to empower these women by giving them a voice in a time of considerable political tension. Not only were they able to draw attention to the rapes of Chinese Indonesian women, but they also exposed severe cases of violence against women in regions of military conflict such as Aceh, West Papua and the former Indonesian territory of East Timor.[19]

The vocal stand of SIP on the situation of women in times of political turmoil raised consciousness on the politics of women's bodies, and it was suggested that women were being used for political ends, commodified and subordinated in the hegemonic and dominant formation of the New Order government. Women who had been depoliticized previously became aware that the concerns of women were in fact closely linked to the intricate game of politics.[20] The work of SIP in unifying women as a collective power centre gave significance to the voice of women: it provided alternative perspectives in a conflict-ridden, heterogeneous and diverse country on the brink of disintegration.

The post-reform era

In the post-reform era after 1998, the strategic use of *Ibu* by feminist activists who had been at the heart of their movement was challenged.

A new position emerged that critiqued the use of unifying identities. Indonesian feminists started to question the construction of women's identity as *Ibu*, pointing out that its unifying force could be construed as potentially repressive to the plurality and fluidity of women's identities in this heterogeneous country. State Ibuism's construction of women's identity could thus be analysed in line with critical feminist argument that 'women are a volatile collectivity in which female persons can be very differently positioned so that the apparent continuity of the subject of women cannot be relied on'.[21]

Ibu was used by SIP as a uniting identity, to include women from various backgrounds, ethnicities, classes and religions. It did, however, mirror the state's ideology of unity in diversity. The politics of feminism employed by SIP activists thus functioned as 'a nation where other women were invited to join without disrupting the ultimate integrity of the nation'.[22] Difference is treated superficially, in an imagined harmony, while excluding the complexities and problematic notions of harmony in difference. The feminist appropriation of Ibuism could thus jeopardize the movement by reinventing the problems created by state Ibuism through forcing the acceptance of a single identity, avoiding the complexities inherent in difference, and prolonging a static ahistorical identity as *Ibu* to the detriment of other identities.

When examined more closely, however, Indonesian feminist political strategy shows a degree of sophistication due to the understanding that *Ibu* is a historically contextualized, temporal identity. In other words, SIP has always seen its activism as a temporary, reactive movement characterized as 'emergency activism'.[23] Its activists understood that an essentialist identity used indiscriminately could create the constraints and disadvantages discussed previously.

Activists succeeded in identifying, understanding and reconstructing the ideology employed by the state. By deconstructing the unifying identity of *Ibu* together with their practice of activism, SIP also demonstrated its level of sophistication by applying it self-reflexively to its activism. The following descriptions of the women's 1999 congress and SIP's first anniversary activities are illustrative of this sophistication. They demonstrate the combination of ideological deconstruction with practical activism in a single process.

During the 1999 women's congress, Indonesian feminists recognized the positive energy of diversity as well as the difficulties inherent in heterogeneous identities. The previous year this congress had been held to create a women's coalition for use as a political pressure group: the initiators were SIP's founder members.[24] During the 1999 congress, one of the important lessons learned was that women's issues cannot be addressed through a 'harmony in difference' approach. Many of the different groups represented by the 500 participants from 26 different provinces had conflicting ideologies and agendas. Throughout the congress, women realized their inability to unite beyond the identity of *Ibu*. Informed by feminist critical thinking, this search for unification rapidly turned into a process of deconstruction of *Ibu*'s identity and, on seeing the results of the congress, it became clear to SIP that the identity of *Ibu* cannot be applied to all women under all conditions.

The limitations of the *Ibu* identity also became clear to SIP when it celebrated its first anniversary. The first activity of this celebration was a seminar entitled 'Redefining the Role of *Ibu* in Society' during which feminist activists said that what was needed was a redefinition of the traditional roles of *Ibu*.[25] Activists are challenging and looking beyond the dichotomy of *Bapakism* (father/man) and *Ibuism* to see a deconstruction of identity, centralized in the idea of the 'in between', for a political purpose.

The second activity to commemorate SIP's first anniversary involved the production of a book in which writers such as Gadis Arivia, Karlina Supeli, Toeti Heraty Noerhadi and Melanie Budianta[26] discussed feminism and *Ibu*, seeing identity as a socially constructed category. They also wrote about its limitations, its contradictions and how they have used it to achieve societal change.

These examples of SIP's participation through congresses, seminars and writings during the post-reform era demonstrate not only the organization's awareness of the limitations of the essentialist identity of *Ibu*, but also its understanding of ideological constructions of identity. Through understanding and practice, SIP activists have participated in a process of deconstruction, critically analysing and moving beyond a hegemonic dominant identity.

Conclusion

Women in Indonesia, and around the world, have the potential to use SIP's experience, learning from its limitations and successes how to continue to empower and create better conditions for women and society in general. Women's movements should move beyond emergency activism. However, in doing so caution needs to be exercised regarding the power of a unifying identity, such as state Ibusim, to constrict and depoliticize women. The Indonesian feminist political movement must continue to question the constructions of identity and truths, not only by the state, but also by its own movement. In so doing, feminists can provide an example of how to see beyond the construction of a nation's hegemonic or dominant identity and contribute to a solution against disintegration – a serious problem in the many heterogeneous and diverse countries of the world.

NOTES

1   The Indonesian woman's role is valued once she has attained the title of *Ibu*. According to the definition in the Echos and Shadily dictionary, *Ibu* has a connotation in Indonesian society of respectability as well as the biological, cultural and social meanings associated with 'mother'. Suseno, F. M., (1981 and translated into English 1997), *Javanese Ethics and World View: the Javanese Idea of the Good Life*, PT Gramedia, Jakarta, p. 52.

2   For other works on state Ibuism and the Indonesian women's struggle see Djajadiningrat-Nieuwenhuis, M. (1987), 'Ibuism and Priyayization: Path to Power?' in E. Locher-Scholten and A. Niehof (eds.), *Indonesian Women in Focus*, Foris Publications, Dordrecht, Netherlands, pp. 42–51; and Robinson, K. (2000), *Indonesian Women: from Orde Baru to Reformasi*, Allen and Unwin, Australia.

3   Indonesia's gender ideology here is understood as resting on stereotypical binary oppositions while placing *bapak* (father/man) as the primary source of power. This binary oppositional theory identifies women as private (domestic) versus men as public (political); women as naturalized (close to nature, emotional) versus men as civilized (rational); also, women are construed as a (biological) sex and not a (socially constructed) gender. Yuval Davis, N. (1997), *Gender and Nation*, Sage Publications, London and Thousand Oaks, New Delhi.

4   State Ibuism also includes the belief in an essential identity or *kodrat*, that combines paternalistic ideology with religious beliefs and social and moral values. According to the *kodrat* belief it is God's will to create women with biological and natural characteristics that are different to men's and that emphasize their responsibility as mothers and wives.

5   McCormick, I. (2003), *Women as Political Actors in Indonesia's New Order*, Monash University, Melbourne, p. 6.

6   Unity in diversity refers to the Indonesian state's ideology *Bhineka Tunggal Ika*,

which describes Indonesia's multicultural nation of over 300 different ethnicities since 1945. McCormick, I. (2003).

7   Political opportunity by definition is a dimension of the political struggle that encourages people to take advantage of spontaneous opportunities to become politically active. See Tarrow, S. (1998), *Power in Movement: Social Movement and Contentious Politics,* Cambridge University Press, USA, pp. 19–20.

8   Because of women's political invisibility and the exclusion of motherhood from the political sphere, their identity as mothers and wives paradoxically enabled them to act and legitimize their demands. Budianta, M. (2003), 'The Blessed Tragedy – the Making of Women's Activism during the Reformasi Years', in Heryanto, A. and S. K. Mandal (eds.), *Challenging Authoritarianism in South East Asia – Comparing Indonesia and Malaysia,* Routledge Curzon, New York and London.

9   Gayatri Spivak's argument (1987) is that if strategic essentialism is practised by the dispossessed themselves, then essentialism can be powerfully disruptive and effective in dismantling structures or alleviating suffering. Hunan, M. (2003), *Dictionary of Feminist Theory* <http://mlhopps.faculty.tcnj.edu/GWWTerms Dict.htm> (last accessed 14 September 2006); and Kilburn, M. (1997), *Glossary of Key Terms in the Work of Gayatri Chakravorty Spivak,* Emory University <http://www.emory.edu/ENGLISH/Postcolonial/Glossary.html> (last accessed 12 September 2003).

10 Women's empowerment here means the processes of making women more aware of their powerlessness and of organizing them to free themselves from the state's control. Hadiwinata, S. (2003), *The Politics of NGOs in Indonesia: Developing Democracy and Managing a Movement,* Routledge Curzon, London.

11 Budianta, M. (1999) 'Suara Ibu Peduli: Pangilan Nurani Warga', in Subono, N. I. (ed.), *Catatan Perjalanan Suara Ibu Peduli,* Yayasan Jurnal Perempuan, Jakarta; and Budianta, M. (2003), in Heryanto, A. and S. K. Mandal (eds.).

12 Sunindyo quoted by Budianta, M. (2003), in Heryanto, A. and S. K. Mandal (eds.).

13 See Wieringa, S. (1988), 'Aborted Feminism in Indonesia: a History of Indonesian Socialist Feminism', in Wieringa, S. (ed.), *Women's Struggles and Strategies,* Gower, Aldershot, for more information about the Indonesian state's construction of women's political groups.

14 McCormick, I. (2003).

15 SIP echoed the students' concerns but added a focus on women's issues such as 'the rising price of basic commodities, health of children and family, the education of the nation and the breakout of violence', McCormick, I. (2003), p.22.

16 McCormick, I. (2003).

17 This *modus operandi* involved systematized planning, the establishment of think-tanks and the involvement of actors: it included targeted raping, burning, looting and the killing of ethnic Chinese so as to incite racial and religious conflict during a political upheaval.

18   Mass rapes targeting the Chinese minority was a tactic within the Suharto New Order government's strategy of using this group as a scapegoat during the 1998 economic crisis.

19   Budianta, M. (2003), in Heryanto, A. and S. K. Mandal (eds.).

20   Oey-Gardiner, M., and C. Bianpoen (2000), *Indonesian Women: the Journey Continues*, Australian National University, Research School of Pacific and Asian Studies, Canberra.

21   Riley, D. (1988), *Am I That Name?: Feminism and the Category of 'Women' in History*, Macmillan, Basingstoke.

22   Ang, I. (2001), *On Not Speaking Chinese*, Routledge, London.

23   Budianta, M. (2003), in Heryanto, A. and S. K. Mandal (eds.).

24   Budianta, M. (2003), in Heryanto, A. and S. K. Mandal (eds.).

25   Nurhadi, T. H. (1999), in Subono, N. I. (ed.), *Catatan Perjalanan Suara Ibu Peduli*, Yayasan Jurnal Perempuan, Jakarta; and Arivia, G. (1999), 'Menjadi ibu tidak selalu semanis madu', in Subono, N. I. (ed.).

26   Nurhadi, T. H., M. Budianta, K. Supelli and N. I. Subono (1999), in Subono, N. I. (ed.); and Arivia, G. (1999), 'Menjadi ibu tidak selalu semanis madu', in Subono, N. I. (ed.).

Part 6

Campaigns as a Means for Movement Building

22

Remobilizing the
Algerian Women's Movement

The 20 Ans Barakat Campaign

Caroline Brac de la Perrière

In February 2002 a few friends were sitting around a kitchen table chatting, as they used to, about the situation of the women's movement in Algeria. These Algerian women, who had been feminist activists for over 20 years, were very concerned about the declining status of women in their country. Violence against women had greatly increased during the 1992–2002 civil war, during which murders, rapes and sexual slavery were perpetrated by armed fundamentalist groups. This violence was aggravated by the way it was perceived – the lens was focused by a conservative educational system and the media – and to a great extent justified on the basis of an extremely retrograde personal status law.

Since 1992 organizations born as a result of the 1989 free association law had seen their actions curtailed, their means decrease, and their memberships dwindle in the face of threats, murders and exile. It had become impossible to sustain and plan work. The only possible action, for those who still had the courage, was to maintain a public presence through statements and protests against religious extremism. These actions were of symbolic importance, since fundamentalists were using any means at their disposal to force women to return to the private sphere. However, this oppression had a limited impact in that it prompted women to react.

The assessment of the women's movement made by *Collectif 95 Maghreb Egalité*[1] in early 2000 was not very positive. The activists who had remained in Algeria were exhausted by the considerable energy required for every move taken in a public sphere constituted by the

unusually violent national context. Activists who had had the opportunity to escape the violence by going into exile were beginning to
recover from the depression that followed the brutal separation from
their families and friends, and the guilt they felt at leaving.

Very few of those who had worked against the ruling of the family
law in the National Assembly in the 1980s were still around. Organizations could not count on the support of the state and political parties.
Nor did they have the organizational capacity to manage support from
international organizations to strategic advantage. While older members
remarked on the almost total absence of youth within the women's
movement, youth complained of the rarity of work being delegated to
them or knowledge shared with them. They were also baffled by the
hermetically distinct discourses and mutually incomprehensible quarrels
between organizations that nevertheless shared the same goals.

The last attempt at collective work was in 1997 when 13 women's
organizations launched a campaign for 'a million signatures for 22
amendments to the family law'. This campaign was considered a failure:
not only was the number of signatures collected disappointing, but
internal discord resulted, with certain groups simply demanding a repeal
of the law. In fact the campaign's failure was mainly due to a profound
lack of trust within the women's movement as a result of a series of
internal accusations. Nonetheless, and despite these problems, it was the
first time in many years that a significant number of organizations had
joined forces to claim equality – even though danger was still omnipresent and all too visible in the series of massacres that took place in
villages around Algiers that year.

The idea for a campaign is born

The Algerian women reminiscing around that kitchen table in 2002
asked themselves how the fight against the infamous family law, which
had remained unchanged since its adoption, could be resumed in such a
context of terror. It would soon be 20 years since it had been adopted
by the National Assembly.

'Family Law – 20 years is enough! 20 years *barakat!*'[2] What a great
slogan and rallying call this would be for the new campaign to unite all
those who wanted to act against the family law! The slogan was particularly appealing since it evoked the end of the war for Algerian
independence when the slogan was 'Seven years *barakat!*'[3] And such a

campaign, the kitchen conference thought, might be a means to unify the women's movement.

Among various possibilities for broadening the scope of the women's movement, a particularly promising option was to look towards Algerians in exile. Many women – and men – who had been part of the women's movement had ended up in exile. (By 1994 10,000 Algerians – mostly artists, intellectuals and progressive business people – had sought refuge in France in the face of death threats from fundamentalists.) These people had never stopped fighting for human rights, and had frequently stayed in contact with organizations in Algeria.

It just so happened that France, with over a million Algerian immigrants, had decided to make 2003 the year of Algeria. Many Algerian artists and intellectuals had already been contacted and a programme of events drawn up. We realized that if we were able to take advantage of this important media event it could provide us with an unexpected opportunity to mobilize public opinion on the human rights situation of Algerian women.

The project began to take shape. It was decided that the campaign had to take place both in Algeria and France and that it should begin in 2003, so as to be in full swing by 2004, the year Algeria's family law would be 'celebrating' its 20th birthday, and, coincidentally, holding presidential elections as well.

Campaign organization, launch and implementation

In 2002, efforts to create a coordinating group and plan a variety of activities between France and Algeria via the Internet were disappointing. Communications were difficult. The need to adopt new strategies and find innovative means to carry out the campaign was recognized. The idea of a song and a video clip thus emerged, and in December 2002 a small group of women living in Dijon, France, created the organization 20 Ans Barakat (twenty years is enough) to provide a legal entity for receiving funds and registering a copyright in France and Algeria.

The organization would also produce campaign tools, but first it embarked on locating as many exiled activists as possible in France and other European countries to inform them of the campaign. Those who were contacted were enthusiastic as the campaign provided them with a means to reinvest in the women's movement in their country of origin.

The idea was to ensure a very flexible campaign coordination that embraced a policy of unrestricted openness and gave free rein to creativity. The primary strategic aim of the campaign was to get every person supporting the idea of equality to feel concerned and involved, ensuring participation by as wide a group of stakeholders as possible rather than the limited and often closed circle of activists for women's rights.

When Internet connections between activists in Algeria and France proved difficult to sustain, a meeting was called in Algiers in February 2003 to bring everyone up-to-date on the proposed initiatives, to examine budgets, and to establish an official campaign launch date.

The official call to join the campaign was made at a press conference in Algiers on 8 March 2003. Six women's organizations became signatories to the campaign in Algeria[4] and a further six in France.[5] In order to obviate administrative complexities in Algeria and difficulties in handling funds from international donors, it was decided that 20 Ans Barakat, in France, would serve as an administrative alternative when it was not possible or desirable for one of the Collectif 20 Ans Barakat, the campaign group of signatory organizations in Algiers, to do so. With these issues resolved, preparations for the campaign could go ahead.

It was now time, as planned, to reach out to the widest possible public via the catchy song and the video clip.[6] Twenty-seven Algerian singers kindly demonstrated their commitment and recorded the song *Ouech eddek yal qadi* (What's happened to you judge?). The lyrics had been written by a group of 20 Ans Barakat members, and the music was composed by an Algerian musician close to the women's movement. The song was aired for the first time on Channel III radio in November 2003, and from December the video clip could be seen regularly on Beur TV, and on the French channel for immigrants along with programmes from Algeria. At about the same time a competition was launched in Algiers by campaign signatories in association with fine arts schools for the most beautiful poster on the life of Algerian women under the family law.

Over 2003 and 2004, diverse activities (concerts, a balloon release, a magazine and advertisements) complemented the more traditional meetings and conferences, press coverage and radio and television programmes. Eleven thousand compact discs and cassettes were distributed throughout Algeria, France and other countries of the Maghreb and Europe. Hundreds of tapes of the video clip were also sent to cinemas to be projected prior to programmed films and to a variety of groups interested in organizing their own women's rights events.

A partial success

The campaign had several goals at the outset. The explicit goals were to ensure the omnipresence of the issue of equality between men and women[7] and to obtain changes in (and preferably the repeal of) the family law. Other objectives were more implicit: for example, the remobilization of women's groups around a simple unifying idea, on the one hand, and the incorporation into the women's movement of those sectors of the population that believe in equality but are not quite sure how to relate to the movement, on the other.

The first objective was achieved. The family code was constantly in the Algerian press, and French media broadcasting from Algeria also covered the campaign.[8] The second objective was only partially achieved. Activists, aware of the influence of the fundamentalists, were not to be fooled. They understood that the government would not repeal the law. However, in February 2005 several amendments were adopted by the national assembly and, among these, three that were of particular importance to women.[9] Although these gains did not meet the expectations of the women activists, they did represent the first breach in Muslim (shari'a) law that hitherto had been considered immutable.

The campaign's success was more limited as far as its implicit goals were concerned. Although it had met with a certain degree of success due to the innovative activities and multiple talents elicited by the campaign, and had attracted a certain number of sympathizers to the cause of women's rights, a weak organizational structure made it impossible to sustain this momentum in the medium and long terms. It was also necessary for us to acknowledge that one of the most important goals for the campaign leaders (after the change in the law) – the remobilization of organizations around a common cause and the reunification and the consolidation of the movement – was not achieved.

The impact on the women's movement

The women and men who participated in the campaign organization consider that the February 2005 amendments to the family code were at least partly due to their efforts. Once the amendments had been passed,

congratulations flowed in from women outside the movement. However, it has been quite common for some feminists who were not
involved in the campaign to omit any reference to it as one of the
possible causes for amendments to the law. Rather than acknowledge
that the actions of some female counterparts might have had a degree of
influence in securing changes to the law, they have preferred to cite the
King of Morocco's changes to Moudouwana,[10] as well as the electoral
campaign and international pressure.

How can we explain why a campaign that had the intention of being
as inclusive as possible, and the funding[11] to carry out virtually all planned
activities, was still unable to unite all Algerian women's organizations?
And why was it that in France the network of Algerian activists
participated in the campaign by disseminating the video clip and selling
CDs throughout the country, but in Algeria many organizations
reported they were unaware of the song or the video clip, and that they
only heard of the campaign through the press? What were the obstacles
that prevented a greater mobilization of the women's movement?

Limiting factors

Some answers to these questions are to be found in the way in which
the campaign developed. In March 2003, when the mobilizing call
went out, the campaign signatories in Algeria, allegedly to maintain
control over the project, did not invite all organizations to participate.

Being the first signatories provided them with a pre-eminence over
the other organizations, who felt they had been relegated to the role of
followers. This was totally unacceptable, especially in view of the poor
relations between organizations at that time. In order to avoid such a
situation, some organizations proposed to distribute the CD and carry
out their own women's rights campaign. However, there were others
who perceived the campaign as an opportunity to settle old scores with
those signatory organizers with whom they had had serious differences
during the 1997 campaign. As a result some very important activists
remained on the edge of the campaign, perhaps helping on some occasions but never fully identifying with it. Others would not participate in
a campaign that might have originated in France.

The campaign did not enable a coming together of all women's
rights organizations, and on occasion became the site of infighting and
the settling of personal differences. It must also be recognized that the

organizations involved have not always been successful in ridding themselves of a certain rigidity in work styles, or indeed of sectarian and
autocratic patterns of behaviour. This became manifest in some
instances as a desire to appropriate the campaign as their own. Even the
group of six signatory organizations 'exploded' at the end of 2004! And,
as mentioned, this has had the effect of distancing younger generations
from the women's movement. Such conflicts also contributed to an
inadequate exploitation of campaign resources, as in the case of the CD
and the musical message, resulting in disappointment for the musicians
involved when their work was not promoted or distributed effectively.

It was difficult for some activists, perhaps due to their age or their
political background, to abandon old working habits and embrace the
campaign as a process of collective decision making and an opportunity
for everyone to contribute their know-how. This sectarianism also
affected relations between activists in Algeria and those living in France.
In fact, from the moment the campaign began in Algeria, the organizations based in France were presented as external supporters – with the
same standing as other well-disposed international groups. While the
campaign should have been perceived as an Algerian campaign irrespective of where the Algerians were located – a situation that would
have given it much more weight – it was presented as an Algerian-based
campaign with 'aid' from French organizations.

All these obstacles had, in fact, been foreseen by the campaign initiators who had even attempted, through all possible means, to mitigate
them by organizing several coordination meetings in Algeria. However,
these turned out to be insufficient. Too few resources had been allocated
for the campaign's coordination. Due to the limited time spent on
organizing the campaign, the coordinating staff – including Algerians
from Algeria and France – had insufficient opportunities to share their
vision of the project and define a unifying strategy. And once the
campaign was in process, it was impossible to establish procedures to
remedy this situation. There should have been, at least, a salaried
coordinator to facilitate communications between the different groups
during the campaign. This coordinator could have travelled between
countries to monitor developments, follow-up on activities, and support
the volunteer activists – who were totally overwhelmed with work.
This would have facilitated partnership building and the involvement of
organizations and individuals, thus helping to unify the campaign.

Another reason why the campaign did not reach its full potential was that none of the women's rights activists who worked so hard to make it a success ever received any form of remuneration. All worked as volunteers, and only a few trips for six-monthly meetings were funded.

The psychological state of activists was one aspect that was completely overlooked. After ten years of violence and terror with the corresponding losses, separations, mourning and stress, it was unrealistic to imagine that continuities of understanding and cooperation could be reinstated so quickly. For example, the considerable difficulties encountered in reaching basic agreements between organizations had much to do with stress and the total absence of tranquillity in the lives of the activists. They had been unable to lay down their arms in the fight against fundamentalism for one moment, and were still in a hypersensitive state that made any form of conflict unbearable. The aftereffects of traumatic situations and experiences need to be taken into account in future similar projects.

Conclusions

Despite the difficulties involved, this remobilization for women's rights on a much larger scale than 1997 was on the whole a very positive experience.

The creativity of the campaign provided a happier note and more dynamism within the women's rights discourse. It also allowed for the inclusion of many new people in the movement. The production of the song and video clip, the important media coverage they generated, the limited mobilization of women's organizations and the amendments to the law all represent hard-earned rewards after two years of immense effort.

The activists involved in the 20 Ans Barakat campaign have concluded that there is an urgent need to identify, analyse and overcome every single obstacle that limited its success. The amendments to the family law were insufficient, and the battle continues for its repeal. It is necessary for the women involved in different organizations that are fighting for their rights to reconsider their discourse, their resources and, above all, their collaborative actions, if they are to improve their chances of success.

It is particularly important that a younger generation of activists be trained in working differently and working together, and that, above all, it is motivated to identify with and become engaged in the women's movement. To this end a project to train young women leaders is currently on the drawing board of some of the campaign militants – because 21 Ans Barakat!

NOTES

1   *Maghrébines pour l'égalité. Auto portrait d'un mouvement* (Maghrébines for equality. Self-portrait of a movement). Synthesis by Caroline Brac de la Perrière for Collectif 95 Maghreb Egalité. Rabat, 2002.

2   *Barakat* means 'enough' in Arabic.

3   The war of independence from French colonialism lasted seven years, from 1954 to 5 July 1962, Algeria's Independence Day. Thirty years later, the ten-year civil war (1992–2002) between the military and armed Muslim fundamentalists began. It resulted in the deaths of 150,000 Algerians.

4   Tharwa Fadhma N'soumer; Association indépendante pour le triomphe des droits des femmes [Independent Association for the Triumph of Women's Rights]; Association pour la promotion et la défense des droits des femmes [Association for the Promotion and the Defence of Women's Rights]; SOS femmes en détresse [SOS women in distress]; Volonté, initiative et engagement [Will, initiative and engagement]; and the Association de femmes victimes du terrorisme, Djezairouna [Association of women victims of terrorism, Djezairouna].

5   Association 20 Ans barakat! [Association 20 Years Barakat!]; New Ways – Atelier pour la vie [New ways – Workshop for Life]; Plurielles–Algérie [Plural-Algeria]; Association pour l'Egalité devant la loi [The Association for Equality before the Law]; Un livre, une vie [A Book, a Life]; Caravane et Association Algériens du Monde [Association of Algerians of the World].

6   The video clip can be viewed at <http://www.bledconnexion.com/wechdek.htm> (last accessed 14 September 2006).

7   Article 31 of the Algerian Constitution stipulates equality between all citizens of both genders.

8   Hundreds of articles were counted in 2003 and 2004.

9   These were (1) the removal of the duty of obedience for the spouse (spouses now have the same duties); (2) guardianship has been given to the divorced mother when she has the custody of her child, and the law on divorce allows women to seek divorce for 'persistent disagreement'; (3) the law on nationality now allows the mother's nationality to be passed on to her child, a very rare occurrence in a Muslim country.

10   The personal status code in Morocco.

11   From the Global Fund for Women (USA), Mama Cash (the Netherlands), Rights and Democracy (Canada), Solifonds (Switzerland), and the Friedrich Naumann Foundation.

23

Advocating Sexual Rights

The Campaign for the Reform
of the Turkish Penal Code

Liz Ercevik Amado

Over the last decade, the women's movement has campaigned success-fully for significant legislative reforms to enhance women's human rights in Turkey. The adoption of a protection order law against domestic violence in 1998, the reform of the civil code to grant women full equality within the family in 2001, and, most recently, the reform of the penal code in 2004 to safeguard women's sexual, reproductive and bodily rights have all been the result of vigorous campaigns by the Turkish women's movement, often against a backdrop of resistance from conservative right-wing governments. The common character-istic of all these campaigns has been that the women's movement has united its forces, and different groups from different regions of Turkey, sometimes with differing visions, have acted in unison to carry out these campaigns. This case study focuses on our experience with the most recent of the above-mentioned campaigns, the three-year Campaign for the Reform of the Turkish Penal Code from a Gender Perspective (2002–4), initiated and coordinated by Women for Women's Human Rights (WWHR)–New Ways (NW). This resulted in a holistic reform of the Turkish penal code, with over thirty amendments protecting the sexual and bodily rights of women and girls.

In 2002, immediately following the reform of the Turkish civil code, WWHR–NW initiated the new campaign. Drawing momentum from the successful civil code campaign, we felt that the women's movement could seize this opportunity to ensure that the penal code reform resulted in the advancement of women's rights and gender equality. The late 1990s and early 2000s have been a period during which a number of legislative reforms were pursued by the government as part of the European Union (EU) accession process. Yet we were well aware that it would take strong and sustained pressure from the women's groups to make women's human rights a priority for Parliament.

Even though civil codes and constitutions are generally considered the primary domains in which women's rights are regulated in national contexts, penal law is in fact also of crucial significance to women's human rights and gender equality. It governs such important issues as violence against women, sexual violence and the regulation of the rights and freedoms of women in the domain of sexual, bodily and reproductive rights. We knew that it was in the penal code that women's human rights violations and discrimination were recognized as actual breaches of law, despite the egalitarian principles upheld in the Turkish Constitution and the newly reformed Civil Code.

The Working Group on the Turkish Penal Code

In 2002, WWHR–NW set up a Working Group on the Turkish Penal Code. This brought together NGO representatives, lawyers, jurists and academics to analyse the current penal code and the draft of the new penal code. Considering the code from a gender perspective, they aimed to determine which provisions were discriminatory and how they should be amended. Three attributes of the working group were later recognized as central to the success of the campaign: its geographical representation; its combination of women's demands with legal perspectives and know-how; and the holistic focus of its methodology.

Members of the working group came not only from Ankara and Istanbul, the two major cities in Turkey, which usually dominate national campaigns, but also from eastern, western and southern Turkey. The members of the working group, mostly bar association and NGO representatives, were active in their regions and knew the legal difficulties faced by women in Turkey's different cities. This provided us with the opportunity not only to compare cases and determine the shortcomings of the current law, but also to debunk claims often made by conservative forces that the women's movement was biased in favour of women in cosmopolitan urban settings and did not reflect the standpoint of women in Turkey as a whole.

The composition of the working group was another major advantage. It included criminal lawyers and academics who were familiar with the intricacies of a legislative system riddled with loopholes for discrimination against women; there were women's groups' representatives with strong feminist perspectives and backgrounds and extensive experience in the field; and there were also lawyers who worked in the women's rights centres of bar associations, dealt with cases on a one-to-one basis, and thus were well aware of the issues of implementation.

During 2002, WWHR–NW organized the working group sessions on a monthly basis. Initially the group analysed the law and the proposed draft, concluding that a holistic approach was necessary to overcome gender inequalities. It was realized that the same patriarchal discriminatory approach that denied women ownership of their bodies, and sexuality, was inherent in the draft law, and that its transformation could only be effected by reforming the penal code's entire philosophy. This entailed shifting the focus of the draft law from one that strives to regulate and control women's sexuality, to one that safeguards sexual rights. Sexual crimes were inadequately named and punished, and were based on the constructs of honour, chastity and so on, while crimes such as honour killing, rape and abduction were legitimized through the sentence reductions allowed for by some provisions. After identifying the articles that legitimized human rights violations and discrimination, the working group proceeded to discuss how these articles should be amended. During this period we analysed international documents and the criminal codes of different countries to help us in the formulation of our amendments. Following research on each article pertaining to us, we formulated a word-by-word amendment, including justifications to explain our own points of view.

The year-long initiative, which represented the first phase of our campaign, was a challenging one. Neither the current penal code nor the draft law recognized sexual crimes as crimes against individuals: they were classified as 'crimes against society', under the sub-section 'crimes against family order and traditions of decency'. In order to overcome the inherent discrimination and understanding that women's bodies and sexuality were commodities belonging to men, family and society, we realized that it was necessary to transform the entire philosophy of the draft law, necessitating an extremely thorough analysis of the complete text.

It was during this process that disagreements surfaced within the working group itself regarding how to formulate amendments. The issues with which we dealt – whether the age of consent, definitions of sexual assault, the rights of sex workers, or discrimination based on sexual orientation – were raised by the different priorities within the women's movement itself and had not previously been of concern or relevance to all members of the group. Consensus thus had to be reached among the working group's own members prior to proceeding with the campaign. This important process was carried out through a series of discussions that considered the perspectives and sensitivities of different group members and sought ways and compromises to resolve them. It provided us with the opportunity to internalize our own demands and stood us in excellent stead when we needed to reaffirm our position as a diverse working group. We thus found ourselves in a stronger position as we had already settled internal differences, and negotiated and answered some of the arguments with which we would subsequently be faced. In particular we were ready to answer the charge that our demands were 'marginal', 'not of concern to women in general', or 'too progressive for society'. We compiled these demands and our word-by-word formulated amendments in a report entitled *The Turkish Penal Code Reform from a Gender Perspective: Women's Demands and Proposed Amendments*. The report, printed by WWHR–NW,[1] was widely disseminated to parliamentarians, NGO representatives and the media by the end of 2002.

Backlash and the launch of a national campaign

We felt we had everything under control and were prepared for the reform process, as the parliamentary commission was only just beginning its review process. We had all our demands ready and formulated. But we were faced with a backlash. Following a political crisis, the three-party coalition led by social democrats resigned and early elections were held in November 2002. A religious, right-wing government assumed power with an overwhelming majority. We presented our report to the new members of Parliament, but our repeated attempts to get an appointment with the Minister of Justice were systematically declined. The new government not only completely disregarded our demands and proposed amendments – the provisions of the new draft law pertaining to women being lifted almost verbatim from the old

Turkish penal code – but also resisted consultation with *any* experts or groups, ignoring our demand for a review of the draft law prior to its submission to Parliament for approval.

In the face of this backlash and resistance, we had to decide how to proceed with our campaign and develop new strategies. The working group initially considered postponing the campaign, or at least withdrawing some of those demands considered more controversial from the government perspective. However, we finally decided against both these compromises and resolved to persist with all our demands and proposals. We realized that unless we took a firm stand and demanded our rights, we would be providing leeway for even more discrimination and rights violations.

We decided to launch a public campaign and broaden the working group into a national platform, so as to place immediate pressure on the new government. The working group became the Platform for the Reform of the Turkish Penal Code, a vehicle for over 30 NGOs countrywide: women's NGOs, human rights associations and lesbian, gay, bisexual and transgender (LGBT) groups. The public campaign was launched in May 2003 with a press conference at which we announced our demands for inclusion in the draft penal code law and drew attention to the continued legitimization of human rights violations and the government's reluctance to respond. The Platform was also publicized, emphasizing that diverse groups throughout Turkey were coming together to advocate for their rights.

It was through the Platform's lobbying efforts that the resistance of the government was gradually broken down. During 2003–4 it closely monitored the work of the Parliamentary Justice Sub-Commission while it was reviewing the draft law, and a number of conferences, meetings and press conferences were held. The Platform received government recognition, and the Minister of Justice, the Head of the Justice Commission and the Minister of Women's Affairs attended the high-level conference organized by WWHR–NW in December 2003.

The efforts of the Platform continued at both the national and local levels. While some members were in touch with Parliament on a daily basis and continuously lobbied the government, the opposition party, EU officials and the Justice Sub-Commission, other Platform representatives organized seminars and press conferences in their own towns and cities.

A variety of strategies were employed. These included finding allies in the Sub-Commission and the opposition party, the use of a press mailing list to keep the media informed of developments, and the issuing of press releases as and when different pertinent articles in the law were discussed. We also took advantage of statements made by conservative jurists and government officials to further our cause. For example, 'Marrying the rapist was a reality of Turkish society', in reference to the provision granting rapists sentence reductions based on the notion that through marriage the woman's 'honour' was saved; and how 'Killing in the name of honour could be justified', in reference to sentence reductions for honour killings. These statements, as well as the accusations by the far-right media painting us as 'immoral', 'indecent' and 'aiming to destroy the moral fibre of society', actually benefited our cause, as they provided us with potent campaign slogans around which we could build resistance and gain public support.

Our intense efforts bore fruit and most of our demands were accepted by the Justice Sub-Commission and included in the draft law. Even our landmark proposal to criminalize discrimination based on sexual orientation was included. One of the unique aspects of the Platform, and a first in Turkey, was that it brought together the women's and the LGBT movements. This was largely due to WWHR–NW's efforts to integrate LGBT groups in the Platform, and the fact that the working group had previously agreed to include and advocate for the proposed amendment on sexual orientation. Even though this provision was later removed from the draft law due to an intervention by the Minister of Justice, the fact that representatives of the LGBT movement were actually able to voice their demands for legislative change before Parliament was an important milestone. As the review of the Justice Sub-Commission was concluded in May 2004, most of our demands were accepted. This was a major achievement considering where we had started back in 2002.

However, the struggle was hardly over. We had to keep advocating right through the final review of the Justice Sub-Commission, to hold the ground we had gained and press for the inclusion of our remaining demands. Even though we succeeded in sustaining the revised draft law, two important reforms were not accepted: the decriminalization of consensual relations of minors between ages 15–18; and the removal of the provision that criminalized sexual orientation.

When voting on the draft law was to take place in Parliament in September 2004, women throughout Turkey mobilized to push for our

remaining demands. Platform members were joined by other platforms
and women's groups from throughout Turkey to push for the remaining demands in a national demonstration on the eve of the vote. The
last-minute proposal by the government to recriminalize adultery –
which had not been a criminal offence in Turkey since 1998 and only
served as grounds for divorce – completely diverted public attention
and overshadowed our principal demands. We thus found ourselves not
only advocating for our remaining demands, but also lobbying for the
withdrawal of the adultery proposal. The fierceness of the struggle led
to a postponement of the vote in the General Assembly before the
government's proposal was eventually withdrawn under pressure from
the women's movement and an adverse reaction from the European
Union.

Campaign results: sexual and bodily rights safeguarded

The draft law, containing over 30 amendments safeguarding sexual and
bodily rights of women in Turkey, was finally passed on 26 September
2004. The new Turkish Penal Code, which states in its first article that
it aims to 'protect the rights and freedoms of individuals', brings progressive definitions and higher sentences for sexual crimes; criminalizes
marital rape; brings measures to prevent sentence reductions granted to
perpetrators of honour killings; eliminates all references to patriarchal
concepts such as chastity, honour, morality, shame or indecent
behaviour; abolishes previously existing discriminations against non-
virgin and unmarried women; abolishes provisions granting sentence
reductions in cases of rape and abduction; criminalizes sexual harassment in the workplace; adequately defines and penalizes the sexual
abuse of children; and considers sexual assaults by security forces as
aggravated offences.

The Campaign for the Reform of the Turkish Penal Code from a
Gender Perspective was very successful. Even though a few of our
demands were not included in the new penal code, we succeeded in
transforming its language and philosophy so as to safeguard sexual and
bodily rights. Given the prevalent conservative climate in Turkey, this
represented a major achievement for the women's movement. However, the process has been challenging, at times draining. Monitoring
the implementation of the law, and raising awareness of the new rights
it safeguards, remains a further challenge.

Obstacles and strategies

In the course of an extensive three-year campaign, internal and external challenges are inevitable. While persistently remaining steadfast and united against resistance from external forces, the Platform had simultaneously to sustain both its unity and the campaign's momentum. As the coordinating organization and campaign secretariat, WWHR–NW played a crucial role in linking and coordinating the actions of the Platform organizations. The length of the campaign sometimes made it difficult to sustain both public attention and the Platform's strength. Nonetheless, efforts were facilitated considerably by the campaign's solid foundation, and the fact that its demands were formulated on the basis of consensual principles that enabled each group within the Platform to pursue advocacy efforts independently around their own lines of work.

The diversity of the groups in the Platform for the Reform of the Turkish Penal Code was highly advantageous and contributed significantly to the campaign. The involvement of organizations from different regions of Turkey, with different visions, provided us with a much stronger case when claiming representation of women's demands throughout Turkey. Furthermore, when approaching parliamentarians or addressing the press, having a platform to support our demands proved to be a major driving point, as no one could rightfully dismiss our demands as 'marginal'. Indeed, when the Prime Minister referred to the demonstration on the issue of adultery prior to the voting on the penal code as 'just the reaction of some marginal women', his comment met with a hostile reception in many quarters.The group demanding further amendments and rejecting the proposal to recriminalize adultery was made up of over 80 organizations and seven platforms from all over the country.

The fact that we started planning early and had clearly defined our objectives was also a major advantage for the campaign. It provided us with a head start, and enabled us to deal more effectively with the last-minute backlash. The planning also meant that we were able to be proactive – formulating our demands before the draft law was finalized – rather than reactive. When the penal code was on the agenda of Parliament's General Assembly and the vote was imminent, we came across many other protesters who discovered to their cost that it was already too late to make any changes.

Having a consensus from the outset meant that we were able to proceed resolutely and approach other groups with concrete propositions. The early resolution of differences within the movement was also vital to the success of the campaign, in which leadership and preparatory work were essential in bringing together heterogeneous groups. Without wide and diverse support it would have been much more difficult to confront the enormous task we faced, increasing the likelihood of failure. As mentioned above, the campaign was also significant in that it brought the women's and LGBT movements together in advocacy for the first time. While the LGBT movement gained visibility and took a major step towards advocating for its own rights, the women's movement became aware of issues of discrimination based on sexual orientation and was thus able to broaden its own agenda. The campaign not only resulted in major advancements for women's rights, but also created a useful model for future campaigns in Turkey. Our determination to promote women's human rights and gender equality was reaffirmed by bringing together so many groups. Even though it was challenging for WWHR–NW to assume responsibility for coordination activities over such a long period, we fully experienced the multiple benefits of acting in unison and coming forward with concrete demands, and we came to understand the importance of standing firm on these. In learning to resolve conflicts among ourselves during the process, we also came to understand the need to seek consensus in pursuing our demands in other forums. Finally, we are aware that implementation of the new penal code to safeguard women's rights as equal to men's is not the end of the road. We will continue to press our demands in other spheres of civil society for holistic reforms to eliminate women's human rights violations and ensure gender equality in Turkey.

NOTE

1   Document available only in Turkish.

24

An Inter-American Convention on Sexual Rights and Reproductive Rights

We're Campaigning!

Elizabeth C. Plácido

We are citizens.
We can decide about the destiny of our nations.
Why, then, would we not decide about our bodies?
Campaign for a Convention

Since becoming involved in feminism seven years ago, I have regularly participated in activities relating to women's human rights and the sexual and reproductive rights of young women and men. So when I heard about AWID's call for papers I thought, 'Great! What a good idea to promote a systematization of the experiences and initiatives of feminist women's organizations.' Young feminists have been making precisely this demand: to learn of our history from those who have been directly involved and who are willing to share their experiences, both good and bad.

Indeed, this chapter aims to share a Latin American and Caribbean experience in linking various women's and feminist organizations to promote the Campaign for an Inter-American Convention on Sexual Rights and Reproductive Rights.[1] It is based on my participation in this initiative as a representative of the Latin American and Caribbean Youth Network for Reproductive and Sexual Rights (REDLAC). Thanks to the invaluable support of the campaign's coordinator,[2] I am able to recount how the campaign developed and to describe the political horizon from which it arose. I also describe some of the strategies that were employed and the actions taken to carry them out, and finally comment on the most salient difficulties and challenges encountered in the process.

For the new generations of feminists and recent arrivals to feminism, the transmission of valuable resources of experience and knowledge contributes to the empowerment and galvanization of new leaderships. These are resources that facilitate the identification of effective strategies, and the development of alliances, political and economic resources, skills, and communications both within and outside the movement. They also provide information on our enemies – the political right and fundamentalists – and represent a means by which we can identify and get to know one another.

Responding to regional threats to Cairo 1994

The campaign was instigated by the Latin American and Caribbean Committee for the Defence of Women's Rights (CLADEM) six years after the United Nations International Conference on Population and Development in Cairo, held in September 1994. It was noted that the efforts of thousands of women who had fought for the recognition of sexual and reproductive rights in the international arena, were experiencing serious setbacks at the local level. For example, in 1998 and 1999 legislation under discussion in El Salvador and Honduras included mandatory HIV-testing for pregnant women, a ban on sodomy, and the elimination of two grounds for abortion, making it totally illegal. Attempts to legislate on life from conception also began to appear, and laws were passed in Panama and El Salvador.

Reflecting on the situation at that time, CLADEM's general coordinator Susana Chiarotti, and founders Gulia Tamayo and Roxana Vázquez,[3] observed that despite advances, international treaties offered no binding guarantees of sexual and reproductive rights, and that no treaty made specific mention of these rights as such. They saw a context in which the global balance was in crisis, our region had been demoted on the agenda of international cooperation, and neo-liberal policies (often restrictive of rights while asserting economic freedom) were taking hold. And then there was, and continues to be, the continuing threat of 'the Bush agenda' with its attempts to remove reference to sexual and reproductive rights from as many agendas and debates as possible.

Asking themselves how much further these issues might be set back,[4] these women perceived the need for a tool similar to the American Convention on Human Rights: an instrument that obliges states of the region to maintain a minimum standard of guarantees. They thus aimed to emulate the process that created the Convention of Belém Do Pará,[5] an earlier victory for the Inter-American Commission of Women, a specialized body of the Organization of American States' System of Human Rights.[6] Sexual and reproductive rights, they felt, should not depend on the whims of politicians and those in government, or those who dispense justice.

With this idea in mind, CLADEM called in Lucy Garrido of *Cotidiano Mujer*, Uruguay's first and only feminist magazine, and together they drafted a preliminary strategy document establishing that the initiative would not belong to just one network or organization: 'Linking more organizations to the initiative is supremely important; to the extent that this is accomplished, it will be a campaign of women – all women – not just CLADEM.'[7] A 'pact of equals' was proposed. It brought together different groups, networks, women's organizations and individual feminists who were not necessarily specialists in sexual and reproductive rights, but who did have a feminist agenda and political abilities that could contribute to the defence of and make the claims for sexual and reproductive rights. In other words, these rights would become an integral part of the feminist cause and a focal point for mobilization around the most revolutionary issues: sexuality and reproduction.

Those called upon included Cecilia Olea and Virginia Vargas of the Centre for Peruvian Women Flora Tristán (Peru); Maria Betania Ávila of SOS-CORPO (Brazil); Rosa María Dominga (Peru); Celita Echer from the Network for People's Education Among Women (REPEM); Nancy Palomino from the Latin American and Caribbean Women's Health Network (RSMLC); Isabel Duque from the Latin American and Caribbean Feminist Network against Domestic and Sexual Violence; as well as a representative of RedeSaúde. These women met with Susana Chiarotti and Roxana Vásquez from CLADEM (Argentina and Peru, respectively) and Lucy Garrido from *Cotidiano Mujer* (Uruguay), and together they formed a regional alliance known as the Grupo de Noviembre[8] to promote the campaign and draft an ethical framework establishing the principles and rules of governance.

The political horizon

From the outset, the perspective underlying the campaign was that processes of democratic construction in our region necessarily involved the challenge of redefining equality and freedom from the standpoint of sexual difference. Feminism in the 1970s involved 'radical questioning of the way in which social relations are structured [and] broke with evidence that upheld the naturalization of inequalities between the sexes'.[9] Our lives are restricted on the basis of sexual difference. In particular, women, young people and children 'have been expropriated of freedoms and autonomies regarding their bodies, definitively damaging their lives',[10] excluding them from public space and denying them recognition as political subjects.

In other words, by drafting new normative frameworks, such as a convention, for the guarantee and protection of sexual and reproductive rights, we will be able to restructure the contents of the concept of democracy as an inclusive form of government. This will enable us to identify the demands and new needs of all people, as well as the connections that exist between the political sphere and the development proposals that affect our sexual practices and reproductive choices.

Organizational strategies to build the campaign

The campaign process was divided into three main phases in each of which different strategies and actions were employed to advance, enrich and strengthen the campaign. The first phase involved the launch of the campaign and the creation of a group of feminist organizations to promote it. The second phase involved three strategic focuses: communications, the conceptual development of the proposal, and the organizational structure that evolved through alliance building. Finally, the third phase involved the actual carrying out of the campaign, during which five mutually reinforcing strategies were implemented.

The first phase was based on six specific activities: the documentation and analysis of international normativity and jurisprudence on sexual and reproductive rights; a survey among feminists and women's organizations to determine how they define sexual and reproductive rights;[11] an analysis of consensus and disagreement over the past 20 years of the feminist movement regarding these rights; the creation of a web page dedicated to the convention;[12] fostering a regional assessment of the current situation of sexual and reproductive rights in legislation, public policies, public opinion and bibliography;[13] and the preparation of promotional materials.

The third regional seminar of CLADEM was dedicated to the campaign and reflections on sexual and reproductive rights.[14] Different feminist organizations and women from the region presented their work and visions for the advancement and defence of sexual and reproductive rights, so as to identify strategies for regional action and motivate participants to become involved in the campaign. This seminar had four important results.

First, points of departure were determined. Although it was recognized that we would not be starting from zero, as some of the ground had already been covered through a series of historical advances in feminism,[15] these required contextualization within each country of the region. A ten-year process was also envisioned, with a gradual accumulation of resources to sustain the campaign. The second outcome was that participants also identified the tensions and challenges that the formulation of sexual and reproductive rights represented for women's organizations, but recognized the importance of maintaining clarity on the non-negotiability of fundamental issues, such as abortion and sexual diversity. Third, some general strategies were identified that allowed for the mapping out of relevant actors in the region, the identification and development of strategic alliances, and the means necessary to construct appropriate communications strategies. Finally, participants made a commitment to adopt the ethical framework and to invite and involve new organizations and networks. For example, the regional networks CFFC (Catholics for a Free Choice), International Gay and Lesbian Human Rights Commission (IGLHRC) and REDLAC joined the regional alliance.

The second phase of the campaign, which continued until the end of 2003, involved three main strategies, the first of which centred on communication. A logo was designed, as well as high-impact slogans such as 'You don't say that, You don't do that, You don't touch that', 'Sex when I want, pregnancy when I decide', and 'Free bodies, secular states'. These were produced on T-shirts, bags, posters, stickers, and other materials distributed nationally and locally, and the web page was also redesigned.[16] The second strategy involved the conceptual development of the proposal and the publication of 14 local/national appraisals carried out as part of the regional appraisal, and a book containing presentations and reflections from the regional seminar.[17] The campaign manifesto was also drafted, along with a series of pamphlets dealing with issues for debate.[18] The third and final strategy carried out during the second phase of the campaign involved the forging of organizational and political alliances in different countries of the region, and campaign launchings during which promotional materials, the appraisals and the book were presented.

The aim of these strategies was to broaden and strengthen the regional alliance, incorporating people and organizations in each country, but also to mobilize people in defence of these rights, and promote

> dialogue with the regional feminist movement, in other words present the idea and convince ourselves of the usefulness or not of the initiative; to present [the campaign] in each country through seminars, in feminist meetings, and within each woman. The result of this phase is many people participating in the idea. It is a core coordinating group made up of feminists from different organizations and networks that meets every November and that comprise the different coordinating bodies formed at the national level.[19]

However, it was the regional alliance that evaluated the strategies implemented thus far in an effort to transmit the ways and perspectives that were being constructed in a clearer and more grounded way, and provided a global view of the process.[20] It was thus that five complementary strategies were envisaged for the campaign's third phase.

The first involved the generation and strengthening of the core regional alliance, for which the Spokeswomen's Workshop was held.[21] This was designed to strengthen national alliances, and create a forum for exchange and training in the use of tools for promoting the campaign. In this manner the 'how' and 'why' of the campaign were reviewed, obstacles and opportunities were explored, participants became familiar with the conceptual definitions of sexual rights and reproductive rights, and decisions were taken on how to establish political alliances and positions on different issues. Strategies to promote a communications campaign were also discussed, and finally, a workplan was laid out to consolidate national/local linkages.[22]

The second strategy involved the creation of a group of core stakeholders who would legitimize the text of the convention. This was accomplished by disseminating the proposal among feminist groups and other local and regional social movements: it went out to youth, lesbian, gay and transgender groups, Afro women, indigenous people, human rights activists and HIV-AIDS campaigners. In other words, the object was to transform the need for promotion and guaranteeing sexual and reproductive rights into an effective social demand.

The third strategy involved the organization of debates so as to generate agreements. Historically, topics such as prostitution, new reproductive technologies, abortion, bioethics and cloning, or transgender issues have caused disagreement within the movement and have not been addressed in any depth. The provision of information and reflection on these issues was considered important prior to generating consensus and mobilizing stakeholders on policy positions, and to this end a regional seminar was held on controversial themes of sexuality and reproduction[23] in which debates and pluralistic reflections were stimulated.

The fourth strategy involved the preparation of the draft convention, and the complementary fifth and final strategy involved convincing governments to support it. The latter gave rise to a virtual debate[24] among organizations, networks and individuals on the campaign manifesto, which in turn fuelled further debate and provided the basis for discussions and guidance on ethical and policy issues to be covered in the text of the convention.

Reflecting on organizational challenges

As in any initiative striving to link actions and actors, difficulties arose. Within the regional alliance, members were involved in different forms and levels of participation. On occasions greater participation on the part of the networks was anticipated, and it was considered that some groups could have been more effective or productive in their actions. This raised issues of degree or level of representativity or legitimacy, and the definition of commitments (work distribution, responsibilities, timetables, etc.) and the allocation of material and human resources. These were found to be directly related to the level of appropriation or sense of 'ownership' that the different networks and organizations themselves had in the campaign.

Other challenges were related to national/local linkages. The political and economic contexts as well as the actual dynamics of the feminist movements in the local/national arena played vital roles in the implementation of the strategies. The campaign could be confined to certain areas and have little or no national impact, and the lack of dialogue on issues still requiring reflection – such as prostitution and abortion – was seen as a limiting factor. There was also an absence of self-criticism within organizations or feminist networks, as well as a fear of linking up with others. The powerful influence of the conservative Church was also viewed as a factor that limited the effective deployment of campaign strategies.

The development of the text for the convention also represented a considerable challenge. It was not simply a question of replicating the process for the Belém Do Pará[25] text, but of recognizing that sexuality and reproductive issues present specific challenges relating to freedom, autonomy and equality; and also of considering how the exercise of sexual and reproductive rights relates to the market and the state. The expectations generated were a measure of the campaign's success. But these also presented new challenges within the regional alliance and among a variety of other stakeholders, rendering the drafting process more complex. It was necessary to consider other initiatives while at the same time differentiating between the core actors and groups who were involved in the drafting of the text and others simply interested in having a greater awareness of the issues under discussion.

Regarding alliances with other movements, we were challenged by different priorities at the conceptual and political levels, as social movements tended to perceive human rights uniquely from the perspective of, for example, 'poverty alleviation' and other issues of 'public interest'. Sexual and reproductive rights were considered superfluous and disconnected from real needs, particularly when it came to the drafting of development proposals in the face of economic crises. It was thus deemed necessary to modify our discourse so as to place greater emphasis on the interdependence of rights and, in this way, increase its relevance for other stakeholders.

Also, some people or groups feared that the final text of the convention would not represent the demands of the core stakeholders, and that the concepts of sexuality and reproduction could be stripped down to their bare conservative and limiting interpretations, forfeiting all advances made since the Cairo Programme of Action[26] and the Beijing Platform for Action.[27] It is clear that the campaign provided great potential for change but also involved considerable risks: 'the risk of doing something of this magnitude for the whole hemisphere represents a political risk, and is difficult at a moment of rising fundamentalism'.[28]

It remains to be said that these and other challenges that are likely to arise will need increasingly effective and innovative strategies that involve each organization or network. To date, the annual meetings of the regional alliance have provided a key space for addressing these. As part of the process of strengthening the movement, commissions have been formed to explore criteria for participation; to draft a second version of the manifesto; and to think of concrete actions that also encompass the visions and needs of young women and men, and include indigenous and transgendered people.

We are halfway there. The challenges we face in ensuring the recognition and exercise of sexual rights and reproductive rights present an enormous hurdle that requires creative thinking, ongoing debate and reflection. The input of all the different groups involved in the campaign will be reflected in a regional normative document protecting sexual rights and reproductive rights. I hope that sharing this experience will contribute to enriching the work of all those feminists around the world who are interested in demanding and defending their rights.

"When you live in a world that denies you your name, your identity, the right to work, the right to harmonize your body, the right to be loved and to love as a member of a family, a couple or a community, any tool that can nourish your hope of change for the better becomes valuable and can make the difference."
Alejandra Zuñiga[29]

NOTES

1   The 'Campaign' included the following organizations and networks: Campaña 28 de septiembre – a regional campaign; Católicas por el Derecho a Decidir (CDD – Catholics for the Right to Decide) – a regional network; Colectivo de Investigación, Desarrollo y Educación entre Mujeres (CIDEM – Collective for Research, Development and Education among Women) – Bolivia; the Latin American and Caribbean Committee for the Defence of Women's Rights (CLADEM); International Gay and Lesbian Human Rights Commission – Latin America Programme – (IGLHRC); *Cotidiano Mujer* – a Uruguayan magazine; the Ecuadorian Foundation for AIDS Assistance, Education and Prevention (FEDAEPS); Flora Tristán, a Peruvian women's centre; the Latin American and Caribbean Women's Health Network (LACWHN); Rede Nacional Feminista de Saúde e Direitos Reproductivos (National Feminist Network for Health and Reproductive Rights), Brazil; Latin American and Caribbean Feminist Network against Sexual and Domestic Violence; Latin American and Caribbean Youth Network for Sexual and Reproductive Rights (REDLAC); Women's Popular Education Network (REPEM-DAWN) – a regional network; and SOS-CORPO – a Brazilian non-governmental organization.

2   Roxana Vázquez, who I thank wholeheartedly for her encouragement, time,

reflections and documentation.

3   Interview with Susana Chiarotti, CLADEM, January 2005.

4   Interview with Susana Chiarotti, CLADEM, January 2005.

5   Also known as the Inter-American Convention on the Prevention, Punishment and Eradication of Violence Against Women. See <http://www.oas.org/cim/> (last accessed 13 September 2006).

6   See <http://www.cidh.org/> (last accessed 13 September 2006).

7   Minutes of the third meeting of the Grupo de Noviembre, Recife, 2002. (See following note.)

8   They referred to themselves as the Grupo de Noviembre (November Group) because they agreed to meet during that month every year to define their actions and strategies. To date the group has met on five occasions.

9   Betania, A. (2003), 'Feminismo y ciudadanía: la producción de nuevos derechos', *Serias para el debate, No. 1, Campaña por la convención de los derechos sexuales y los derechos reproductivos*, Lima, Peru, p. 63.

10 *Manifiesto. Primera versión (para el debate)*, Campaña por una Convención Interamericana de los Derechos Sexuales y los Derechos Reproductivos, Lima, 2002. Produced by the Campaign's core coordinating group and available on line at <http://www.convencion.org.uy/menu1-07.htm> (last accessed 20 September 2006).

11 De las Casas Mónica, *Sexualidad y Reproducción en los sistemas universal e interamericano de derechos humanos*, CLADEM, Lima, 2000. The result of this systematization is available on the campaign's website.

12 See <http://www.cladem.org> (last accessed 16 September 2006).

13 For which appraisals were conducted from August 2000 to May 2001 in 14 countries of the region: Argentina, Bolivia, Brazil, Colombia, Chile, Ecuador, El Salvador, Honduras, Mexico, Panama, Paraguay, Peru, Puerto Rico and Uruguay.

14 Held in November 2001, in El Pueblo, Peru.

15 We refer to theoretical and conceptual developments about the body, identities and human rights, and to the results of the strategic experiences and policies carried out in the region.

16 See <http://www.convencion.org.uy> (last accessed 13 September 2006). This is the Campaign website that is hosted in Uruguay.

17 CLADEM (2002), *Derechos sexuales y derechos reproductivos, derechos humanos. Tercer seminario regional*, CLADEM, Lima, Peru.

18 *Serias para el Debate* (Series – Issues for Debate) with works on themes related to sexual rights and reproductive rights. Four issues have been published from 2003 to August 2005.

19 Interview with Lucy Garrido, *Cotidiano Mujer*, March 2005.

20 *Plan Marco 2003-2006*, internal Campaign document.

21 Organized by *Cotidiano Mujer*, Flora Tristán, REDLAC and the Campaign coordination. Extracted from Plácido Elizabeth, *Memoria Taller de Voceras*, working document, May 2004.

22 At the time of writing, activities are planned in Brazil, Colombia, El Salvador, Paraguay, Panama, Peru, Bolivia, and Costa Rica. Activities or 'launchings' have already taken place in Argentina, Uruguay, Honduras, Puerto Rico and Mexico.

23 The seminar was titled Prostitución/trabajadoras del sexo. Nuevas tecnologías reproductivas. Transgeneridades: un debate a partir de los derechos sexuales y los derechos reproductivas (Prostitution/sex workers. New reproductive technologies. Transgender issues: a debate on sexual rights and reproductive rights). It was organized by SOS-CORPO, the Instituto Feminista para la Democracia, Católicas por el Derecho a Decidir, International Gay and Lesbian Human Rights Commission, and CLADEM. Information extracted from *Un debate a partir de los derechos sexuales y los derechos reproductivos*, Lima, Peru, September 2005.

24 Organized by RSMLAC, Santiago de Chile, October 2004.

25 This is the familiar term used in referring to the Inter-American Convention on the Prevention, Punishment and Eradication of Violence against Women, approved in 1994 in the city of Belém do Pará, Brazil, by OAS member states.

26 The main agreement resulting from the United Nations International Conference on Population and Development, held in Cairo, 1994.

27 The main agreement of the United Nations Fourth World Conference on Women, held in Beijing, 1995.

28 Interview with Lucy Garrido, *Cotidiano Mujer*, March 2005.

29 Psychologist and sexologist, transgender activist, cofounder of the now-defunct Grupo Eon, Inteligencia Transgenérica and currently collaborating with the Grupo Opción Bi … Sexualidades Diversas.

25

A Matter of Life or Death

Campaigning to Build Support for the Defence of Women's Rights in Nigeria

Titi Salaam

Why is it so difficult to build an international women's movement? We must recognize our femaleness and see through the existing versions of femininity which surround us.[1] We need to increase awareness to render the campaign for building a feminist movement more viable, while recognizing that oppression is common to many of us as women[2] and is independent of other circumstances such as race, class, and sexual orientation. Although lack of structure within the movement is sometimes considered a weakness, it could also be seen as its greatest strength in that it continues to grow in directions that cannot always be predicted. Whatever the size of the feminist movement, hard work and self-sacrifice by its members are qualities that are indispensable if we are to emancipate women from the shackles of patriarchy.

The underlying assumption of this chapter is that justice and peace, two principles of feminist leadership, are those that are required to replace injustice and violence. Another feminist principle of leadership involves embracing and sharing the skills and knowledge of individual women, and providing opportunities for all women to develop their leadership potential.[3] As members of a feminist organization we invest power and trust in our leaders in the expectation that they will draw upon feminist practices and processes in our joint effort towards equality and inclusion. What drives the individual in this process of leadership is not what she may stand to gain personally but what the entire movement stands to gain from a collective course of action.[4] The goal of feminist leadership is to create a value-based culture that will benefit both leaders and followers.

The current situation in Nigeria makes it even more compelling to invest in building positive leadership within the feminist movement and reduce social, economic and political tension among its members. We may hope that our feminist groups will be problem-free or that we will create an inclusive environment by virtue of our collective work. However, we need to recognize that we have different leadership experiences and that our practices are informed by traditional hierarchical power structures. As advocates of feminism, we need to explore and discuss our ideas and experiences of leadership to avoid falling into negative behaviour patterns within the movement. Effective strategies to strengthen the movement are also required at different levels to avoid fragmentation. Finally, we must ensure that the feminist agenda is heard and addressed by other civil society groups such as trades unions, small farmer organizations and youth movements.[5]

The feminist principle of accountability is also essential to building and maintaining unity and a healthy, active, equality-seeking movement. We should hold ourselves accountable to one another and to the global women's movement and in this way improve and strengthen our collective efforts towards peace, equality and justice. In this case study, which is based on my own personal experience of the women's movement in Nigeria, I analyse one instance of the promotion of women's rights and movement building that has attempted to put all these aforementioned principles into practice: the Women Advocates Research and Documentation Centre (WARDC).

This organization is a non–profit, non–governmental advocacy organization established in May 2000 to promote women's human rights, equity and social justice in Nigeria. The mission of WARDC is to advance education, research and self-development among women and promote gender justice and equality in policies, laws and social relations. The vision of the organization is to have a peaceful society free from all forms of discrimination against women and girls, with structures that protect the fundamental human rights of all and in which everybody within the organization works vigorously in unity towards genuine democracy and development. The organization has its head office in Lagos and a branch office in Kaduna State, in central northern Nigeria. The section below discusses the participation of WARDC in creating greater awareness on women's issues related to the building of a feminist movement in Nigeria. Specific mention is made of the role played by our organization in the campaign for women's human rights under the shari'a law imposed in northern Nigeria.

Shari'a law and women's rights violations in northern Nigeria

Nigerian Muslims number approximately 50 million, an estimated 42 per cent[6] of the total population according to the 1991 census. The greatest density of Muslims is to be found in the northern part of the country, with a lower density in the central and western parts and a relatively sparse population in the east of the country. The twelve northern shari'a states have higher densities of Muslims than the southwest and eastern states.

Shari'a is an Arabic term, which literally means a road that leads to a watering place.[7] Since water brings about life and sound health, shari'a, in its figurative sense, symbolizes many aspects of life. Islamic fundamentalists have adopted shari'a as a code of conduct that 'ensures salvation from evil and deviant behaviour'. Islam requires total submission to the will of Allah, and Muslims see shari'a as synonymous with Islam. In other words, the two are one and the same.

In 2000, a significant legal process under this law caused the mobilization of numerous women's groups. Safiya Tugartudu Hussein, a 30-year-old woman, was arrested in December that year and charged at the Upper Shari'a Court, Gwadabawa, Sokoto State, for allegedly committing adultery and having sexual intercourse out of wedlock. Safiya was sentenced to death on the grounds of her pregnancy, confessional statement and admission to having sex with Yakubu Abubakar, a Muslim divorcee.[8] He was also arrested but later released when he denied the charge and no evidence was forthcoming. This event, in addition to hitting international headlines, triggered the launch of the Safiya Must Not Die Campaign (SMNDC).

In 2002 the Safiya campaign became the Coalition Against Injustice when two other young girls, Hafsat and Amina, were also sentenced to death by stoning by the Sokoto and Katsina Shari'a courts for similar offences. Hafsat was sentenced to death, but her case did not attract international attention as she was set free almost immediately. Amina Lawal was sentenced to death on 15 January 2002. The coalition, made up of over 30 organizations, undertook several activities to save the lives of Safiya, Hafsat and Amina.

The SMNDC and the Coalition Against Injustice[9]

First, as one of the groups leading the campaign, and subsequently as the Coalition Against Injustice, we issued press releases to the media, held press conferences and organized a letter of protest that was signed by the 30 coalition members and sent to the governors of Sokoto and Katsina states and to the country's President, Olusegun Obasanjo. A peaceful walk was staged in the city of Lagos, and the 2002 International Women's Day was dedicated to Safiya. Campaign materials, including T-shirts and leaflets, helped to create more awareness of the situation of the three young women and the stand that was being taken against their death sentences. All these activities helped focus world attention on Nigeria.

By November 2001 we had already organized a public lecture to assess the situation of the human rights of women in northern Nigeria, with the purpose of analysing the Safiya Tugartudu case. This was followed by an expert meeting in February 2002 with Safiya's lawyer and other Islamic clerics to discuss the procedures in Safiya's case and the protection of women's rights under shari'a law in northern Nigeria. Ten experts on shari'a law from northern Nigeria also met to discuss the rights of women under Islamic law. The book *Protection of Women's Rights under Shari'a Law: Safiya Tugartudu Hussein – A Case Study*[10] was one of the outcomes of these meetings.

In October 2002, a workshop was organized by WARDC and the Women's Aid Collective (WACOL)[11] in Abuja to identify and develop strategies for intervention. During the workshop we developed and adopted a programme of action to respond to issues of women's rights under shari'a law. This workshop led to a national conference held in Abuja in 2003 organized by WARDC and WACOL on Women's Rights and Access to Justice under the shari'a law in northern Nigeria. Attracting representatives from other African countries and parts of Asia, Islamic scholars were able to share their experiences of the application of shari'a law in their respective countries, and the conference resulted in the publication of *Shari'a Implementation in Nigeria: Issues and Challenges on Women's Rights and Access to Justice.*[12]

The internal organization of the coalition

Women from all walks of life were involved in the coalition's campaign. It was very important for us to guarantee that there was unity in our diversity during the campaign process. The diversity of the group was its strength as each of the 30 organizations was involved according to its area of specialization. We were able to build on our differences and find strength in our alliances to unite against Islamic fundamentalism. We were committed to achieving internal democracy in the campaign group. In essence, we tried to ensure that every woman in the group had an equal chance to participate, assume responsibility and develop her potential. We successfully used persuasive approaches in times of conflict during discussions that generated heated debates – as, for example, when considering the name change of the Safiya Must Not Die Campaign to the Coalition Against Injustice. We decided to use a persuasive approach as we were more interested in what the group stood to gain collectively than in individual achievements. The ideological basis of feminism provided us with the means to offset the differences that we faced during the campaign. The resolution of internal friction in this way made it easier to take a solid stand when dealing with conflict outside the movement.

Our management strategy involved cooperation and collective action in power sharing, and directly contributed to the efficiency of the campaign group as a viable social movement that was prepared to stop the stoning to death of Safiya and Amina. The alliances and networks established during the campaign formed the basis of subsequent initiatives: a clear example of this was a meeting held in Maduguri to deliberate on the building of a women's movement following the 2004 Nigeria Social Forum meeting.

Results of our initiatives

The overturning of the death sentences was the result of joint efforts and pressure put on the Katsina and Sokoto state governments by the Coalition Against Injustice, international organizations and the media. Our success in this respect demonstrated the effectiveness of joint action and the importance of developing a common platform for social change. The involvement and interest of stakeholders at the international level was also considered to be a positive step as it contributed significantly to the building of the international feminist movement. Nonetheless, involvement at the local level is essential to strengthen the international movement. According to feminist writer Alda Facio, if feminists could succeed in consolidating a strong international feminist movement, firmly rooted at the local level, women would be in the best position to unite all groups against any common cause that divides them.[13]

There were, nonetheless, some women's groups that declined to cooperate with WARDC. This was directly related to the scarcity of funding and resulted in the duplication of effort. It is also important to mention that the increasing reluctance of funding agencies to make institutional grants continues to be a major challenge for WARDC and is a factor that seriously limits the organization's capacity to meet its goals.

Lessons learned

I believe that the introduction of the shari'a law in northern Nigeria as a mechanism for dealing with complex social problems such as prostitution, adultery and crime has been a total failure. More importantly, I have observed that shari'a law is only applied to criminal offences in Nigeria, while social welfare has been ignored by the state governors. To date, the activities of the Coalition Against Injustice have shown that the victories relating to the shari'a cases are only temporary ones, as judgements of the shari'a courts continue, and will need to be opposed by ongoing, non-violent protests and the support of local and international campaigns.

International organizations and the media have a significant impact on local and national injustice: in these particular cases direct pressure was put on President Obasanjo, who was plagued wherever he went with questions on the fate of Amina and Safiya. This became an embarrassment to Nigeria and the governors of the states of Sokoto and Katsina. Despite the overturning of the death sentences in the cases of Amina, Hafsat and Safiya, shari'a court judges continue to have no qualms in sentencing a woman to death by stoning for exercising a right to sexual privacy. This case has demonstrated the importance of solidarity and joint action at all levels. The international dimension is of particular importance due to the power that can be harnessed and brought to bear on abuses of women's human rights such as those in Nigeria. Such power is needed if we are to reconstruct masculinity and femininity and change the present patriarchal world, ensuring that women are respected as human beings. This is one of the current challenges facing the international women's movement.

Conclusion

I propose that international solidarity is necessary to build a feminist movement that fights against patriarchy, and that action by women on a massive scale in the form of strikes and different types of protests should become an integral part of this struggle. From my perspective, the first strategy for change is to involve everyone, the privileged and non-privileged, the oppressed and those who benefit from freedom, as well as victims and the perpetrators of abuse in all its forms. Women and men, irrespective of class, race, ethnicity or sexual orientation, need the support of the feminist movement in the fight against oppression.

The second strategy involves, as previously mentioned, the practice of feminist principles of leadership, and especially the principle of accountability, among those who hold a stake in the women's movement: out of this comes a true sense of ownership alongside a willingness to improve the lot of all stakeholders.

Some questions come to mind regarding advances in the women's movement. Why is it that we do not wish to discuss our differences? Why have we refused to build on our supposed weaknesses as women? And how can we ensure that more people become agents of change? As an advocate of feminism, I believe that through resistance we free our hearts and our minds from patriarchal betrayals; and that leadership begins by laying claim to important questions and by promoting public discourse on issues that divide us. Any woman is in a position to lead a revolution in her own life and to join in revolutionary movements at different levels.

NOTES

1   Rowbotham, S. (1973), *Woman's Consciousness Man's World*. Penguin Books, Harmondsworth.
2   Tuttle, L. (1986), *Encyclopedia of Feminism*, Facts on File Publications, New York, p. 360.
3   Women Advisory Council on the Status of Women, Newfoundland and Labrador, 'The Feminist Principle of Accountability',
    <http://www.pacw.com/ pdf/accountable.pdf> (last accessed 3 March 2005).

4   Ciulla (1998), p. 15, cited in Albert, A. O. (2003), *Mainstreaming Positive Leadership in Conflict Transformation in Nigeria*, Centre for Social Science Research and Development, Lagos, p. 48.

5   Santiago, M.M., 'Building Global Solidarity through Feminist Dialogues' at <http://www.isiswomen.org/pub/wia/wia2-O4/mari.htm> (last accessed 21 June 2006).

6   Thomas-Emmeagwali, G. (1994), 'Islam and Gender: The Nigeria Case', in C. Fawzi El-Solh and J. Mabro (eds.), *Muslim Women's Choices: Religious Belief and Social Reality*, Berg Publishers, United States of America, p. 73, cited in T. Salaam, (2005), 'Exploring Women's Rights Under Sharia Law in Northern Nigeria: The Burden of Safiya and Amina', unpublished MA thesis.

7   Quattan, M. (1996), *Tarikh al-tashri'al-Islamiy, Maktabatul-ma'arif.* Lagos, Riyadh, pp.13–14, cited in Bashir, Y. I. (2003), 'Application of the Shari'a Penal Law and Justice System in Northern Nigeria: Constitutional Issues and Implications', in J. Ngozi, M. T. Ladan and A. A. Afolabi (eds.), *Sharia Implementation in Nigeria: Issues and Challenges on Women's Rights and Access to Justice.* Women Aid Collective Enugu, WARDC, Lagos. See T. Salaam (2005), 'Exploring Women's Rights Under Sharia Law in Northern Nigeria: The Burden of Safiya and Amina', unpublished MA thesis.

8   Salaam, T. (2005), 'Exploring Women's Rights Under Sharia Law in Northern Nigeria: The Burden of Safiya and Amina', unpublished MA thesis.

9   The Safiya Must Not Die Campaign (SMNDC) subsequently became the Coalition Against Injustice. All references to the latter include previous activities also carried out by SMNDC.

10 WARDC and Friedrich Ebert Stifttung (2002), *Protection of Women's Rights under Sharia Law: Safiya Tugartudu Hussein – A Case Study.* WARDC, Lagos.

11 A Nigerian NGO. See <http://www.wacolnigeria.org> (last accessed 19 September 2006).

12 Ezeilo, J., M. T. Ladan and A. Afolabi-Akiyode (eds.) (2003), *Sharia Implementation in Nigeria: Issues and Challenges on Women's Rights and Access to Justice.* WARDC, Lagos.
    See http://www.boellnigeria.org/sharia_implementation.html> (last accessed 19 September 2006).

13 Alda Facio (2003), 'The Empire Strikes Back: but Finds Feminism Invincible', paper presented at the Seventh Annual Dame Nita Barrow Lecture, Toronto, Canada, November 2003.
    See <http://www.awid.org/publications/facio.pdf336>

26

The Evolution of Discourse

The Campaign to Change Family Law in Morocco

Alexandra Pittman
with Lucero González and Margaret Schellenberg[1]

One of the key features in determining a social movement's success or failure is the ability to create a sense of shared beliefs and values.[2] Establishing a common discourse is one way that a group can establish this sense of shared identity. Groups undergo a reflexive learning process where activists utilize various cultural tools, including earlier histories of their own struggles, to forge new visions of the future. Religion, politics, and societal norms can be transformed into cultural tools for the purpose of group mobilization.

This chapter explores the means by which the Moroccan women's rights movement has integrated socio-political traditions of the past and present with their 'subversive' claims for the future in the campaign to alter the Moudawana or Personal Status Code (that is, family law). Specifically, the roles of religion, politics and cultural traditions will be examined as the bases from which activist women borrow and reinterpret their rights.

History of the Moudawana

Feminists in Morocco have been engaged in a struggle for equality since their country's independence from France in 1956. In 1957 and 1958, the Moudawana, a family code based on Islamic law that defined the rights and obligations of men and women in personal situations, was instituted. The Moroccan traditional family law was based on *fiqh*, the Muslim law that governs all aspects of private life at the political, religious, economic and social levels. The Moroccan family code developed within a traditional patriarchal framework that granted unequal rights to men and women and limited women's full public participation in a range of social, economic, political and religious activities.[3] The Islamic law superseded Moroccan constitutional law that granted equality to all citizens. According to the former Moudawana (1957/8–2004), some of the restrictions on women's rights relate to seeking divorce, retaining custody of children in the case of divorce, and inheritance. More generally, the laws tended to view women not as autonomous individuals but as adult minors under the guardianship of males.[4]

Traditionally, conservative Islamists have used religion as a means to legitimize patriarchal social structures.[5] However, women's rights activists argue that the Koran has been misinterpreted and usurped by conservative Islamists.[6] Activists have attempted to place the *fiqh* within an historically evolving framework in order to reinterpret traditional laws and align these with current socio-political values.

Moving to an equality discourse

Gender inequality has not only been present on a religious level. Throughout Moroccan history, there has been a lack of gender aware- ness[7] with issues of development, democracy and human rights being traditionally resolved by men.[8] This has contributed to an environment in which feminists struggle for national legitimacy in political realms.

Starting in the 1960s a first generation of activists, with an equity- based agenda, made several unsuccessful attempts to reform the Moudawana. These attempts continued through the 1980s[9] when the prominent discourse emphasized that women, as counterparts of men, should have access to the same political space on the basis of their skills. This argument for equity in the late 1980s was relatively short-lived and quickly gave way, with the emerging moves toward economic liberaliza- tion and increased democratization,[10] to a rights-based approach.

Within this second generation of activists, feminist organizations began to play a central role in shifting socio-legal norms. Initially these organizations were closely affiliated with political parties, but over time they evolved to become partially or completely autonomous from partisan structures. Examples of such organizations are the Union de l'Action Feminine (UAF) and the Association Démocratique des Femmes du Maroc (ADFM), which focus on urgent matters of gender

discrimination, civil rights, violence against women and sexual harassment.[11]

The activities of the feminist organizations specifically relate to the
mobilization efforts for changes to the Moudawana. Feminist arguments emerged calling for equality between men and women as a fundamental prerequisite for achieving a democratic society that is respectful
of human rights.[12] This strategic shift served a variety of purposes. Not
only did it outline a clear and tangible rights-based vision, but it enabled
feminists to take advantage of current political sentiments, as the country
was committed to moving toward more democratic social structures.

Strategies for change

Activists focused on three fronts to galvanize changes to the Moudawana: mobilizing the grassroots, creating inter-organizational networks,
and establishing a persuasive discourse.

At the grassroots level, some people began charging that Moroccan
NGOs were elitist. In response to these criticisms, many NGOs reached
out to the grassroots in order to diversify their base, and activists were
thus able to mobilize a sizeable constituency for women's equality at the
grassroots through targeted campaign efforts. Not only did this shift in
campaign tactics quell some Moroccan women's sense of disenfran-
chisement, but the grassroots also became a powerful political force that
eventually could be used to help tip the balance in favour of feminists.

Two examples illustrate these grassroots mobilizations. The first wave
of mobilizations occurred during 1987–1993. On 3 March 1992, the
UAF, through its newspaper *8 Mars*, launched a campaign to obtain a
million-signature petition in favour of reforming the Moudawana. This
petition was a great success, with the first legal reform being made in
1993. While superficial, it was a crucial step as 'Once something was
removed from the Moudawana text, the halo of sacredness that surrounded the text was also removed. The Moudawana stopped being
divine and started to become a law that could be changed and
amended.'[13]

The second wave of mobilizations occurred between 1999 and
2004. One example of a particularly successful mobilization effort was
the 2000 protest in Rabat. During the protest, tensions swelled when
tens of thousands of women and men marched the streets to demand
changes in women's status.[14] A counter-march was held simultaneously

in Casablanca by conservative Islamists and contributed to the creation of an extremely tense political situation as the two movements were very charged and passionate. However, these grassroots tactics used by women activist organizations worked remarkably well as the grassroots put pressure on the government to make gender equality a main priority in Moroccan politics and legislation.[15]

Creating networks for change

Further pushing their agenda for change, women's associations actively participated in the development of the National Plan for the Integration of Women in Development (PANIFD)[16] that integrated the tenets of the Beijing Platform for the protection and promotion of women's rights. Seven of the 200 measures in the PANIFD were related to the revision of the Moudawana. The first socialist government took power in 1999 and Prime Minister Abderrhamane el-Youssoufi publicly supported the action plan in March of that year. However, pressure from conservative Islamists, who argued that the plan was against Islam, caused the government to withdraw its support.

The women's rights activists immediately moved to ensure that these seven measures remained in the public discourse and, to this end, a PANIFD support network[17] was established. The network was made up of 200 human rights, women's rights, and development associations committed to supporting and promoting the measures set out in the plan.

In 2001, after the Rabat march, King Mohamed VI invited a delegation of 40 women from different NGOs, political parties and trades unions to share their opinions on women's issues. A few weeks later the Printemps d'Egalité network[18] was formed to coordinate mobilization efforts to change the Moudawana including the drafting of legislation, organization of information sessions, grassroots mobilizations and lobbying sessions with parliamentarians. This network demanded changes in the Moudawana, which included eradicating marital tutorship, increasing women's age of marriage to 18 (the same as that established for men), allowing women the right to divorce, establishing equality in marriage and abolishing polygamy.

Printemps d'Egalité sent King Mohamed VI a memorandum with their propositions and demands for change in the Moudawana. The current and past efforts of Printemps d'Egalité were successful in mobilizing an official response from the King as he established a Royal

Commission. The commission responsible for the reform of the Moudawana[19] was comprised of theologians, lawyers, sociologists and doctors. It met regularly between 2001 and 2004 and received delegations of women representatives from local women's NGOs as well as other social and political actors.

Interpreting equality through the Koran

Efforts to change the Moudawana were pragmatic from the outset: religion is part of daily life and thus had to be taken into account. The feminist activists' aim was to demonstrate that equality could be reached in a Muslim country.[20] However, feminist organizations encountered staunch opposition throughout their campaign and mobilization efforts. One conservative Islamist slogan, 'Islam is in danger', roused passions and moved people to form a formidable counter-feminist movement. A campaign using persuasive discourse to raise awareness of the necessity to defend women's rights in Moroccan society thus became imperative.

Printemps d'Egalité launched an advocacy and awareness-raising campaign that targeted different groups. Part of the campaign focused on the Royal Commission. The activists advocated change to the Moudawana based on the tenets of equality between men and women expressed throughout the Koran. Further, the activists insisted that such changes be passed through Parliament, in keeping with the democratic process.[21] Nouzha Guessous, a (female) member of the Royal Commission, drew attention to charges that some campaigners were anti-Muslim and 'forced Morocco's intellectuals and women's organizations to redefine their proposals very carefully and within an Islamic frame of reference, and prove they were grounded in Arab/Muslim culture, not dictated by the West. I think this was the most important tactical change in the whole battle.'[22]

Using the Koran to justify the need for equality between the genders became of utmost importance in the face of the conservative Islamic backlash. In order to address these issues, the Collectif 95 Maghreb Egalité, a coalition of women's activist organizations, intellectuals, leaders and researchers in three countries – Algeria, Tunisia, and Morocco – wrote the *Dalil pour l'égalité dans la famille au Maghreb* (Manual for Equality in the Family in the Maghreb).[23,24,25] The *Dalil*[26] addressed issues relating to the status of men and women in the family codes in each country, and presented sociological, human rights, religious and legal arguments for changing family law.

Feminists used the *Dalil* to juxtapose the burgeoning democratic frameworks with the dire social and legal situations of women, and a main argument of their discourse was that democracy could not be achieved without equality between all citizens. Highlighting the discourse of the Koran and its tenets of equality between men and women thus became a high priority in a Moroccan democratic society, together with public education on the necessity of women's rights.

The media as a conduit for public discourse

The Printemps d'Egalité campaign also targeted the public through the media and awareness-raising campaigns. Between 2002 and 2003 efforts included the dissemination of four real case histories of Moroccan women of different ages and backgrounds. These were adapted by Printemps d'Egalité so people could identify with the situations of these women and relate to the inequalities and injustices to which they were subjected.[27] Three case studies from the campaign follow. Samira, who is 15 and married, wanted to become a teacher. She inquired: 'Why did I have to quit school? For getting married … my father chose someone for me. I had to obey. I don't have the choice…. I wanted to become a school teacher….' Sixty-five-year-old Yamna, who has five children – four of them small – is homeless, and commented: 'After all these years, I don't understand…. Yes, I refused to share my house with another [woman], but not to be thrown out on the street, this is unjust.' And, finally, Kenza, a 32-year-old engineer and a battered wife, asked: 'I work. I pay my taxes. I assume my responsibilities at home. All the same, my husband beats me regularly. So why do I not have the right to ask for a divorce?'

One objective of these cases was to provide the public with the motivation for and the rationale behind reforming the Moudawana. The case studies humanized the current Moudawana laws by bringing to life the sorrows, hardships and injustices that Moroccan women face on a daily basis. Using Yamna's case as an example, after her statement, the association reiterated the need for changes in the code to eradicate polygamy so that women like her have their rights protected and are not arbitrarily excluded and humiliated after years of marriage. Printemps d'Egalité provided contact information along with information on the Royal Commission's activities in revising the Moudawana. The current political and legal opportunities that existed as a result of the Royal Commission's investigations were highlighted in campaign materials, giving the sense that change was not only necessary but indeed possible.

The case ended with the slogan, 'Building a democratic Moroccan society depends on respect for women's rights.' In using this slogan, the country's political and social goals were leveraged in favour of the necessity of equal rights for women.

Campaign results

In September 2003, the Royal Commission presented Parliament with the results of its investigations and its recommendations. With efforts proving fruitful, on 3 February 2004 the legislation to change the Moudawana was unanimously passed by Parliament and then passed on to King Mohamed VI for his endorsement. The main legislative changes to the Moudawana included

- the abolition of marital tutorship;
- the elimination of the principle of obedience to the husband;
- the establishment of joint responsibility between husbands and wives within the family;
- the offer of opportunities for mutual spousal divorce;
- the establishment of 18 as the legal age for marriage for both men and women alike;
- the expansion of legal guardianship rights for women (at 15 years of age children have parental choice and if a woman remarries she can have custody of children until they reach seven years of age);
- judicial discretion was to be applied in cases of polygamy; and
- inheritance from maternal grandfathers as well as from paternal grandparents was allowed for grandchildren.

Among the most important of these changes was the abolition of marital tutorship, which meant that Moroccan women became autonomous.

Entrenched norms

After all these changes, feminist struggles were far from over as modifications to the Moudawana would not have a direct impact on Moroccan women's lives. Certainly, the legal groundwork created the space and opportunity for greater social change and equality in Morocco. However, a considerable struggle lay ahead as the public's perception of and mindsets regarding women's equality had not changed. More importantly, many women remained unaware of their newly acquired rights.[28]

It was thus in May 2005 that ADFM launched a media public awareness campaign for television, radio and the written press to combat the lack of awareness of the Moudawana reforms and stimulate change in the public discourse.[29] The aim of the campaign (carried out in both the Moroccan languages, French and Arabic) was to educate the general public in women's rights, gender equality and the new changes in the Moudawana. Six main social problems were the focus of ADFM's campaign: domestic violence, divorce, expulsion, sexual harassment, matrimonial tutorship and gender discrimination in the workplace. The campaign was clear and simple in its aim to educate the public on the newly acquired rights of women in the family. For example, after seeing the advertisement on domestic violence once or twice, a person is well-informed on new changes to the Moudawana. The campaign reinforced the message that women do not have to accept domestic violence and that laws exist to defend their rights. In this way, the media became a conduit for disseminating critical public information regarding the new legal changes to the Moudawana that had been catalysed by the feminist activists.

Lessons learned: strengthening and broadening the movement

In many ways, culture dictates the constraints and opportunities that women face and how they respond to injustice. Certainly, any attempt to understand women's struggles in terms of equality is incomplete without an analysis of the social, political and religious landscape in which individuals are socialized. In the case of women activists, it is necessary for them to have an understanding of the cultural elements within their society so as to be able to transcend and transform them.

Islam and its basic tenets of equality provided activists with the moral and philosophical framework for their movement and have enabled them to re-interpret the Koran and traditional Islamic law in favour of women's equality within the social, political and economic spheres. The Printemps d'Egalité and Collectif 95 were thus able to respond to religious opposition with a redefinition of the significance of equality in a democratic society.

The media were utilized as a powerful means to inform the public of the necessity of reforming the Moudawana. It was in this way that the new rights-based discourse, supported by an Islamic philosophy, was able to be articulated effectively and reproduced for the benefit of the general public. The juxtaposition of the burgeoning democratic, economic, and technological advancement of the country with the extreme gender inequalities offered a powerful and persuasive argument for the necessity of legal and social change. In addition, after legal changes were instated, the media became an ally for disseminating the new education campaigns about women's enhanced rights.

Lessons learned: strengthening and broadening the movement with the grassroots and through networking

While the Royal Commission provided the activists with a significant socio-legal front, women's rights activists' work at the grassroots afforded them the opportunity to mobilize large segments of the population as well as reaching some of its marginalized groups.

Grassroots campaign efforts, such as the million-person petition to reform the Moudawana and the 2000 Rabat protest, mobilized a significant number of supporters for legal change to the Moudawana. The strength of the grassroots involvement was used by activists and policy makers as leverage and as socio-cultural support for legal change to the family law.

In addition, the joint efforts of the PANIFD, Printemps d'Egalité and the Collectif 95 networks, and the establishment of a common vision, broadened support for the campaign that reached across feminist groups, across the country, and beyond national frontiers to reach the Maghreb.

Using politics to strengthen and broaden a movement

The interactions of civil society, the grassroots and political leadership all influence the ways in which institutional and legal change can be achieved. Although this chapter has focused primarily on the institutional and legal aspects, the influence and power of political leadership cannot be ignored.[30]

The success of the feminist discourse in changing the Moudawana appeared to reach political leadership at the highest levels. In 1999 after ascending to the throne, and in 2003 in a speech addressing Parliament, King Mohamed VI asked, 'How can society achieve progress, while women, who represent half the nation, see their rights violated and suffer as a result of injustice, violence and marginalisation, notwith-standing the dignity and justice granted them by our glorious religion?'[31] This catalysed a process of change that included appointing a number of high-profile women to political positions within the government, establishing a Royal Commission to investigate changes to the Moudawana, as well as receiving the delegation of 40 activists and political leaders. Ultimately, King Mohamed VI, in justifying changes to the women's status code with reference to the Koran, gave women's equality the necessary religious legitimacy.

The women's movement in Morocco used a reflexive and respon-sive cycle of rights-based and Islamic discourse to achieve legislative changes for the benefit of women. The evolution of networks, the passion of the grassroots activists, the strategic use of socio-political landscape within the country and the preparedness to adapt of the campaign's discourse to change the Moudawana ultimately led to the strengthening of the movement. This powerful integration created the circumstances in which profound social change had the opportunity to flourish.

ACKNOWLEDGEMENTS

I would like to offer my warmest gratitude to the Women's Learning Partnership for the funding of this project. Mahnaz Afkhami, Rakhee Goyal, Anna Workman, Anne Bwozemi and Lisa Basalla have been particularly kind and gracious in supporting this work.

I would also like to thank ADFM for their tremendous work and passion. In particular, I would like to express my appreciation to Rabèa Naciri for your hospitality, your detailed feedback and revisions, and access to ADFM's documents and past mobilization efforts – I appreciate all of your insights. Amina Lemrini, thank you for being so generous in giving time for interviews and for sharing your experiences – I have learned so much. I offer a warm thanks to Rabèa Lemrini for the many hours you spent editing and providing feedback on this chapter – you have been so helpful. Thank you to my wonderful adviser and friend, Dr Ali Banuazizi, at Boston College, for your superb guidance. I offer my endless gratitude and love to my friend and editor, Sunnee Billingsley. Finally, a huge thanks to David Magone for your unconditional love and encouragement.

NOTES

1   In association with the Association Démocratique des Femmes du Maroc (ADFM).

2   Banaszak, L. A. (1996), *Why Movements Succeed or Fail: Opportunity, Culture, and the Struggle for Woman Suffrage*. Princeton University Press, Princeton, New Jersey.

3   Lemrini, A. (2004), *Association Démocratique des Femmes du Maroc and the Campaign to Change the Moudawana*. Maghreb Roaming Institute, Marrakech, Morocco.

4   Lemrini, A. (2004), *Association Démocratique des Femmes du Maroc and the Campaign to Change to the Moudawana*. Maghreb Roaming Institute, Marrakech, Morocco.

5   Interview with Amina Lemrini, Association Démocratique des Femmes du Maroc, 27 April 2005, Rabat, Morocco.

6   Collectif 95 Maghreb Egalité (2003), *Dalil pour l'égalité dans la famille au Maghreb* (Dalil for equality in the family in the Maghreb), Editions Collectif 95, Rabat.

7   Daoud, Z. (1993), *Féminisme et politique au Magreb*, Eddif, Casablanca.

8   Eddouada, S. (2001), *Feminism and Politics in Moroccan Feminist Non-Governmental Organizations*. Retrieved online 1 December 2004 from <http://www.postcolonialweb.org/poldiscourse/casablanca/eddouada2.html>

9   Interview with Amina Lemrini, Association Démocratique des Femmes du Maroc, 27 April 2005, Rabat, Morocco.

10 Naciri, R. (1998), 'The women's movement and political discourse in Morocco', UNRISD's Contribution to the Fourth Conference on Women, UNRISD.

11 Naciri, R. (1998), 'The women's movement and political discourse in Morocco', UNRISD's Contribution to the Fourth Conference on Women, UNRISD.

12 Naciri, R. (1998), 'The women's movement and political discourse in Morocco', UNRISD's Contribution to the Fourth Conference on Women, UNRISD.

13 Lemrini, A. (2004), *Association Démocratique des Femmes du Maroc and the Campaign to Change to the Moudawana*. Maghreb Roaming Institute, Marrakech, Morocco.

14 Interview with Amina Lemrini, Association Démocratique des Femmes du Maroc, 27 April 2005, Rabat, Morocco.

15 Eddouada, S. (2001), *Feminism and Politics in Moroccan Feminist Non-Governmental Organisations*, Mohamed V University, Rabat, Morocco. Retrieved online 1 December 2004 from <http://www.postcolonialweb.org/ poldiscourse/casablanca/eddouada2.html>.

16 In French, the Plan d'action pour l'intégration des femmes au développement (PANIFD).

17 In French, known as the Réseau d'appui au PANIFD.

18 The network was initially composed of nine women's organizations, but eventually grew to thirty.

19 An initial Royal Commission to reform the Moudawana was created in 1993 by King Hassan II, but it did not include any female members and did not receive feminist organization delegations. Due to the conservative make-up of the first commission, an impasse was reached and no decision could be made. However, it put the issue of gender equality and Moudawana reform on the political and legal agenda.

20 Interview with Amina Lemrini, Association Démocratique des Femmes du Maroc 27 April 2005, Rabat, Morocco.

21 Lemrini, A. (2004), *Association Démocratique des Femmes du Maroc and the Campaign to Change the Moudawana*. Maghreb Roaming Institute, Marrakech, Morocco.

22 Kristianasen, W. (2004), quoting Nouzha Guessous, in *Islam's Women Fight for Their Rights* (retrieved online 12 December 2004 from <http://faculty-staff.ou.edu/L/Joshua.M.Landis 1/blogger/archive/2004_05_03_archive>.)

23 There were five main non-governmental human and women's rights organizations involved in the founding of the Collectif 95 and its efforts to change the family law. In Algeria: Association pour la Promotion des Droits des Femmes (APDF) (Association for the Promotion of Women's Rights); and Association Indépendante pour le Triomphe des Droits des Femmes (AITDF) (Independent Association for the Victory of Women's Rights). In Morocco: Association Démocratique des Femmes du Maroc (ADFM) (Democratic Association of Moroccan Women). In Tunisia: Association Tunisienne des Femmes Démocrates (ATFD) (Tunisian Association of Democratic Women); and Association des Femmes Tunisiennes pour la Recherche et le Développement (AFTURD) (Tunisian Women's Research and Development Association).

24 Collectif 95 Maghreb Egalité (2003), *Dalil pour l'égalité dans la famille au Maghreb* (Dalil for Equality in the Family in the Maghreb), Editions Collectif 95, Rabat.

25 In 2005, the *Dalil* was translated into English by Women's Learning Partnership.

26 A *dalil* is a type of technical reference manual for activists and activist lawyers.

27 Printemps d'Egalité (2002), public awareness campaign to change the Moudawana.

28 Interview with Amina Lemrini, Association Démocratique des Femmes du Maroc, 27 April 2005, Rabat, Morocco.

29 ADFM (2005), 'Stop aux violences contre les femmes. Campagne d'information sur les nouvelles dispositions du Code de la Famille' (Stop violence against women. Information campaign on the new nature of the Family Code), press conference, 27 April 2005.

30 Bunce, V. (1981), *Do New Leaders Make a Difference?* Princeton University Press, Princeton, New Jersey.

31 King Mohamed VI (2003), Speech Delivered by H. M. King Mohammed VI at the opening of the Parliament Fall Session. (Retrieved on 15 November 2005 from <http://www.mincom.gov.ma/english/generalities/speech/2003/ ParliamentFallSession101003.htm>.)

EDITORS AND CONTRIBUTORS

Editors

Lydia Alpízar Durán is a Costa Rican feminist activist who lives in Mexico City. She participated actively in youth organizing and mobilization around the 1991–2 Earth Summit process and was coordinator of the Earth Council's Youth Programme. She coordinated the international project 'A Young Women's Portrait Beyond Beijing '95' and the publication *Our Words, Our Voices: Young Women for Change!* Lydia is co-founder and adviser to Elige, the Youth Network for Reproductive and Sexual Rights (Mexico), and co-founder of the Latin American and Caribbean Youth Network for Reproductive and Sexual Rights. She has been on the Board of Trustees of the International Committee for the Peace Council since 1996, is a member of the Board of Directors of the Global Fund for Women, and of the International Council on Human Rights Policy. Lydia is a sociologist and a former participant in the 2003 Human Rights Advocates Training Program of the Center for the Study of Human Rights, Columbia University. She has worked with AWID since 2003 as Manager of the Feminist Movements and Organizations Programme, and has recently been appointed as the organization's new Executive Director.

Noël Payne was born in England and is a naturalized Costa Rican. Prior to moving to Costa Rica in 1986 she worked for ten years for the World Conservation Union (IUCN). In Central America she undertook various consultancies for IUCN and the Dutch Development Programme in the field of education for sustainable development in the public sector, and then joined the Earth Council in 1994. Since 1996 she has been an activist and alternative entrepreneur promoting the development of the Costa Rican organic movement. Throughout her twenty years in Central America she has worked as a freelance translator and editor for a wide range of international organizations – with an emphasis on sustainable development, private enterprise, peace, human rights, and the environment – and private companies that are world leaders in the area of corporate social responsibility and sustainable development.

Anahi Russo is a Mexican-Canadian anthropologist. She is currently a PhD student in Women's and Gender studies at Rutgers University. She previously worked with AWID as a research assistant, contributing to organizational strengthening and movement building. She also worked on the Gender Equality and Youth Programme at the Women's Institute of Mexico City's local government. In 2004, she was part of the organizing committee of the Sixth Lesbian Feminist Encounter of Latin America and the Caribbean. Her current research interests concern gender and sexuality in Latin America, the global women's movement and social change.

Contributors

Raquel Avilés Caminero was born in Valdepeñas, Spain. She holds a degree in clinical psychology from the Universidad Complutense de Madrid. Her work experience involves internships at the University of Aachen's Psychiatric, Neurology and Psychotherapy Clinic, and the Alexianer Krankenhaus Day Clinic, also in Aachen, Germany. She is now a German resident living in Hamburg where she currently works for Amnesty for Women, providing psychological guidance to and coordinating a self-help group of migrant women from Latin America.

Verónica Baracat is Argentinian and holds a degree in administration and a master's degree in gender and development from the London School of Economics. Since 2002 she has held the position of training specialist at the Latin American chapter of the International Gender and Trade Network. She participates in the design and implementation of projects within the

Training Programme on Gender and Trade, and also coordinates workshops on social issues, particularly those relating to women. As a consultant to various government programmes in Argentina, her most recent post was Unit Head of Operations of the Families for Social Inclusion Programme financed by the Inter-American Development Bank.

Jennifer Beeman is Research and Training Coordinator at the Conseil d'intervention pour l'accès des femmes au travail, a women's organization based in Montreal, Canada that promotes respect for the rights and access to decent work of women workers. She was previously a researcher for over eight years at the Équipe de recherche sur la culture organisationelle des groupes de femmes (ERCOF). She has a master's degree in sociology from the University of Quebec at Montreal.

Camelia Blaga lives in Sibiu, Romania. She has a BA in the English and Romanian languages, has studied women's rights in Sweden and Austria, and worked with projects relating to women since 1998. In 2002, while working for a local NGO, she produced one of Romania's first women's TV shows that addressed issues such as violence against women and women's public participation. In 2004 she founded the Association for Gender Equality and Freedom, which provides counselling to women and girls and promotes feminist values, especially among youth.

Caroline Brac de la Perrière was born in Algeria and is a psychologist and a specialist in contemporary Maghreb history. As a women's rights activist she was obliged to flee Algerian fundamentalist violence in 1993. She was the coordinator and later director of the international coordination office of the International Solidarity Network of Women Living under Muslim Laws from 1995 until 1999, and a member of the Collectif 95 Maghreb Egalité organization for twelve years. Her concern for women's rights and peace issues led her to join other women activists in Mediterranean countries in establishing the New Ways International Alliance for Social Innovation. In 2002, she was the France–Algeria coordinator of the 20 Ans Barakat campaign against the family code in Algeria. She is also the author of several books and articles on women's rights in the Maghreb.

Phyllida Cox is of English nationality. While living in Buenos Aires, Argentina, for two years she researched policy issues relating to sexual and reproductive health and rights and volunteered to be the Argentinian focal point of the International Gender and Trade Network. She is currently carrying out postgraduate research at the African Gender Institute in Cape Town, South Africa that involves anthropological fieldwork on masculinities and sexual and reproductive health in urban Xhosa communities. She also does advocacy work on women's health policy issues for a local non-governmental organization.

Ann Crews Melton holds a degree in religion and gender studies from Austin College in Sherman, Texas. She served as co-moderator of the National Network of Presbyterian College Women from 2002 to 2003, during which time she founded a womenspace spirituality group on her campus. Ann staffed the National Office of Women's Advocacy at the Presbyterian Church (USA) from 2003 to 2005. She is currently employed as Development Associate at Temple Israel in Boston, Massachusetts.

Andrea D'Atri is Argentinian and holds a post-graduate degree in gender studies. She has worked as a university professor and currently works in gender-oriented communications with a radio programme and an electronic newspaper. As an activist she is a member of Argentina's Socialist Workers' Party, and she was also one of the founders of the Centre for Professionals in Human Rights and of Pan y Rosas. She currently contributes to the work of the Institute for Socialist Thought where she offers seminars and conferences in her areas of expertise.

Emilienne de León holds a bachelor's degree in international relations from the Universidad Nacional Autónoma de México and has over 15 years' experience working as a consultant to Mexican NGOs and women's groups in strategic planning and institutional development. She has been Semillas's Executive Director since 2002, is on the Board of Directors of the Women's Funding Network, is co-chair of the International Network of Women's Funds, a board member of the Mexican NGO Movimiento Ciudadano para la Democracia, and a member of Mexico's Red de Investigadores. In 2005 she received the annual Women's eNews prize presented to women who are 'changing the world with vision, passion and power'.

Monika S. W. Doxey is a PhD student in anthropology at the Research School of Pacific and Asian Studies of the Australian National University (ANU). Her thesis is related to the well-being of Indonesian women migrants in Australia. She has assisted in a variety of research projects at ANU's departments of Anthropology and Humanities, Gender, Culture and Sexualities, as well as at the university's National Centre for Epidemiology and Population Health. Monika's research interests include gender and cultural representation, migration, identity, transcultural/transnational marriages/relationships, well-being and adaptation, violence against women, the feminist movement and political identity.

Leona M. English is associate professor of adult education at St Francis Xavier University, Nova Scotia, Canada. She researches women in development, gender and non-profit leadership, and spirituality of adult educators. Her recent publications include the *International Encyclopedia of Adult Education* and the *Spirituality of Adult Education and Training*. She is currently working on a series of articles on women, power and knowledge.

Liz Ercevik Amado has been working with Women for Women's Human Rights (WWHR) – New Ways, an independent women's NGO based in Istanbul, Turkey, since 2002. She was also joint coordinator (2002–4) of the Campaign for the Reform of the Turkish Penal Code from a Gender Perspective. She has prepared and edited several WWHR-New Ways publications including *Sexual and Bodily Rights as Human Rights in the Middle East and North Africa: a Workshop Report* and *Human Rights Training Programme for Women (1995–2003)*.

Danielle Fournier is the coordinator of field placements and of the certificate in community organization at the School of Social Work at the University of Montreal. She teaches community organization and applied ethics. Her research interests include the practices of the women's movement and management models developed by women's groups. She sits on the boards of several women's groups.

Lise Gervais is a social worker and has worked in non-profit community groups as a practitioner, a trainer and a coordinator, notably in youth, popular education and women's groups since 1979. She has also collaborated on research projects developing increased knowledge of community and women's groups and improving women's lives and their access to equality. She is currently the coordinator of the group Relais-Femmes.

Amanda Mercedes Gigler was born in the US and has been involved in the country's grassroots women's movement for more than 15 years. In 2001 she moved to Mexico City and in 2003 joined Semillas's resource development staff to cultivate relationships with foundations and corporations, and two years later she assumed the post of coordinator of the organization's resource development programme. She also serves as a volunteer leading workshops on self-esteem, basic job skills and market research for first-generation Latin American immigrant women in San Francisco. Amanda holds a double major in comparative literature and inter-disciplinary studies at the University of Berkeley, California.

Lucero González is a Mexican sociologist and photographer. She became involved in the student activist movement in Mexico in the late 1960s. Her contributions as a feminist and human rights activist and as a photographer have been recognized in various Mexican forums. She is a member of the Mexican Academy for Human Rights, a founding member of Semillas and of the Grupo de Información en Reproducción Eligida (GIRE), and an adviser to the Global Fund for Women. She is currently President of Semillas's board of directors. In 2005 Lucero received an award of distinction from Semillas's board in recognition of 15 years of dedication to the organization's development.

Nancy Guberman was director of the Équipe de recherche sur la culture organisationelle des groupes de femmes (ERCOF), a group of professors and activists that produced several studies on the women's movement in Quebec, Canada, including the one from which her essay is taken. She is Professor of Social Work at the University of Quebec at Montreal and a board member of several women's and community groups.

Shahnaz Iqbal, is a human rights activist and holds a master's degree in history from the University of Punjab, Pakistan. She works with Shirkat Gah, the Women's Resource Centre, as coordinator of the Women Law and Status Programme. Her main activities involve research and capacity building in legal and gender awareness, and violence against women for target groups. She also facilitates local, national and international advocacy initiatives. She is an active participant in campaigns and solidarity actions initiated by the Joint Action Committee for People's Rights, a coalition of civil society groups, and in other forms of lobbying on issues related to women's rights.

Jocelyne Lamoureux is professor of sociology at the University of Quebec at Montreal. She has carried out extensive research on social movements and citizenship, has written many books and articles on these subjects, and is a well-known speaker in Quebec. She has been actively involved with groups promoting the rights of sex workers.

Jinock Lee is South Korean and a PhD candidate in the Department of Politics and International Studies, University of Warwick, United Kingdom. Her thesis on global economic restructuring and gender politics in South Korea examines how gender has been one of the foundations of the globalization process. Part of her research was carried out while volunteering for the Korean Women's Trade Union where she was able to assist in the organization of a union of university-subcontracted women cleaning workers.

Adriana Medina Espino was born in a rural community in the state of Michoacán, Mexico. She is a sociologist with a master's degree in gender studies. Among her most memorable experiences so far are the lessons learned from rural migrant children in the Consejo Nacional de Fomento Educativo, with indigenous women in the K´inal Antzetik organization, with young people in the Universidad Autónoma Metropolitana-Azcapotzalco, and her work in the Women's Institute of the Government of Mexico City.

Pramada Menon is a co-founder and Programme Director of the Indian non-governmental organization Creating Resources for Empowerment in Action (CREA). She has worked in the development sector in that country for the past eighteen years as an activist, a trainer, a planner, an implementer and an administrator. She was the Executive Director of Dastkar, a registered society working to ensure sustainable livelihoods for traditional craftspeople. Her work over the years has focused on issues related to sexuality and sexual rights, livelihoods, gender and development, violence against women, and organizational development. She is on the board of a number of Indian non-profit organizations including Dastkar, TARSHI (Talking About Reproductive and Sexual Health Issues), Janani and the North East Network. She also serves on the Advisory Council of the Global Fund for Women.

Yamini Mishra is an Indian feminist activist. She has worked with different organizations on a diverse range of issues. Her contribution to this publication was written while she was working with the Asia Pacific Forum on Women, Law and Development in Chiangmai, Thailand. Yamini is now back in India working with the Centre for Budget and Governance Accountability in Delhi, trying to integrate a gender perspective and feminist principles in the work of the centre.

Nicholas Pialek is currently a PhD student at the University of Oxford. He will submit his thesis in 2006. His doctoral work focuses on how organizational culture influences policy uptake in development organizations. More specifically his research discusses the issue of gender mainstreaming. He has conducted the majority of his fieldwork in Oxfam GB.

Alexandra Pittman is an independent consultant and evaluation specialist focusing on organizational development, gender and social change. In June 2004, she obtained her EdM in international education policy from Harvard University. She is currently a doctoral student in cultural psychology at Boston College where she also serves as Assistant Coordinator for the Middle Eastern and Islamic Studies Program. Her current research includes a collaborative evaluation project with activists at the Association Démocratique des Femmes du Maroc and the Women's Learning Partnership; the research explores the effectiveness of the Leading to Choices leadership programme on participants' conceptualization of the self, as well as its impact on their participation in the family, community, and professional life. Alexandra is also conducting research on the trends of discourse in women's rights movements in the Global South as a means of building and strengthening these movements.

Elizabeth Plácido is a Mexican sociologist and a member of the Mexican chapter of the Latin American and Caribbean Committee for the Defence of Women's Rights. An enthusiastic cinema-goer, coffee drinker and admirer of Remedios Varo (a Mexican painter), she enjoys wandering on the campus of the Universidad Nacional Autónoma de México contemplating the full moon. *Persona y Democracia* by María Zambrano has been her bedside book over the last few years.

Kelsey Rice is an associate of the National Network of Presbyterian College Women, a network of collegiate Christian feminists from all over the United States. Her work takes her around the country, speaking on the role of young women in the Christian church. Kelsey has written articles and essays for *My Red Couch, and Other Stories on Seeking a Feminist Faith*; *Presbyterians Today*; *Horizons: The Magazine for Presbyterian Women*; and *Church and Society*. A graduate of Whitworth College in Spokane, Washington, USA, Kelsey lives in Louisville, Kentucky.

Sol Viviana Rojas was born in Bogota, and graduated in psychology from Colombia's Universidad Javeriana in 1996. This was followed by a master's degree in gender studies at the Central European University in Budapest, Hungary. She has worked as a psychologist, researcher and consultant in social affairs and development education in organizations such as the Jesuit Refugee Service and the Colombian Fund for Scientific Reaearch. She currently lives in Hamburg, Germany, where she works for Amnesty for Women and the European Network for Transnational HIV/STI Prevention among Migrant Sex Workers.

Dalia Sachs is a senior lecturer at the Department of Occupational Therapy of the University of Haifa. She is an activist in feminist and peace organizations, such as Women in Black and the Women's Coalition for Peace, where she promotes equal representation for women from different backgrounds. She established a project at Isha L'Isha, the Haifa Feminist Center, for the promotion of health and welfare among elderly women. Her current research focuses on the lives of women in conflict areas and the importance of women's participation in peace negotiations.

Hannah Safran is a peace and feminist activist turned scholar after years of working at Isha L'Isha, the Haifa Feminist Center. Her recently published book, *Don't Wanna Be Nice Girls: The Struggle for Suffrage and the New Feminism in Israel,* is centered on the history of the Jewish suffrage movement in the 1920s and Israel's new feminist movement of the 1970s. Her current research focuses on aspects of feminist organizing with specific emphasis on lesbian women and the women's peace movement. She participates in promoting new feminist ventures, helping women achieve economic independence and freedom from violence.

Titi Salaam is Nigerian and has been active in the women's rights movement since 2001. She has a combined honours degree in history and English from the Obafemi Awolowo University, Ile Ife, and a masters degree in gender and peace building from the University for Peace in Costa Rica in 2004. Having previously worked with Nigeria's Women Advocates Research and Documentation Centre, she currently holds the post of Programme Officer of the Conflict Management Project with the Heinrich Böll Foundation in Lagos. Titi has carried out extensive research on the trafficking of women for prostitution, the non-violent struggle of women in the Niger Delta, women's human rights under shari'a law in Northern Nigeria, women's political participation in Nigeria, and the role of women in conflict resolution and peace building.

Norma Sanchís is an Argentinian sociologist, specializing in public policy with a gender focus in the fields of economic development, the labour market, local development, small business, credit and international trade. She is a consultant in development projects financed by UNIFEM, UNICEF, OAS, IADB and the World Bank. She is joint Regional Coordinator in Latin America, in charge of training in the International Gender and Trade Network. She was also responsible for the design and implementation of the Virtual Seminar on Gender and Trade.

Margaret Schellenberg is a US citizen who has lived in Mexico City since 1996 and worked as a development consultant with various Mexican non-profit organizations, including Semillas, where she was a staff member between 1998 and 2003. She previously held the positions of director of the FEMAP Foundation in El Paso, Texas and director of resource development for FEMAP in Ciudad Juárez, Chihuahua, Mexico. She was also founder and co-coordinator of the Border Awareness Program, and co-director and founder of the Center for New Creation, a non-profit organization located in Arlington, Virginia. Margaret graduated with a BA in philosophy and a master's in inter-disciplinary studies, with a focus on Latin American studies.

Margalit Shilo is a professor teaching at the Land of Israel and Archeology Studies Department, Bar Ilan University, Ramat Gan, Israel. She is a specialist in the history of the Jewish community in pre-state Israel (the nineteenth and twentieth centuries). Her recent book: *Princess or Prisoner? Jewish Women in Jerusalem 1840–1914* was published in Hebrew by Haifa University Press and received the Bahat Prize; it was published in English in 2005 by Brandeis University Press.

Nalini Singh has an Indo-Fijian ethnic background and grew up in the Fiji Islands. She graduated with a bachelor's degree from the University of the South Pacific in 2001 with a major in development studies, having previously studied at the Australian National University in Canberra, Australia. Nalini is currently Programme Officer at the Thailand-based Asia Pacific Forum on Women, Law and Development (APWLD), in charge of the Labour and Migration and Women's Participation in Political Processes programmes. Nalini's main interest is development and she hopes to continue using her training and experience in the promotion of human rights and social justice.

Yusmidia Solano is based at the Institute of Caribbean Studies, at the Universidad Nacional de Colombia on the island of San Andrés. Her studies focus on the participation and contribution of women to social, political and economic affairs in Colombia, and particularly in the Caribbean region. She has participated in the formation of various womens' organizations such as the Corporación de Mujeres Orocomay (a Colombian NGO), the Women's Network of the Caribbean region of Colombia, the National Women's Network, and the Women for Peace Initiative.

Mary Olivia Tandon is a Barrrister-at-Law. She served on the Bench in the High Court of Uganda from 1964 to 1970, and lectured in law at the University of Dar-es-Salaam, Tanzania, between 1972 and 1979. When Zimbabwe achieved independence she moved to Zimbabwe, where she worked for three years as a legal adviser to the Ministry of Legal and Parliamentary Affairs. She was also involved in rural development in Zimbabwe and Southern Africa for twelve years. During this period she was also an activist in women's and human rights issues.

Trees Zbidat-Kosterman is Dutch and has been living in Sakhnin, a Palestinian town in the north of Israel, since 1993 with her Palestinian husband and two daughters. She previously carried out social work with mainly Moroccan and Turkish immigrant women and second-generation immigrant youth and political asylum seekers in Utrecht, Holland. She also studied Arabic. After moving to Israel she started working for the Al Zahraa women's organization in 1998 as a resource development and public relations officer. She has also contributed many articles about Palestinian women to Dutch magazines and is a member of the advisory council of the Global Fund for Women (GFW) in San Francisco, advising GFW's board on grants for Israeli/Palestinian women's organizations.

INDEX

20 Ans Bakarat organization,
223-4, 228-9
Ávila, Maria Betania, 241
abortion, 36, 243, 245;
clandestine, 21; right to, 17-18
Abubakar, Yakubu, 252
accountability, feminist principle,
42, 251
acronyms, language of, 80, 82, 84
Activism and Development,
India, 115-16
activism: decision for, 72;
fundraising, 107; older models,
7; volunteer, 227-8
adolescent girls, issues of, 112
adultery: death sentence
campaign, 252, 252;
recriminalising proposal, 237
advocacy, 7, 100; campaigns, 115
affirmative action, 40
Afghanistan, US-led war, 37
Agenda of Women for Peace,
Colombia, 184
ageism, 46
agunoa, abandoned Orthodox
Jewish women, 29
Ahoti organization, 206
Aid organizations, pressures from,
37
Al Zahara organization, 190,
193-8
ALEG, (Association for Gender
Equality and Liberty),
Romania, 159-60; Gender
Equality Festival, 163, 165;
young people focus, 161
Algeria: civil war, 221; family
code amendments, 225-6
alienation, mechanisms of, 71
alliances, 246; choice of
collaborators, 40; development
of, 240, 242; regional, 244
American Convention on
Human Rights, 240
Amina, 254-5
Amnesty for Women (AfW),
Hamburg, Latin American
section, 141, 143-4, 146-7;
volunteer professionals, 142
Arab Democratic Party, Israel,
193
Argentina: December 2001
protests, 15; women's
information network (RIMA),
19
Arivia, Gadis, 215
Armanca, Brândua, 163

arranged marriages, 172
Association Démocratique des
Femmes de Maroc (ADFM),
259, 265
Association for Women's Rights
in Development, 1, 3, 7-9,
239; Feminist Movements and
Organizations Program, 2
Autodefensas Unidas de
Colombia, paramilitaries, 185
awareness-raising; campaigns,
163; groups, 10

backlash, anti-feminist: subvert-
ing of, 235
Beijing: Fourth World
Conference on Women, 7;
Platform for Action, 37, 246,
261; 'plus' review processes,
174
Belém Do Para, 246
biographies, working women
struggles, 22
Brukman textile factory, Buenos
Aires, 15; worker recuperated,
16, 17
budgets, 69
Budianta, Melanie, 215

Cairo Programme of Action, 246
Caleta Olivia, political prisoners,
20
Campaign for an Inter-American
Convention on Sexual Rights
And Reproductive Rights,
239
Campaign for the Reform of the
Turkish Penal Code, 230
campaigns, 9; advocacy, 115;
awareness-raising, 163;
differences resolution, 238;
manifestos, 245; momentum,
237; training in promotion of,
244
Canadian International
Development Agency, 137
capitalism, patriarchal, 16, 18
Casablanca, conservative
Islamists, 261
Centre for Peruvian Women
Flora Tristán, 241
'checklists', 80
Chiarotti, Susana, 240-1
childcare, trade union issue, 154,
155
Christianity, theological
spectrum, 50

citizenship, 68; issue of, 58;
training for, 76
co-responsibility, 6
Coalition Against Injustice,
Nigeria, 252-5
Coalition of Women for Peace,
Israel, 201
Collectif 95 Maghreb Egalité, 221,
262, 265-6
collective cause, living for, 63
Colombia: armed conflict, 181;
National March of Women
Against the War, 183;
syndicated unions, 182
Commission of Inquiry on
Women, Pakistan, 173
common good, defining of, 74
communications strategy, 187
conflict, organization fear of, 92
'consensus', 93-4; blocking, 49;
false, 62; 'group', 61; model,
5; process, 233
cooperation: cooperatives, 151,
153-4; fragility of, 201; inter-
organizational, 205
Cotidiano Mujer, 241
counter-feminist movement,
Morocco, 262
CREA, Mexico, 111-12, 116;
Community-Based Leadership
Programme, 110, 113-15, 117;
support organization, 113
Creating Resources for
Empowerment in Action,
India, 109

danger, for Algerian women, 222
Days of Activism Against Gender
Violence, Pakistan, 174-5
decision making processes, 5, 68,
72, 75, 121, 187; collective
coordinators, 227; consensus
model, 44, 49, 88-9;
experience, 156; feminist
perspective, 119; gender-
biased, 194-5, 197;
independent evaluation, 42;
majority vote mechanisms, 5;
SIPAM, 61; structures, 62;
youth inclusion, 162
'democracy', 67; organizational,
68; participatory, 57
Democratic Women's
Movement, Israel, 192
'depression', 142
development institutions, 4, 39;
professionals, 110

discourse: establishing common, 258; gender and development, 79; hermetically sealed, 222
discrimination, criminalizing proposal, 235
dispute resolution processes, 171, 173
distance-learning, difficulties, 125
division of labour, gendered, 153
divorce, 265; denial of, 29, 31
domestic violence, 170, 230, 265
dominant codes, subversion of, 58
Dominga, Rosa María, 241
Dominican Republic, Trujillo dictatorship, 20
donor agencies, 3; aid agency pressures, 39; international, 101, 105–6, 224; Mexico, 99; relationship with, 8; women, 102–4; Zimbabwe withdrawal, 137; see also, funding
Duque, Isabel, 241

e-learning, specialists, 123
e-mail, debate via, 124
East Asian economic crisis 1997, 150, 153
Echer, Celita, 241
economic development, gender sensitive, 120
education, 195; through participation, 171; see also literacy
egalitarian practices, rigid, 60
El Salvador, 240
El-Youssoufi, Abderrhamana, 261
Eliahu, Mordechai, 29
Elige, Youth Network for Reproductive and Sexual Rights, 107
elites, local power structures, 171
'emergency activism', 214, 216
empowerment, 67, 72, 74; courses for/on, 194, 196; cycle of, 100; leaders, 110; literacy acquisition, 133; model of, 46; process, 69, 71, 73, 195
'equal representation', system, 201, 203, 205; 'quarters policy', 200
equality, gender blind, 160
essentialism, strategic, 211
European Union, 141; Turkish accession process, 231
'exclusion', Colombian women, 183–4
exhaustion, feminist comrades, 41
'experts', 80; expertise demystification, 75; gender, 82–4

Facio, Alda, 254
family laws, 172; Algeria, 222–3, 225, 230; Morocco, 258–64
Federation of Korean Trade Unions, 153
Federation of Women for Equal Rights, Israel, 32
Fels, Anna, 46
feminism: experienced knowledge, 239; movement, 36; North American organizational literature, 71; political strategy, 214, 216; rights-based approach, 259–60; see also organization(s), feminist
feminists: bosses, 38; collegiate Christian, 45; lesbian, 201; Romanian view of, 159; veteran, 91
Femrite, Ugandan Women's Writers Organization, 136
FENARETE project, 141
First International Kolech Conference, 28
Foucault, Michel, 87–8
Fourth World Conference on Women, Beijing 1995, 7
framing, 79
Freeman, Jo, 6
friendships, organizational limitations of, 60
fundamentalism, 1, 17, 21, 225, 246; fight against, 228; Islamic, 254; resurgence of, 36
funding, 39, 63, 134; absorption with, 16; access to, 8; approach imposition, 10; government, 88, 92–3, 142; Mexico crisis, 105; plans, 106; results oriented, 40; see also donors
fundraising, 101, 103, 162, 196; model for, 99; training in, 107

Garrido, Lucy, 241
Gelman, Yehuda, 28
gender: and development discourse, 79; discrimination, 116; ideologies, 210; knowledge enclave, 80; 'machinery', 7; mainstreaming, 58, 78–9, 81–5; political, 84; terminology, 79–80; work discrimination, 265; Zionist equality myth, 202
Gender and Development Peace Corps, 165
Gender and Trade Virtual Seminar, 121
Gender and Trade Work, Latin American chapter (LAGTN),

119, 121; web page, 125
German language: classes, 145; migrant command of, 141
Global Fund for Women, 101, 107, 137
Gong Theatre for Children and Youth, 163
Gonzalez, Daniel, 81
grant making, 103–4
groups, attendance fluctuations, 145
Guessous, Nouzha, 262

Haifa women's coalition, 206
Halakhah (Jewish law), 26–8
Hamburg, women migrants, 140
Haq, Zia-ul, 167
Heraty Noehadi, Toeti, 215
hierarchy, sources of, 46
Hindi language, resource materials, 113, 116
HIV/AIDS, 137; women with, 58
Hivos, Dutch Institute, 134, 137
'home managers' cooperatives, 151
Honduras, 240
'honour killing', 174, 194, 236
household economics, political domain, 211

ibu (motherhood) identity, 209; deconstruction, 214–15
Ibuism, Indonesian state ideology, 212; feminist appropriation, 213–14
identity(ies): constructions of, 216; 'hyphenated', 207; reconstruction, 209; strategically essentialized, 211
IMF (International Monetary Fund), 37
International Gender and Trade Network, 120
inclusion, organizational: climates of, 94; fiction of, 92
India: criminal code, 116; development strategies, 110, 115; fundamentalist groups, 36; leadership positions, 111; women, 112
Indian Association of Women's Studies, 115
Indonesia: economic crisis 1998, 210–11; women's crisis centre, 213
Indymedia, 19
inequality, economic, 200
information: access, 115; sharing of, 68
Iniciativa de Mujeres pr la Paz, Colombia (IMP), 181-3, 187-8

Institute for Rights, 115-16
institutional memory, loss of, 3
'institutional secrets', 61
intentionality, 51
Inter-American Commission of
   Women, 240
interest groups, right wing, 1
international agreements,
   implementation need, 7, 240
International Conference on
   Population and Development,
   37
International Criminal Court
   (ICC), US undermining, 37
International Day of Action for
   Women's Health, 2, 17
International Gay and Lesbian
   Human Rights Commission,
   243
International Meeting of Women
   Against War 2004, 185
international trade: civil society
   non-involvement, 120; gender
   perspective, 123; social impact,
   119
International Women's Day, 169,
   195, 253; 1975, 167; 2002, 16;
   2004, 18
International Women's Year
   1975, 167
Internet: limited access, 125; use
   of, 18, 223-4
Intifada: first, 203; second, 205
Iraq, fundamentalist groups, 36;
   US-led invasion, 37; women
   against invasion, 17
Islam: conservatives, 37, 261-2;
   law, 167, 252-3, 258-9, 265
Israel: Defence Force (IDF), 31;
   feminist movement, 26-7,
   200, 207; Jewish state
   establishment, 190-1; Jewish
   settlement expansion, 193;
   post-1967 occupations, 192;
   ruling elite, 202; Supreme
   Court, 27; women's peace
   movement, 203, 205

Japan, Constitution Article 24, 37
Jewish Orthodox Feminist
   Alliance (JOFA), 27
jirga, 173
Joint Action Committee for
   People's Rights, Pakistan, 174

Kaduna State, Nigeria, 251
Kamir, Orit, 31
Karimanzira, David, 135
Kayan organization, 206
Kehat, Hanna, 28, 30
Kellogg Foundation, 101, 107
King Mohamed VI, Morocco,
   261, 267

Kitson, Norma, 135
Knafo, Vicki, 205
Knesset, Arab members, 196
Kolech, Israeli Religious
   Women's Forum, 27-8;
   opposition to, 31
Koran: conservative
   misinterpretation, 259; gender
   equality reading, 262-3, 265
Korean Confederation of Trade
   Unions, 150, 153
Korean National Confederation
   of Women, 153
Korean Women Workers'
   Associations United
   (KWWAU), 150-1, 153;
   Equality Line service, 152
Korean Women's Associations
   United, 153
Korean Women's Trade Union
   (KWTU), 150-3; 88 CC
   Division, 156; manuals, 155;
   women friendly model, 154

labour: gendered division of, 153;
   irregular workers, 152; rights,
   206
Lagos, 251, 253
language, issues of, 204
Lanteri, Julieta, 22
Las Libres organization,
   Guanajuato, 107
Latin America: economic
   policies, 123; electronic
   networking, 125; fundraising,
   99; philanthropy, 102; trade
   agreements, 124; women's
   movement, 119
Latin American and Caribbean
   Committee for the Defence of
   Women's Rights (CLADEM),
   240-2
Latin American and Caribbean
   Women's Health Network,
   241
Latin American and Caribbean
   Youth Network for
   Reproductive and Sexual
   Rights (REDLAC), 239, 243
Law, Eric H.F., 48
leaders: identification of, 204;
   training of young, 229
leadership: allowances for, 63; as
   dynamic quality, 111;
   capacities building, 110;
   control of, 62; courses, 197;
   development spaces, 46;
   experiences of, 251; internal
   consolidation, 60; issues of, 5;
   non-hierarchical models, 48,
   50; older women, 6;
   programme, 113; shared, 45;
   styles, 7, 91; transfer processes,

64; women positions, 111
'legal consciousness', 168-70,
   175; advice, 143
literacy issue of, 133-4, 168
lobbying, 93, 234
loyalty, as organizational obstacle,
   63
'Lucian Blaga' University, Faculty
   of Journalism, 163

MacArthur Foundation, 101
'majority rules', ethic of, 47
majority-vote mechanisms, 5
Malaysia, fundamentalist groups,
   36
management: boards, 73;
   structures, 69
marginalized peoples, voices of
   mutual invitation,, 48
marital laws, Orthodox Jewish,
   29; Moroccan abolition, 264
maternal mortality, 58
matriarchs, feminist
   organizations, 38
media, the, use of, 224, 265-6;
   communications strategy, 187;
   promotional materials, 243;
   public communications, 102;
   publicity, 162
meetings: attendance, 144-5;
   confidence in, 155; participant
   subsidies, 204
Meir, Golda, 190
Mexico: feminist organization,
   57; international donors, 105;
   local women's philanthropy,
   101-2; stratified class structure,
   103
migrant women, 140-1, 143-7
militancy, limits of, 63
minimum wage: campaigns for,
   153; issue of, 152
Mirabel sisters, assassination of,
   20
Mizrahi Jewish Women, 200,
   202, 206
Moravians, 45
Moudawana (Personal Status
   Code), Morocco, 226, 258-9;
   change campaign, 260-2;
   Royal Commission on, 263-4
movement building, 4, 9-10
Mugabe, Robert, 137
Mujeres en Alianza, Colombia,
   186
Mujeres Inviertendo en Mujeres
   (MIM), 102-3, 106
mystique, gender work, 82

National Network of
   Presbyterian College Women,
   USA, 44-5, 47, 49;
   Coordinating committee, 51

National Network of Women, Colombia, 186
National Plan for the Integration of Women in Development (PANFID), Morocco, 261, 266
National Women's Meeting, Rosario 2003, 17-18
Ndebele language, 135, 138
negotiations, skills in, 186-7
neighbourhood assemblies, Argentina, 15
Network for People's Education Among Women (REPEM)
NGOs (non-governmental organizations), 10; competition between, 113; elitist accusation, 260; stakeholders, 39
Nigeria: shari'a law, 252-3, 255; Social Forum meeting 2004, 254
non-violence, Gandhian principles, 41
Norwegian Agency for Development Cooperation, 134, 137

Obasanjo, Olusegun, 253, 255
Olea, Cecilia, 241
one-upwomanship, 41
Open Society Institute, 107
Operation Siriri, 186
oral narrative, 133; recording of, 134
organization(s), feminist: accommodation of 'outsiders', 74; autocratic patterns of behaviour, 227; autonomous, 259; Christian, 49; development, 78; economic sustainability, 101, 137-8, 164, 181; exit strategy for members, 64; fear of internal conflict, 62, 93; feminist values, 5-6; fictional readings of, 94-founder members' relationship, 59-60, 63, 94; generational differences, 222; history of, 10; informal social activities, 144; language choice, 143; marginal women, 99; non-hierarchical, 50; participants 'user' status, 74; processes, 38, 40; skills of, 73; strategic planning, 42, 59, 104; terms for membership, 75; see also leadership
Organization of American States' System of Human Rights, 240
Oslo Agreement, 203
outreach programmes, 168-175; by world of mouth, 143
Oxfam GB, gender issue, 78-85

Pakistan: Constitution, 169; fundamentalist groups, 36; peace rallies, 174
Palestine, extended family structure, 191
Palomino, Nancy, 241
Pan American Health Organization manual, 143
Pan y Rosas, Argentina, 15-18; no funding of, 21
Panama, 240
parliamentary systems, 47
participation: equality, 62; learning, 88; mechanisms, 64; methodology, 183, 187
partnership building, 164-5
Pastrana, Andrés, 182
'paternalistic practices', 75
pay, 63, 93; flat structures, 90, 94
Peace Corps, 161-3
petitions, 260, 266
philanthropy: concept of, 101; progressive models, 102
Platform for the Reform of the Turkish Penal Code, 234, 236-7
political prisoners, campaigns for, 19-20
polygamy, 263
post-structuralism, 87-8, 94
poverty: alleviation, 112; women, 110
power, disciplinary, 87; dynamics, 4; equalizing tools, 45; issues of, 5; micro-practices, 88; subordination mechanisms, 71; technologies of, 89, 91; understanding of structures, 175
pregnancy, adolescent, 20-1
Printemps d'Egalité network, 261-2, 265-6
proletarianization, Palestine, 191
psychological counselling service, AfW, 142
publishing, 132

Quebec, women's movement, 68

Rabat, 2000 feminist protest, 260
race, issues of, 47
rape: Chinese Indonesian women, 213; crisis centres, 206; marital, 236
Red MIM del Campo, Jalisco, 107
RedeSaúde, 241
Reinhelt, C., 75
religion: extremism, 221; feminist theologians, 50; institutions, 4, 46
report writing, 169
representation, issue of, 245;

identity groups, 207
resource materials, availability, 117
Revolutionary Armed Forces of Colombia (FARC), 182, 185
Rhodesian Literature Bureau, 132
rights: -based discourse, 266-7; human, 100, 112; interdependence of, 246; women, 8, 39, 104
rituals, egalitarian, 51
Robert's Rules of Order, 47
Roman Catholic Church, 37, 45; Catholics for a Free Choice (CFFC), 243; fundamentalist sectors, 17
Romania: 1989 Revolution, 159; women's franchise, 160
Rosario, Argentina, 17-18

Safiya Must Not Die Campaign, 252, 254
Sakhnin, Israel, 193; women from, 194
Salas, Wendy, 104
sectarianism, 226-7
self-criticism, absence of, 245
self-surveillance, 90-2
Semilla (Seeds) organization, Mexico, 99, 101, 103, 106; economic sustainability, 100; public communications strategy, 102; strategic planning, 104
seminars, 243
Seoul Women's Trade Union, 150
sexual and reproductive health, 58, 111-12, 115
sexual and reproductive rights, 235, 241-2, 246; as effective demand, 244; Bush agenda, 240; formulation of, 243; right to privacy, 255
sexual crimes: criminalized, 236; Turkish legitimation, 232
sexual harassment and abuse, Orthodox Jewish women, 29-30
Sexuality and Rights Institute, India, 116
shared experience, assumptions of, 61
Shaheen, Wafaa, 193
Shakdiel, Leah, 27
Shiran, Vicky, 203
Shirkat Gah, India, 168, 170-1; Women Law and Status (WLS) programme, 167, 173
Shona language, 135, 138
Sierra de Oaxca, weaving cooperative, 100

SIPAM (Salud Integral para la Mujer), 57-8, 64; decision-making, 61; disagreements, 62; egalitarian practices, 60; founders withdrawal/ leadership crisis, 59
skills: acquisition of, 76; enhancement, 114, 116; organizational, 145; writing, 134
social protest, 'criminalization' of, 19
social welfare, cuts, 205
songs, use of, 224, 226, 228
SOS-CORPO, Brazil, 241
specialists, e-learning, 123
Spivak, Gayatri, 211
Spokeswoman Workshop, 244
sponsorship, 164
stereotypes, Romanian gender, 160
storytelling, 88; employment experience, 155; oral, 133-4
Suara Ibu Peduli, Indonesia (SIP), 209, 212
Suharto, 209, 211-12; New Order state, 210; resignation, 213
Supeli, Karlina, 215
support networks, 142, 146-7
Swedish Federation of State Workers, 182, 187
Swedish International Development Agency (SIDA), 182, 187

Tamayo, Gulia, 240
TAMPEP project, 141
TARSHI, Indian NGO, 116
tasks, distribution of, 62
Tel Aviv University, 193
telephone counseling, women's employment, 152
The Tyranny of Structurelesness, 6
tokenism, 47
Torah, the, 29; study institutions, 25-6; values, 28
trade agreements: negotiations transparency lack, 120; social mobilization around, 124
trade unions, 4; domestic workers, 154; irregular workers, 152; rules and procedures, 155
tradition: repressive use, 132; young people influenced by, 160
training: activists, 228; campaign promoting, 244; local paralegals, 170-2; on sexuality,

116; skills, 196; trainers, 120-1, 197
truth: fear of, 92; regime of, 89-90
Tugartudu Hussein, Safiya, 252-5
Turkey, Penal Code, 230-4, 236

UN (United Nations), 112, 173, 198; Children's Fund (UNICEF), 135; constitution, 169; Development Fund for Women (UNIFEM), 122, 197; International Conference on Population and Development, 240; Security Resolution 1325, 182
Union de l'Action Feminine, Morocco, 259-60
United Methodists, 45
University of Salisbury, 132
University of Uppsala, 182
University of Zimbabwe, 132
urban-rural disparity, 134
Uribe, Alvaro, 185
Uruguay, feminist magazine, 241
USA (United States of America), ICC undermining, 37
Utar Pradesh, India, 114

Vásquez, Roxana, 240-1
Vanangana organization, India, 113
Vargas, Virginia, 241
'victims', 74
video cassettes/clips, use of, 174-5, 224, 228
Vienna tribunal 1993, video of, 174, 175
VIF Coalition, 165
violence against women, 111, 145, 172-5, 195, 200, 213, 221; Algeria, 221; domestic, 170, 230, 265; protection group, Guajuato, 100
virtual training/education, 121, 125; methodology, 122;seminars, 119-20, 123-4
Voice of Concerned Mothers, Indonesia, 210

war mentality, post 9/11, 185
Weaver Press, 138
white privilege, issues of, 47
women: Algerian exiles, 222-3; demonstrations, 212; double oppressions, 202; education issue, 194; free trade treaty impact, 120; income generation, 131; India, 112; lesbian, 203-4, 206; media

representation, 162; Palestinian in Israel, 190; prisoners, 136; rabbinical lawyer training, 26; shelters, 75, 206; state depoliticization, 210; violence against, *see* violence; 'Westernized accusation against, 132, 175; writing by, 133; young, 46, 49; Zimbabwe freedom fighters, 136
Women Advocates Research and Documentation Centre (WARDC), Nigeria, 251, 253, 255
Women for Women's Rights-New ways (WWHR-NW), Turkey, 230-8
Women in Black movement, 185
Women in Writing, South Africa, 136
Women's Aid Collective (WACOL), Abuja, 253
Women's Emancipatory Constituent, Colombia, 181-5
Women's Initiative for Peace, Colombia, 186
Women's Link, Korea, 153
Women's Peace Conference, Stockholm 2001, 182
Women's Rights and Access to Justice, 253
women's rights, funding, 39, work for, 8
women workers: biographies, 22; job insecurity, 151
work, differing responsibilities, 90
workers in organizations, interests of, 75-6
Workers without Employers movement, Argentina, 16
World AIDS Day, 173
World Bank, 37
WTO (World Trade Organization), 37

Yeivin, Esther, 32

Zimbabwe: Land Reform Policy, 137; Social Welfare Act, 133; women freedom fighters, 136
Zimbabwe Women Writers (ZWW), 131; creation of, 132; economic sustainability challenge, 137-8; legal identity need, 133; membership growth, 134; publications, 136; reviewer feedback, 135